John Dewey's Pragmatic Technology

The Indiana Series in the Philosophy of Technology

Don Ihde, general editor

John Dewey's Pragmatic Technology

Larry A. Hickman

INDIANA UNIVERSITY PRESS
Bloomington and Indianapolis

Library of Congress Cataloging-in-Publication Data

Hickman, Larry A.
    John Dewey's pragmatic technology/Larry A. Hickman.
       p.   cm.—(The Indiana series in the philosophy of technology)
    Bibliography: p.
    Includes index.
    ISBN 0-253-32747-4
    1. Technology—Philosophy. 2. Pragmatism. 3. Dewey, John, 1859–1952. I. Title. II.
Series.
T14.H44   1990
601—dc20   89-45418
                                                          CIP

     1 2 3 4 5 94 93 92 91 90

Contents

Editor's Foreword

Indiana University Press is proud to launch the Indiana Series in the
Philosophy of Technology with the following trio: *John Dewey's
Pragmatic Technology,* by Larry A. Hickman; *Technology and the
Lifeworld: From Garden to Earth,* by Don Ihde; and *Heidegger's
Confrontation with Modernity: Technology, Politics, Art,* by Michael
Zimmerman.

The Indiana Series is the first North American series explicitly
dedicated to the philosophy of technology. (There are other series
relating philosophy and technology, particularly those that collect
interdisciplinary articles, but none of these has been devoted to the
development of a new subdiscipline within philosophy.) Broadly
conceived, it nevertheless will address a wide variety of issues relating
to technology from distinctly philosophical perspectives. Philosophically,
our approach will be pluralistic, and this is evidenced in our first round of
books. The traditions of both American pragmatism and Euro-American
trends are evidenced.

Our trio is timely. We begin with radical reappraisals and
interpretations of the two early twentieth-century philosophers who
made questions of technology central to their thought: John Dewey and
Martin Heidegger. And we are also beginning with a systematic
reformulation of a framework and set of questions regarding technology
in its cultural setting in *Technology and the Lifeworld.* Later we will be
adding topics of a more thematic nature, including books on
"Engineering Birth," "Big Instrument Science," "Media and Rationality,"
"Technological Transformations of Perception," and many others.

Our goals are to include philosophically critical, historical, and
interpretive studies as well as original and topical ones within a
perspective that is balanced, reasoned, and rigorous regarding the
emergent field of the philosophy of technology.

With *John Dewey's Pragmatic Technology* we are also trying to balance the beginning of our series. While it must be admitted that others have heretofore dominated what has become a North American philosophy of technology—including the dystopians Jacques Ellul and Herbert Marcuse, and also Martin Heidegger, who made technology central to his thought—John Dewey's prior instrumentalism has often been overlooked.

Yet Dewey is, par excellence, the American "father" of the philosophy of technology. Larry Hickman demonstrates this here in his insightful reappraisal of Dewey in the context of the philosophy of technology. The result is a tour de force with respect to Dewey. Hickman shows Dewey's relevance to many of the most contemporary questions involving modern science and technology. Long before it became fashionable in history-of-technology circles, Dewey described and analyzed the interconnection of science and technology and, simultaneously with Heidegger, argued for a precedence of technology over science, based, in Dewey's case, upon a pragmatic theory of action.

Philosophers as diverse as Richard Rorty and William Barrett have recognized Dewey as the American philosophical revolutionary who, even before Wittgenstein and Heidegger, moved philosophy into the postmodern period. Larry Hickman takes this appreciation a step further and places Dewey in the very midst of a high-technological culture. Dewey is seen as critic, appreciator, and expositor of the unique kind of "instrumentalism" that has evolved in contemporary life. Considering Dewey in the context of his more recent peers, Hickman addresses the now-crucial issues of technological determinism, the technology/science interface, and, above all, the question of the role of the philosopher in our social and political, technologically textured world.

Here, then, is a most original piece of Dewey scholarship, combined with a penetrating critique of technological culture. It is located precisely between the extremes of utopian and dystopian thinking and displays both the balance and engagement required by the conversation with technology. The key metaphor, coined by Hickman, is *responsible technology*. One can see immediately how such a notion meshes with the valuation of community and democracy, which also play crucial roles in Dewey's thought. By bringing both Dewey and these issues up to date, Hickman clearly broadens the field of the philosophy of technology.

DON IHDE

Acknowledgments

There are many people without whose help this book could not have come to fruition. The advice of my colleague John J. McDermott has been of inestimable value. My department head, Herman Saatkamp, provided unquestioning logistical support and constant encouragement. The advice of Peter Manicas and Ralph Sleeper helped get the project off on the right foot. Ralph Sleeper, Paul Durbin, Gregory Moses, Elizabeth Porter, Gregory Pappas, and Richard Martin read early drafts and provided suggestions that have helped clarify the final product and render it more readable.

My work at the Dewey Center at Southern Illinois University was rendered both efficient and pleasurable by Jo Ann Boydston and her staff, and especially by Tom Alexander, who served as host during my visit to Carbondale. Dan Unger helped with bibliographical searches, and Wayne Riggs and Ed Gabrielsen undertook the tasks of proofreading and reference checking with patience and diligence.

This book was made possible in part by a grant (RH-20844-87) from the Division of Research Programs of the National Endowment for the Humanities, an independent federal agency. For their help in obtaining matching funds from the College of Liberal Arts of Texas A&M University, I am indebted to Dean Daniel Fallon and to Associate Dean Arnold Vedlitz.

Introduction

When I began to think seriously about writing this book, my colleague John J. McDermott provided a metaphor that has since proved invaluable. Dewey's work, he suggested, is an elaborate spider's web, the junctions and lineaments of which its engineer knows well, and in and on which he is able to move about with great facility. But for the outsider who seeks to traverse or to map that territory, there is the constant danger of getting stuck.

A proficient introduction is, to be sure, a map of the territory under discussion. But it must also offer general information about the area covered by the map, the routes of travel that converge upon it, its importance to neighboring regions, and how to return home once the visit is finished.

In this case, the territory is John Dewey's critique of technology, an enterprise he carried out during more than half a century and on more than 13,000 published pages. Major points of interest include his radical reconstruction of the debates between idealists and realists on matters of ontology and epistemology; his characterization of the history of science and technology, and of their present relations to each other; his insistence that theory is a kind of practice; his treatment of social and political publics as technological products; and his insight that the fine and the vernacular arts are essential parts of the technological continuum. The major feature of Dewey's technological landscape is his contention that what lies beyond theory and practice, and what allows them to have commerce with one another, is the production of testable artifacts, among which he includes both those things popularly called "mental" and those popularly called "physical." Dewey's critique of technology is above all a critique of the production of novel and testable artifacts.

The roads that lead to and from Dewey's critique of technology provide connections to American studies, to the history and philosophy of science, to aesthetics, and to social and political theory. I have attempted to provide way markers for each of these avenues within each chapter.

As a further guide, and because not every reader will have the critical edition of Dewey's works at hand, I have provided two sets of citations for references to Dewey's major works. Page references to the first volume of *The Later Works* (LW1), for example, are accompanied by references to *Experience and Nature* (EN). Where I have cited only the critical edition, it is either because the essay in question was not reprinted before its inclusion in the critical edition or because it was not reprinted in any collection of Dewey's works that might now be readily available.

In an attempt to make the way as smooth as possible, I have also provided an appendix that contains two pagination keys to those of Dewey's works that I have cited. The first key lists, in chronological order and by the page range within the critical edition, each of Dewey's works that I have cited. To each of the items in this column there corresponds a reference to a precritical-edition imprint of that work. The second key lists cited precritical-edition imprints alphabetically. To each of these imprints there corresponds a range of pages within the critical edition.

Chapter 1 constitutes an attempt to locate Dewey's critique of technology with respect to his times, his places, his style, his students, and even some of his critics. I have argued that his critique of technology resists location even within the best current taxonomies of technology, such as those proposed by Carl Mitcham and Robert Mackey, and by Alexander Borgmann. The feature of Dewey's critique of technology that renders it unique is his contention that tools or instruments cut across traditional boundary lines such as those between the psychical and the physical, the inner and the outer, and the real and the ideal. This idea, which Dewey cultivated and nourished until it grew into a methodology, was Dewey's instrumentalism.

The focus of chapter 2 is Dewey's theory of inquiry. Its thesis in brief is that inquiry was reconstructed by Dewey as a productive skill whose artifact is knowing. He argued that knowing is characterizable only relative to the situations in which specific instances of inquiry take place, and that it is an artifact produced in order to effect or maintain control of a region of experience that would otherwise be dominated by chance. Knowing is thus provisional: when conditions change, further inquiry may be called for if control is still required. A corollary of this view is that the goal of inquiry is not epistemic certainty, as it has been taken to be by most of the philosophic tradition since Plato, but instead a matter of ongoing interaction with novel situations by means of constantly refashioned artifactual tools. Unlike most philosophers of technology, Dewey held the view that technological instruments include immaterial objects such as ideas, theories, numbers, and the objects of logic (such as logical connectives). His instrumentalist account of inquiry rejected both realism and idealism on the grounds that neither position was capable of developing an adequate understanding of the function played in knowing by tools and media of all sorts.

Chapter 3 treats Dewey's work on aesthetics as part of his critique of technology. Dewey contended that the division between the "fine" and the "practical" or "industrial" arts has largely been the result of an infelicitous divorce of ends from means. Where ends and means interpenetrate and inform one another, however, the application of *techne*, or productive skill, in the arts leads to enriched experience, whether the art product be a painting or a pair of shoes. Dewey argued that the *work* of art is neither identical to nor a property of what is normally called the art product. He also denied that the work of art is entirely a function of the experience of the perceiver or user of such art products. Appreciation is for Dewey no less an act of technological production than is the construction of what is to be appreciated. The *work* of art is the transaction between the art product and its appreciator, and is itself a process of producing new artifacts, both tangible and intangible.

Chapter 4 is an examination of Dewey's treatment of the history of technology. Since Dewey's primary interest was philosophy, his account may be read as a history of the *philosophy* of technology, within which he isolated three stages. In its first stage, Greek philosophers demeaned the work of the artisan, but at the same time appropriated his models as the basis for their grand cosmological schemes. Plato relocated productive skill in a supernatural realm, and Aristotle treated a hypostatized nature as Grand Artisan. Dewey argued that because of their lack ᴏɪ interest in experimentation and instrumentation, and because of their preoccupation with the contemplation of what they regarded as fixed and finished essences, the Greeks had not so much *science* as the *idea* of science. Dewey viewed what he took to be the second major period of the philosophy of technology, the one that extended from the decline of Roman civilization to the beginning of the Renaissance, as exhibiting little more than "failure of nerve." Philosophy and technology were treated during that period primarily as avenues of access to the supernatural. The successes of the period that followed, the age of scientific technology that began in the seventeenth century, were due to increased use of instrumentation, a novel emphasis on public experimentation, and a *de facto* abandonment of the substance-accident metaphysics of Aristotle. Further advances in scientific technology will, Dewey suggested, involve the explicit and conscious rejection of the Aristotelian model as well as the extended application of the methods of scientific technology, especially to the social sciences.

Chapter 5 treats Dewey's view of the relations among theory, practice, and production. Aristotle's hierarchy of ways of knowing placed theory in a superior position with respect to practice and production, and made practice in its turn superior to production. Dewey inverted this hierarchy, suggesting that the interpenetration of theory (or ideas about things to be done) with practice (or the doing of things) is made meaningful only when novel tools and solutions are produced. Dewey thought that the production of tools of a wide variety is essential to properly controlled inquiry, and that such tools include theories, hypotheses, and novel habits. He argued that one of the great impediments to successful inquiry is the taking of the tools he termed inference, implication, and reference as entities existing in their own right prior to inquiry. Among inquirential tools once used but no longer needed, Dewey counted what have been called "the principle of cause and effect" and "the principle of necessity." These principles, he argued, are required neither for framing and using scientific laws, nor for the more properly philosophical task of understanding how such laws work. Dewey thus described science as a type of productive technology—that is, as an activity that even in its most abstract form, in the realm in which abstract mathematical significance is manipulated, involves constructed artifacts that are tried and tested, proximately within a realm of abstract possibilities and ultimately with respect to existential situations.

In chapter 6 I have undertaken an analysis of Dewey's treatment of what has been called "technological determinism." I have attempted to put this complex of issues, which is also commonly referred to as the "autonomous technology debate," in its widest perspective in order to underscore the uniqueness of Dewey's contribution to it. To that end I have developed an analysis of the several varieties of historical and economic determinism advanced by Karl Marx, as well as the view of Jacques Ellul, which I have called "technological gridlock," and the view of Langdon Winner, which I have called "technology without a core." Dewey rejected all forms of determinism, including technological varieties. He argued against traditional attempts to hypostatize a "will" that is capable of being either free or bound, and he characterized as unscientific positions that hold that there are inevitable historical "forces" at work. He argued that technological conditions form the *necessary* but not the *sufficient* conditions for technological progress; and that ultimate responsibility for the future lies not in the abstract laws of history (Marx), or in a reified technological "system" (Ellul), or in hope for supernatural intervention (Ellul), but in concrete decisions made by human beings, both singly and in groups.

In chapter 7 I have examined some further social and political ramifications of Dewey's critique of technology. Dewey rejected the traditional structural distinction between the individual and the social, and put in its place a functional distinction between what is private and what is public. Dewey's reconstruction of the idea of technical progress grows out of his discussion of the private and the public, and is of particular importance to his wider public philosophy. He was a leader in the successful attempt mounted by progressives in the 1890s to wrest evolutionary metaphors from Spencerian conservatives, arguing that they had held an untenable dualism between what is natural and what is ethical. I have concluded this chapter with an analysis of some of the attacks made upon Dewey's work from the left, particularly by C. Wright Mills and Reinhold Niebuhr.

The final section is a brief epilogue in which I have attempted to tie together some of the broader themes of the book by means of a single metaphor: responsible technology. I have argued that of the three giants of twentieth-century philosophy—Wittgenstein, Heidegger, and Dewey—only Dewey took it as *his* responsibility to enter into the rough-and-tumble of public affairs, and only Dewey was able to construct a responsible account of technology. To ignore this aspect of Dewey's work, as some self-styled "neopragmatists" have done, is to remain on the periphery of what Dewey regarded as his life's work.

Abbreviations

Citations of the works of John Dewey are to the critical edition published by Southern Illinois University under the editorship of Jo Ann Boydston. At the time of this writing (1989), complete are the five volumes of *The Early Works, 1882–1898* and the fifteen volumes of *The Middle Works, 1899–1924*. *The Later Works, 1925–1953*, eventually will include seventeen volumes; as of the fall of 1989, fourteen have appeared. Volumes fifteen and sixteen are promised for December 1989, and volume seventeen is in preparation. Citations will be made in what has come to be the standard way: the initials of the series are followed by volume and page numbers. Abbreviations for the critical edition are

EW   The Early Works (1882–1898)
MW The Middle Works (1899–1924)
LW   The Later Works (1925–1953)

Abbreviations for other commonly used editions, including those not yet replaced by the critical edition, are listed in the appendix.

John Dewey's Pragmatic Technology

Chapter One: Locating Dewey's Critique of Technology

> When the instrumental and final functions of
> communication live together in experience, there
> exists an intelligence which is the method and reward
> of the common life, and a society worthy to
> command affection, admiration, and loyalty.
> (LW1:160;EN:169)

I

John Dewey's concern with technology pervades his published work.
From his early days at the University of Michigan in the late 1880s until
his last published work in the 1950s, Dewey formed his fundamental
philosophical insights in response to the problems and opportunities of
the developing technological society in which he lived as an active
participant. While still at Michigan he came to view the problems of
technology and the problems of philosophy as inseparable. Throughout
his career his philosophical arguments were illuminated by means of a
rich inventory of tools, machines, and hardware. Late in his life,
"technology" became a synonym for his very method of inquiry.

It is the central thesis of this book that inquiry within technological
fields—among which he included science as well as the fine and the
vernacular arts—formed the basis of and provided the models for
Dewey's larger project: his analysis and critique of the meanings of
human experience.[1] And it is no overstatement to say that his critique of
technology was the warp on which the weft of that larger project was
strung.

It is therefore remarkable that Dewey is not generally known for his
critique of technology. It is true that it was only after Dewey's death in
1952 that professional philosophers in America and Europe began to
think systematically about technology and to organize themselves into
societies to promote such research. But standard anthologies of the
philosophy of technology[2] still do not include Dewey's essays, nor has
his work on the subject yet been the focus of more than a few isolated
interpretive essays.[3] A survey of publications in American studies and

American philosophy reveals a similar situation: Dewey has not generally been read as having set out a philosophy of technology.[4]

Some of the responsibility for this situation may have been Dewey's own, for he concentrated his critique of technology in no single work. His books on ethics, logic, aesthetics, education, religion, and political philosophy are clearly marked as such, and there is at least a healthy debate concerning whether *Experience and Nature* is a book about metaphysics.[5] But there is no *locus classicus* for Dewey's account of technology.[6]

Fault may also lie with Dewey's students and disciples. Almost without exception they failed to see that the version of pragmatism he called "instrumentalism" was his lifelong critique of tools and media of all sorts. Of that group, apparently only Sidney Hook and C. E. Ayres grasped this basic feature of instrumentalism. Hook's neglected Ph.D. dissertation, *The Metaphysics of Pragmatism* (published in 1927, the year the fifteen millionth Model "T" Ford rolled off the assembly line) caught Dewey's work in midstride. It nevertheless remains one of the best sources of insight into what Dewey meant by "instrumentalism." Few of Dewey's other colleagues or disciples seem to have understood that term as Dewey himself understood it, namely as a cognate of "technology."

No less overlooked and underrated than Hook's dissertation are the works of C. E. Ayres. *Science: The False Messiah* (which appeared in 1927, the same year as Hook's dissertation and Dewey's *The Public and Its Problems*), *The Industrial Economy* (1952), and *Toward a Reasonable Society* (1961) represent Ayres's attempts to construct along instrumentalist lines a theory of political economy appropriate to technologically based democracies. Taken together, these works of Hook and Ayres constitute the only sustained treatments of this fecund area of Dewey's thought.

It is to some extent possible to account for Dewey's preoccupation with technology in terms of the milieu in which he lived and worked. He came to prominence as "America's philosopher"[7] during a period that Charles Beard termed "the machine age." "In his hands," wrote Beard, "a branch of wisdom once deemed esoteric acquired a practical ring; in fact it conformed very closely to the requirements of an age committed to machine production, science, and progressive endeavor."[8]

The innovations of the machine age, the cultural changes through which Dewey lived and that influenced his thinking, shed light on Beard's assessment. His first essay was published in 1882, the year that Thomas A. Edison designed his first hydroelectric plant in Appleton, Wisconsin; his last appeared some seventy-two years later, shortly after his death in 1952, a year also visited by the explosion of the first hydrogen bomb and the first mass production of the birth-control pill.

At the time of Dewey's birth in 1859 the United States was in the last stages of what Lewis Mumford has called the "eotechnic" period of technology. Wind, water, and animals were still the primary sources of power. Wood, in addition to powering steamships and railway locomotives, was the principal material of construction. The year of Dewey's birth was also the year that the first oil well was drilled in Titusville, Pennsylvania.

By 1900, however, when Dewey was in the middle of his ten-year term at the University of Chicago, Americans had moved firmly into Mumford's "paleotechnic" phase of coal and steel. They had "mastered the mechanical equivalent of 65,000,000 horses. Four million units of this new power eased the farmers' burdens. Railroads accounted for 24,000,000 horsepower as contrasted with less than 2,000,000 in 1860, and the stage had been set for automotive power to become . . . dominant . . . by 1910."[9]

By the time of Dewey's death in 1952, America was the undisputed leader in what Mumford called the "neotechnic" age of electricity and synthetic materials. America had moved, and had helped move the world, into the age of nuclear fission.

But the fact that Dewey's milieu was a technologically active one fails to provide a sufficient reason for his abiding interest in the subject. There were other philosophers with whom Dewey shared the places and times of the American machine age, but who exhibited scant interest in its public objects and events. Of the major figures of the classical period of American philosophy, for example, Dewey was the only one to engage actively in the cultural events of his lifetime. Both C. S. Peirce and William James were in their twenties during the American Civil War of 1861–65. But Peirce wrote nothing at all about that national trauma, and James's remarks were confined to an oration in 1897 on the occasion of the dedication of a monument.[10] The conceptual origins of the machine age in America have been traced by Swiss historian of technology Siegfried Giedion to Oliver Evans's mechanized grain mill built in Redclay Creek, Pennsylvania, in 1784.[11] But neither Peirce (1839–1914) nor James (1841–1910)—nor, for that matter, Royce (1855–1916) or Santayana (1863–1952)—seems to have regarded such matters as bearers of philosophical import.

For Dewey, however, philosophical inquiry, like any other form of inquiry, takes place as part of, and is directed toward, specific times and places. No major American philosopher, with the possible exception of Dewey's student Sidney Hook, has been more diligently committed to this ideal. As Dewey wrote in 1938, "We always live at the time we live and not at some other time, and only by extracting at each present time the full meaning of each present experience are we prepared for doing the same thing in the future. This is the only preparation which in the long run amounts to anything" (LW13:29–30;EE:51).

The machine age of which Beard wrote, and through much of which

Dewey lived, gave birth to two highly mechanized world wars concerning which Dewey was anything but silent. But it also gave rise to the locomotives, power plants, microscopes, radios, automobiles, agricultural implements, and even the humble pedals and skates that Dewey's readers find around every turn. These and hundreds of other technological artifacts concentrated his attention and furnished him with illustrative materials. He was concerned with how tools and instruments come to be, how they change human experience, and what they portend. But even more fundamentally, he sought to demonstrate that the methods and means by which technological inquiry takes place *are* the methods and means by which all knowing, in its "honorific" sense, is generated (see LW12:73;LTI:67).

In this area of his work as well as others, Dewey demonstrated outstanding tenacity with respect to the development, refinement, and recasting of his ideas over time so as to render them intelligible for the diverse audiences that constituted his reading publics.[12] His theory of inquiry, for example, which I shall argue was from first to last an account of technological method, was for the most part developed in essays and books published between 1903 and 1938. But it is adumbrated in his essay on "Moral Theory and Practice," published in January 1891 (EW3:93–109), and in his syllabus for "Introduction to Philosophy," offered at the University of Michigan in 1892 (EW3:230). Its development continued to occupy him until his death some sixty years later.

In his 1891 essay Dewey posed ethics as a type of problem in engineering. In his syllabus of 1892 he characterized the theory of inquiry, or logic, as "the general theory of science" (EW3:230), by which he meant experimentation that progresses only as it develops and utilizes ever more precise instrumentation. He argued in the 1892 syllabus that it is the task of logic to look backward at already complete experiments, by which he meant the manipulation of experience by means of instrumentation of all appropriate types, in order to resolve such experiments into their constituent factors. In his last letter to Arthur F. Bentley, dated 9 April 1951, he wrote that if he got the needed strength, he would like to write "on *knowing* as the way of behaving in which linguistic artifacts transact business with physical artifacts, tools, implements, apparatus, both kinds being planned for the purpose and rendering *inquiry* of necessity an *experimental transaction* . . . ."[13]

Some of Dewey's work was directed toward the interests of other professional philosophers, some to educators working in primary and secondary schools, some to students of philosophy, some to the "intellectual" community in general, and some to the general public. But his prodigious ambition with respect to creating and sustaining these diverse constituencies led not just to his national prominence; it may also be responsible for the formidable difficulties confronted by those who attempt to get an overview of his massive published work.

II

Dewey's ambition with respect to creating and maintaining diverse audiences may also account for his somewhat controversial style. Dewey's style (or, as one of his students remarked, "his lack of it"[14]) has at times been a stumbling block to recognition of the revolutionary character of his insights and proposals.

In *The Golden Day*, Lewis Mumford characterized Dewey's style as "fuzzy and formless as lint."[15] One of the anonymous authors of the file on Dewey compiled by the Federal Bureau of Investigation during the 1940s remarked, somewhat less generously, that "[r]eading him is a task."[16] Perhaps least generous of all was H. L. Mencken, who called Dewey "the most dreadful writer ever heard of."[17]

More sympathetic was the assessment of Stephen Toulmin that Dewey's style was "loose limbed and colloquial."[18] And John J. McDermott, with even greater sympathy, suggested that "Dewey was very wary of the seductive character of language and strove to avoid the use of the flamboyant phrase, choosing rather to make his point in the 'plain style.' "[19]

But whereas Mumford was so offended by Dewey's style that he was almost invariably oblivious to his insights, Toulmin and McDermott saw that form and content were for Dewey parts of a single fabric. Even though most of Dewey's work on his theory of inquiry, for example, was done during a time when philosophy was becoming increasingly formal and symbolic, the fact that his own presentations continued to be discursive was not due just to happenstance or force of habit, but to what he took to be the nature of the material he had chosen to treat.

Dewey's remarks in the preface to his 1938 *Logic: The Theory of Inquiry* are typical of his justifications of this predilection. There, he suggested that adequate symbolization of logic must follow a "general theory of language in which form and matter are not separated," that logic "depends upon prior institution of valid ideas of the conceptions and relations that are symbolized," and that without such discursive preparation, "formal symbolization will (as so often happens at present) merely perpetuate existing mistakes while strengthening them by seeming to give them scientific standing" (LW12:4;LTI:iv).

True to his distaste for dualisms and his penchant for avoiding extreme positions, Dewey's style exhibits neither the ornateness characteristic of most of the philosophical literature of his early and middle periods nor the bare-boned, low-content formalism that came to be the fashion in philosophical circles during his later period. It is reminiscent instead of what was characteristic of American-made tools of the machine age: functional simplicity designed for tasks at hand.

As I have already indicated, however, Dewey's design strategy was not without its difficulties. Novice or unsophisticated tool users tend at times to mistake simplicity for commonness or lack of adequacy.

Perhaps that is why tools that are poorly designed and constructed often sport superfluous frills and come in brightly colored packages. It is also true that the designer of a new tool that does the work traditionally done by an old and familiar one (but in a radically novel and more efficient fashion) had better be chary of calling the new device by the name of the old one.

Regardless of how one assesses his style, however, one thing is quite clear: Dewey steadfastly refused to obey the rules of the philosophical games played during the several periods of his long professional life. Early, when building systems was the norm, he refused to be a builder of systems. Later, when finding logical fallacies and "category mistakes" in the arguments of one's critics and opponents became stylish, he was still out of step. What in fact characterized his philosophical style from first to last was a plainspokenness that veiled the extent to which he undercut and then reconstructed the assumptions of his opponents and critics, and this in a way that was so radical that his opponents more often than not missed the point of his critiques of their works.[20]

III

One measure of the extent to which Dewey undercut traditional assumptions about technology is found in the fact that his work has to this day not been adequately addressed, even by the best and most complete taxonomies of the subject. One of the most reliable maps of this rugged and treacherous territory has been constructed by Carl Mitcham in his seminal essay "Types of Technology," published in 1978. In its "narrow" sense, Mitcham suggests, technology is the disposition and manipulation of materials by technically trained experts. To proponents of this view, including many engineers, technology is a realm of tools, machines, and electronic devices overseen by mechanics, engineers, and programmers. Typical questions within this domain are: "What is the best material with which to construct some artifact? What is the most efficient procedure for producing a particular product or bringing about a desired effect? How can materials and energy be combined to create new inventions?"[21]

As used by historians and social scientists, however, "technology" normally has a much broader meaning. It includes the narrow sense, to be sure, but is extended to include "all making of material artifacts, the objects made, their use, together with their intellectual and social contexts."[22] In this usage, for example, premodern pot making is counted as a form of technology because of its obvious connections to modern forms of technology such as industrial ceramics, and because the social conditions associated with earlier pot making are continuous with the production and use of such artifacts today. Mitcham suggests that "in the history of technology, which is the primary social science study of technology, technology has sometimes been defined so as to refer even to the making of nonmaterial things such as laws and languages—although in practice this definition has not been widely utilized."[23]

Mitcham's own suggestion is that the term "technology" is not univocal, but that there is a certain primacy connected with its use to refer to the making of material artifacts. He even proposes that "the term be stipulated to refer to the human making and using of material artifacts in all forms and aspects."[24] Mitcham correctly sees the history of philosophy as almost exclusively concerned with human *doing*, and he thinks that this fact may be responsible for the somewhat tardy and grudging attention that philosophers have given to technological matters, which are matters of *making*.

Despite his disclaimer regarding the exclusion of nonmaterial things from the realm of technology, however, Mitcham's work exhibits a somewhat hesitant tendency to include such immaterial things as laws and languages within the domain of technological artifacts. This tendency, however ambivalently expressed, aligns Mitcham almost uniquely among contemporary philosophers of technology with the position developed by John Dewey in the initial decades of this century.[25]

Mitcham has argued that properly philosophical accounts of technology operate somewhere between the narrow and broad domains just described. As opposed to the "first-order" questions posed by engineers and historians, however, philosophers of technology concern themselves with "second-order" issues such as the nature and meanings of technology, and its structural and functional aspects.

In the introduction to their now-classic *Philosophy and Technology*, Mitcham and his colleague Robert Mackey isolated three basic groups of philosophical approaches within this middle field: (1) those that analyze technology as a problem of epistemology, (2) those that consider technology from an anthropological standpoint, that is, in relation to the nature of human life, and (3) those that treat technology as "the defining characteristic of thought and action in modern society."[26]

In terms of these distinctions (and by way of preview), Dewey's own position may be characterized as follows. First, he attempted to undercut the epistemological position by arguing that technology has to do with experience in a wider sense than could be contained even in the broadest of epistemological accounts. He argued that one of the principal fallacies in the history of philosophy was the taking of "cognitive knowledge" as paradigmatic for all human experience. He further contended that there are vast areas of human experience, including some in which technological activities take place, with which knowing has no business. As Ralph Sleeper has convincingly argued, inquiry is for Dewey more a matter of logic than of epistemology.[27] In other words, Dewey was not so much interested in a theory of certain knowledge as he was in a method of inquiry by means of which perceived problems could be solved.

Second, Dewey was acutely aware of the place of technology within the larger concerns of human life. In this as well as other matters, Charles Beard's assessment was essentially correct: Dewey "waited assiduously on the new revelations of science, listened to the changing voices of psychology, and gave to his thought the semblance of vitality and motion that accompanied the flow of all things."[28]

Dewey was forever seeking to establish connections and continuities between humble quotidian technological practices and their refined, enriched manifestations.[29] In his account of inquiry he argued for the continuity of inquiry from mundane affairs through science, logic, and metaphysics. In his treatment of the production of art and aesthetic experience his metaphor was that of a mountain peak: "Mountain peaks do not float unsupported; they do not even just rest upon the earth. They *are* the earth in one of its manifest operations. It is the business of those who are concerned with the theory of the earth, geographers and geologists, to make this fact evident in its various implications. The theorist who would deal philosophically with fine art has a like task to accomplish" (LW10:9–10;AE:3–4).

Third, Dewey did not think technology "the defining characteristic of thought and action in modern society." Because of his characterization of the ways in which meanings are generated and in which they function, and because of his appreciation of the complexity of human society, he rejected the view that *any* characteristic of modern society could adequately define it. He was, however, careful to distinguish those activities within modern societies that are productive of expanded meanings and significances from those activities that are "mechanical" in the infelicitous sense of that word; that is, in the sense in which means and ends have been divorced from one another, and meaningfulness has been lost, forfeited, or abandoned. Unfortunately, however, as Dewey well knew, the term "technological" has been utilized for both kinds of activities. This fact served as one of the primary motivations for his attempt to reconstruct the term.

IV

Even attempts by other philosophers to refine Mitcham and Mackey's taxonomy have failed to make a place for Dewey's critique of technology. Utilizing their work as his point of departure, Albert Borgmann discerned what he takes to be three conjointly exhaustive approaches to second order, or philosophical, questions about technology.[30] He terms these views "substantive," "instrumentalist," and "pluralist."

Substantive approaches, such as the one advanced by Jacques

Ellul,[31] reify technology by treating it as a force in its own right. They seek "to give a comprehensive elucidation of our world by reducing its perplexing features and changes to one force or principle. That principle, technology, serves to explain everything, but it remains itself entirely unexplained and obscure."[32] I shall deal more fully with Ellul's views in chapter 6; but for now it is correct, even if something of an oversimplification, to say that he views technology as artificial and autonomous, as exhibiting exponential self-augmenting growth, as having complete power of determination over other cultural manifestations such as art and religion, and as rendering human beings increasingly impotent with respect to control over their lives.

Borgmann suggests that "instrumentalist" approaches are both more familiar and offer a more perspicuous view of technology. These views are "historicist" (in one of the many senses of that word) in that they attempt to display a "continuous historical thread that leads from our ensemble of machines back to simple tools and instruments."[33] Borgmann divides instrumentalist views into three further types:

1. "Anthropological" views treat human beings fundamentally as tool users and makers of artifacts.
2. "Epistemological" views are those whose primary focus "is not the development of humans and their tools but . . . the methodology that modern technology embodies as a way of taking up with reality, particularly in distinction to scientific procedure."[34]
3. "Rational value determinism" is the view that the determination of what guides value formulation within technology is itself a rational undertaking. Since Borgmann thinks that instrumentalist views treat technology as "value neutral," it is a matter of some interest that he nevertheless holds that "rational value determinism" is a form of instrumentalism. "If technology is at bottom a mere instrument," he suggests, "the inquiry of *what guides* technology becomes a task in its own right. The determination of the guiding values is sometimes held to be a matter of rational inquiry. 'Rational value determinism' is therefore by implication a species of instrumentalism."[35]

Borgmann's final category comprises what he calls "pluralist" approaches. This is a family of positions which might also be called "sociological," in the sense that each is characterized by its attempts to describe the complex of trends, attitudes, and forces that are termed "technological" even in a loose sense. Borgmann's view is that for pluralists such as Victor Ferkiss[36] there is no overall pattern of technology, but rather a continually shifting network of technological phenomena that comprises numerous countervailing forces.

Though one would have expected to find Dewey listed as an

advocate of what Borgmann calls the instrumentalist view (since that was Dewey's name for his own position), Borgmann does not mention him in that (or in any other) connection. In fact, Dewey's account of technology fits comfortably in none of the three categories that Borgmann thinks are conjointly exhaustive.

Dewey's is not a substantive view because he continually and explicitly rejected reification of all sorts. Dewey's well-known antifoundationalism with respect to the traditional problems of metaphysics, his contention that certainty is both illusive and not required for satisfactory knowing, and his constant insistence that nouns such as "mind" and "knowledge" be treated as gerunds rather than substantives all militate against an interpretation of his view as a substantive position.

Nor is his view "pluralist" in Borgmann's sense. Even though Dewey was not unaware of the enormous diversity of cultural manifestations we call technological, his work went beyond the tagging, cataloging, and comparing that often delimit such approaches. Ever the reformer, Dewey did not shy away from working out critical proposals regarding the reconstruction of technological inquiry; he thought that such proposals should be developed for all technical-cultural manifestations that are living and momentous.

Was Dewey, then, an instrumentalist in Borgmann's sense of that term? At first glance, and because Dewey used the term "instrumentalism" as one of the designations for his own philosophical method, this would appear to be the case. But further analysis reveals adequate grounds for locating Dewey's position outside this category as well.

It is true that Dewey thought that there is a historical thread from the simple tools and implements of our ancestors to the complex machines of contemporary life. There is a vestige of a bent stick in the most up-to-date plowing equipment. In contrast to the position taken by Heidegger and to Borgmann's own neo-Heideggerian position, however, Dewey thought that the experimental tools and methods produced by seventeenth-century science and further developed during the first industrial revolution did not so much constitute a radical break in the progress of inquiry as they did a giant step forward for inquiry.

Dewey repeatedly insisted that his account of inquiry was based on a genetic method that took development over time as an essential component. Since human beings are within and part of nature, the development of intelligence with respect to the control of human environments in order to effect increased meaning and significance within those environments is for Dewey emergent within nature. And though he was not reluctant to admit that there have been periods of stagnation and retrogression in the history of intelligent control of environing situations, he also thought that the history of the development of the tools and artifacts by means of which such control has been effected has generally been cumulative.

Dewey's position also fails to exhibit the other marks that Borgmann thinks characterize instrumentalism. First, human beings are in Dewey's view certainly more than simply tool makers and tool users, although they are that. They engage in myriad activities that may be loosely termed "aesthetic" in the sense that they involve primitive and uncritical delight. Their interests are also directed toward those experiences Dewey calls "consummatory"—that is, experiences in which appreciation has been sharpened and significance has been expanded by means of critical inquiry in order to extend them far beyond anything that might be called a primitive pleasure. Dewey specifically associates tool use in its most important sense with knowing, but he just as specifically indicates that there are portions of experience in which tools are used habitually and transparently, that is, without reflective interaction with them.

This is one of the aspects of Dewey's view that is incompatible with strict versions of the *homo faber* thesis. There are, he emphasized, areas of human experience with which knowing has no business. In Dewey's view, human beings find themselves in situations and exhibit responses that are much richer than would be characteristic of forms of life in which the construction and use of tools was the highest good. Dewey thought that tools are most often developed to solve some specific existential problem. But it was also his view that the construction and use of tools is a part of the richness of human experience, and that tool making and using may be a means of enrichment of those areas of human experience in which knowing is not operative. Tools and machines have their own momentum: they have consequences that were never intended.

Second, it is true that Dewey held that value determination is rational, but in a sense quite different from Borgmann's use of that phrase. For Borgmann, rationality is apparently something cognitive, and set over and against experimental activities we call technological, setting the goals of more properly technological activities and informing them with meaning. This view provides the basis for his contention that science and technology are fundamentally different enterprises. But Dewey rejected the notion that rationality is purely cognitive, and he viewed science as a type of technology. He reconstructed "rationality" as "intelligence"—the formulation and testing of ends that are proposed in the context of, and grow from, experimental activities.

Intelligence is for Dewey not something over or against technology, but a characteristic of technology in its honorific sense. In other words, when what is commonly called technology fails to be intelligent, it does not, strictly speaking, deserve the name "technology." It should instead be termed repetition of habitual behavior, acquiescence to the temptation of personal gain in economic or political spheres, or perhaps even laziness or stupidity.

Dewey's critique of technology is not instrumentalism in the ordinary sense, in which ends are established, revealed, or inherited, and then means to reach them are sought. Dewey never tired of arguing against acquiesence to fixed and final values or ends, and against default to unconditional or supernaturally transcendent goals. He proposed instead that goals be treated as "ends-in-view"—ends that are alive and active only as they exhibit continuous interplay with the means that are devised and tested in order to secure them. Insofar as he utilized the term at all, transcendence was for Dewey a kind of projection into the future, not something read out of eternity or something given once and for all by the authors of the "classics" (as some writers of best-selling books and champions of "great books" programs would have it).[37]

Analysis of means and ends thus becomes, in Dewey's view, an analytical exercise performed *after* the fact of successful inquiry, for the purpose of separating out elements of a total inquirential situation in order to produce within it still further meaning and significance. Far from being just given in experience, means and ends in Dewey's view are themselves constructed as tools of analysis from enriched experience once experience becomes the object of reflection.

Third, perhaps the most glaring difference between Dewey's position and the kind of instrumentalism sketched by Borgmann is that Borgmann's instrumentalists, like his substantivists and pluralists (and, for that matter, like Borgmann himself), restrict the domain of technological instruments to tangible artifacts that are extra-organic. They do this by distinguishing as different tangible tools and hardware on one side, and conceptual means or ideas on another. It was Dewey's view, however, that the tools and artifacts we call technological may be found on either side of what he argued was an extremely malleable and permeable membrane that separates the "internal" from the "external" with respect to the organism only in the loosest and most tentative of senses.

In *Experience and Nature* Dewey specifically identified ideas as artifacts. "The idea," he contended, "is, in short, art and a work of art. As a work of art, it directly liberates subsequent action and makes it more fruitful in a creation of more meanings and more perceptions" (LW1:278;EN:301). As I have indicated, he was already in the 1890s treating ethics as a kind of engineering problem. And as early as 1916 he compared the construction of logical entities to the development of agricultural implements, suggesting that instruments, including tools and works of art, provide an alternative to the entities that have traditionally been placed in compartments labeled "physical," "psychical," and "metaphysical."

Consider the bare possibility that tools and works of art give the key to the

question at hand: that works and tools of art are precisely the sought-for
alternative to physical, psychical and metaphysical entities. On this
possibility, the ignoring of the characteristic features of this kind of thing is
responsible for the unsettled and persistent controversy. Manufactured
articles do not exist without human intervention; they do not come into
being without an end in view. But when they exist and operate, they are
just as realistic, just as free from dependence upon psychical states (to say
nothing of their not *being* psychical states) as any other physical
things . . . . They are simply prior natural things reshaped for the sake of
entering effectively into some type of behavior. (MW 10:92)

It was further his view that "logical distinctions and relations may
be purely methodological, and yet not 'mental' in the traditional sense of
mental. They may well be . . . the tools of a safeguarded research and
the results *qua* results of such investigation" (MW 10:93).

Borgmann thinks that the position taken by instrumentalists is
"shortsighted"[38] and that it "does not constitute a proper theory of
technology"[39] because its treatment of tools and instruments as value-
neutral "is congenial to that liberal democratic tradition which holds that
it is the task of the state to provide means for the good life but wants to
leave to private efforts the establishment and pursuit of ultimate
values."[40]

This might be true of what may be called "naive" instrumentalism,
or what Langdon Winner has called "straight-line" instrumentalism. But
it is not true of Dewey's instrumentalist version of pragmatism. Many of
those who have hurled stones at technology from the ivory towers of
the humanities have misidentified all or most technology as straight-line
instrumentalism. William Barrett's remarks on technology in *The Illusion
of Technique* provide a good example. Technology is for Barrett
"*embodied technique* . . . and technique reaches its limits precisely at
that point beyond which real creativity is called for—in the sciences as
well as the arts."[41] Barrett's definition of technique is in fact one that
offers a good description of the straight-line instrumentalism of pre-
seventeenth-century crafts: "A technique is a standard method that can
be taught. It is a recipe that can be fully conveyed from one person to
another. A recipe always lays down a certain number of steps which if
followed to the letter, ought to lead invariably to the end desired. The
logicians call this a *decision procedure*."[42] But as Dewey repeatedly
reminded us, technology is much more than the straight-line
instrumentalism with which Barrett wished to identify it.

In the chapters that follow, I shall have much more to say about the
differences between Dewey's instrumentalism and naive or straight-line
instrumentalism. For the present, however, it should be said that Dewey
did not treat tools and instruments as value-neutral but rather as
teeming with values and potentialities that form the basis for intelligent
selection of ends-in-view, or things to be done. Moreover, regarding

Borgmann's criticism that the straight-line instrumentalists tend to want to leave to private interests "the establishment of ultimate values," it should be remembered that Dewey's critics on the political right never tired of attacking him for his call to intelligent planning—the engendering and testing of goals and ends—at the most comprehensive of public levels.

Far from taking the position of the straight-line instrumentalists that Borgmann characterizes so well—that technology constitutes a value-neutral tool that is equally pliable in the hands of political moderates or in those of extremists of the left or right—it was Dewey's contention that the failure of political programs such as those undertaken by the European Fascists of the 1930s was due precisely to their misunderstanding of the values implicit in the situations that gave rise to their tools and in which they utilized them. Political inquiry, because it is one important form of assessing and choosing the most desirable among these values, was for Dewey a form of technological inquiry, though not the highest or primary form of *techne*, as it was for Plato. It is simply one area of human experience, which requires successful instrumental inquiry if it is to generate satisfactory consequences.

V

Carl Mitcham has argued that philosophers are also properly concerned with the "structural" and "functional" aspects of technology. "Structure," for Mitcham, has to do with the search for a "real definition of the essence of technology that can be seen to underlie or be exemplified in its various modes and manifestations."[43] In terms of function, he thinks that an adequate philosophical critique of technology must distinguish between what "goes on internally in man, that which is part of his bodily activity and thus his social involvement, and that which becomes in a sense part of and interacts with the natural world by taking on a life of its own independent of his immediate bodily action. This corresponds to the distinctions between technology-as-knowledge, technology-as-process, and technology-as-product—or thoughts, activities, and objects."[44]

In this definition technological objects include utensils, apparatus, utilities, tools, machines, and electronic devices. Technological activities include invention, design, making, operation, and management. Mitcham suggests that "the functions of planning, teaching, consulting, and systems engineering cut across these various distinctions."[45] Finally, technological "thoughts" include for Mitcham (a) unconscious sensorimotor awareness of how to make or use some artifact; (b) technical maxims or rules of thumb, such as "cookbook recipes" of the form "to get A, do B"; (c) descriptive laws of the form "if A, then B"; and (d) technological theories that relate or provide an explanatory framework for descriptive laws.[46]

It is possible to see in Mitcham's account the vestiges of one that is considerably older. Aristotle, too, distinguished among (inner) theoretical sciences such as mathematics, (social) practical sciences such as ethics, and (artifactual) productive sciences such as poetry. A full account of the very different ways in which Aristotle and Dewey treated these matters will be part of chapter 5. For the present, however, the following should be noted. For Aristotle, the theoretical sciences were regarded as superior to those that are practical and productive (1026a20),[47] and the practical sciences were regarded as superior to those that are productive (1064a10).[48] But because Dewey rejected the Aristotelian view that objects, ends, or principles are fixed and finished, cognitive or theoretical exercises are for him more than mere contemplation of static entities. They become special tools of activities that are practical. And since practice that is intelligent (as opposed to rote or lazy) involves the constant production of new artifacts, including "internal" artifacts such as refined habits, production takes precedence over and becomes a guide to practicality.

Despite the fact that Dewey and Aristotle shared an approach to philosophy that has been termed both naturalist and functionalist, in the matter of the classification of these "sciences" Dewey turns Aristotle on his head. Dewey goes beyond theory and beyond praxis to production: his concern is with the making and testing of new entities including extra-organic tools as well as goals and ideals.

In addition to the "intellectual component" that is most commonly taken as "internal" with respect to technology, Mitcham sees a second internal function, which he calls "technology-as-volition." From this vantage point " . . . technologies seem to be tied up with every imaginable will, motive, love, desire, need, intention, affection, choice, etc."[49]

This post-Aristotelian category may be traced at least as far back as book 5 of Francis Bacon's *The Dignity and Advancement of Learning*. It is there that Bacon asserts that "the doctrine concerning the Intellect . . . and the doctrine concerning the Will of man, are as it were twins by birth. For purity of illumination and freedom of will began and fell together; and nowhere in the universal nature of things is there so intimate a sympathy as between truth and goodness. The more should learned men be ashamed, if in knowledge they be as the winged angels, but in their desires as crawling serpents; carrying about with them minds like a mirror indeed, but a mirror polluted and false."[50]

Whereas much of the philosophical tradition since Bacon posits two things or faculties—namely, intellect and will (sometimes, as in the work of Hume, called reason and passion)—Dewey characterizes the situation quite differently. Human beings operate on the basis of habits that are learned as the result of previous inquiry, whether their own or that of someone else, and they are able to marshal those habits in the pursuit of projected ends, which he calls ideas. Dewey thus rejects attempts to reify intellect and will. He substitutes a functional account for a structural one, eschewing in the process all varieties of faculty psychology.

Dewey treated this matter in his 1922 *Human Nature and Conduct*, where he developed at considerable length his reasons for rejecting those positions, such as Bacon's, that have hypostatized the "will." He argued that what is commonly called "will" is but a complex of habits, which in turn are "demands for certain kinds of activity . . . and . . . constitute the self. In any intelligible sense of the word will, they *are* will. They form our effective desires and they furnish us with our working capacities" (MW14:21;HNC:25).

Habits are in their turn characterized in terms of rich technological metaphors: the toolbox (MW14:22;HNC:25), the flywheel, and the mainspring (see LW2:334–35;PP:159). Dewey contrasted tools passively arrayed in a toolbox to tools in active use. To think of habits as tools in a box is to treat them as objects, not as tools. We can certainly think of habits in this way, as having certain structural features; but in their function as tools, rather than as objects in a box, they have their meaning only in their use, and they are used only in conjunction with concrete situations. Habits are dynamic, supplying inner tension, like mainsprings, and, like flywheels, they also supply the momentum necessary for continued activity even in the absence of stimuli that call for innovative thinking.

If structure gives way to function in Dewey's account of tools, including the tools we call habits, it is also the case that the diremption of inner and outer gives way to attention to a total situation. Eye, arm, and hand may be treated structurally, as objects: in use, however, they function as tools for grasping and handling. But grasping is an activity that when actively engaged resists attempts to separate that which grasps from that which is grasped: " . . . Whenever they are in action they are cooperating with external materials and energies. Without support from beyond themselves the eye stares blankly and the hand moves fumblingly. They are means only when they enter into organization with things which independently accomplish definite results" (MW14:22;HNC:26). What is grasped and what grasps may be analyzed *after* grasping has been attempted or accomplished, and *on the basis of* that functional activity. But Dewey argues that to say (as is common in philosophical treatments of technology) that there exists *before* that activity takes place something essentially grasping and something essentially grasped, is to commit what he terms "the philosophic fallacy": the taking the results of inquiry as prior to it.

Chapter Two: Knowing as a Technological Artifact

> Inference, or the use of things as evidence of other
> things, is a constant and important function of
> behavior, as much so as any other in life. This is a
> minimum statement, suffering from exaggerated over-
> caution. If such acts as walking, plowing, eating,
> blacksmithing, etc., need and evolve distinctive
> instrumentalities, organs, structures, for their
> prosecution, especially for their *successful*
> prosecution, the presumption is strongly in favor of
> the statement that the operation of inference has its
> own peculiar characteristic tools and results.
> (MW10:92)

I

Techne, the ancestor of "technology," was used by Greek
contemporaries of Plato and Aristotle to designate any productive skill.
More specifically, the term was used in a demotic sense as "a kind of
professional competence as opposed to instinctive ability (*physis*) or
mere chance (*tyche*)."[1] *Techne* was thus used to designate a realm of
activity that occupied a place between two extremes: the order of
nature (or supernature) and the disorder of chance. For the Greeks,
productive skill was said to act with respect to both extremes.

For Aristotle and Plato alike, *techne* was said to imitate nature by
modifying and bringing to completion natural events and objects for the
sake of human purpose and use. At the same time it was said to
perform the quasi-divine function of establishing order where there had
been only chance. Although Aristotle found much in Plato's treatment of
techne with which to disagree, it is clear that both men would have
accepted this general characterization of the term.

In addition to its intermediate position between nature and chance,
techne stood, for the Greeks, between two other extremes. Since it
involved knowledge and ability directed toward production and
construction, it occupied "a sort of intermediate place between mere
experience or know-how, *empeiria*, and theoretical knowledge,
episteme."[2] Unlike *episteme*, technology did not have to do with the

immutable. Instead, productive knowledge was thought to concern the processes of becoming and what comes to be. Unlike *empeiria*, productive skill was said to go beyond the loose associations retained in memory, and to be concerned with more than just particular instances and their connections. In his rich paraphrase of Aristotle, Wolfgang Schadewaldt contrasted productive skill with its opposite, *atechnia*: "Thus *techne* is expressly defined as a knowledge and ability which has come about by habit, i.e. has passed into flesh and blood, and which is directed to a producing, but in connection with a clear course of reasoning concerning the thing itself, which the man of mere experience does not have in view. A knowledge that is likewise productive but which, however rich and diverse it may be, has a false idea of the thing itself remains simply *atechnia*, blunder."[3]

Techne was for the Greeks a pro-duction, a leading toward, and a con-struction, a drawing together, of various parts and pieces in order to make something novel. *Techne* was thus central to the thought of the Greeks in the sense of having been an important element in their form of life. But it was also centrally located for them between state of nature and finished artifact, between necessity and chance, and between theoretical certainty and unstructured experience.

Technology in the sense of "active productive skill" is likewise a central element in John Dewey's philosophy, but in ways that constitute a radical departure from the thought of the Greeks. For one thing, he rejected Aristotle's foundationalism. Aristotle treated theoretical knowledge—*theoretike*—as knowledge of what could not be otherwise.[4] Dewey argued instead that absolute certainty and immutability are chimerical. He thought that belief in existential necessity, necessity apart from thought, amounted to a kind of superstition. He contended that the construction of theories is a special case of the use of productive skill, that is, a special type of technical production. But he also argued that Aristotle's practical knowledge, *praktike*, when it is divorced from real production, becomes humdrum and lifeless. Active productive skill is thus, for Dewey, at center stage because it includes and informs both the theoretical and the practical whenever and wherever they are effective.

Dewey also rejected the Greeks' essentialism. Aristotle held the view that there are essences to which qualities are appended or in which they inhere.[5] By hypostatizing both essences and qualities (at least according to one long tradition of interpretation), Aristotle was able to pigeonhole them into a grid constituted horizontally by his ten categories—one for substance and nine for its accidents or properties—and vertically by degrees of abstracted generality. Each of the categories, whether of substance or of accident, contains individuals, species, genera, and so on, right up to the most general genus. It was Dewey's contention that far from being prior to and informing thought, Aristotle's realm of essences and accidents in fact arose *from* thought, that it was itself a tool of thought, a technological artifact.

Active productive skill also took its place in Dewey's thought as a means by which he could, in his role as opponent of unresolved dualisms of all sorts, place human experience *in medias res*. Active productive skill offered Dewey a key to understanding the place of human beings within and at the cutting edge of the activities of nature. He thought that it provides the only successful means by which lived experiences can be brought to fruition and made meaningful, and by which problematic situations can be resolved. The activities that Dewey called technology were for him a busy intermediary, a liaison between the resting places we call doubt on one side and resolution on the other.

Techne was for the Greeks active only in the sense that it was the application of a body of skills that was regarded as more or less stable. But technology was for Dewey an active method of generating and testing new skills, as well as reconstructing old ones.

II

Nowhere is Dewey's treatment of technology more insightful than in his radical reconstruction of traditional theories of knowledge and his replacement of them with a theory of inquiry. It is no overstatement to say that for Dewey properly controlled inquiry exhibits the most general traits of all other types of productive skill and that its artifact, knowing, exhibits the most general traits of all other successful artifacts.

In 1903 Dewey and several of his students at the University of Chicago published a collection of essays that they called *Studies in Logical Theory*. The four essays that Dewey contributed formed the basis for another book on logic, *Essays in Experimental Logic*, entirely his own and published in 1916.

In the first sentence of his introduction to the 1916 volume Dewey furnished the key to understanding those essays. It was to be found, he suggested, in "the passages regarding the temporal development of experience" (MW10:320;EEL:1).

Dewey's account of experience begins in terms that are existential: human beings are constantly engaged in immediate or "nonreflective" experiences. While certain intellectual elements may intervene in such experiences, they are primarily constituted by complexes of other qualities that are, as he puts it, "objects of esteem or aversion, of decision, of use, of suffering, of endeavor and revolt, not of knowledge" (MW10:322;EEL:4).

These noncognitive experiences—to call them "qualities" would be to give them sharper definition than they possess, as well as to open the door to confusing them with Aristotelian qualities or accidents—may subsequently be the objects of inquiry. It is possible, and even a common practice, to read the results of inquiry back into these original experiences so as to conclude that there were well-defined qualities, sense data, or objects already present prior to inquiry. Initially, however, it is engagement and not reflection that characterizes an individual's involvement with these noncognitive experiences.

What are the significant traits of these nonreflective experiences? First, their various factors hang together and are "saturated with a pervasive quality" (MW10:322;EEL:5). Having the flu, being involved in a political campaign, putting an overstock of canned tomatoes on sale, going to school, being caught up in a romance—each of these experiences, Dewey suggests, exhibits features that are not the business of inquiry. Insofar as they are organized, these experiences are the result of inquiry that is previous, not present. These experiences may be called immediate and aesthetic.

Second, these experiences have what Dewey calls "focus and context." "Movement about an axis persists, but what is in focus constantly changes" (MW10:323;EEL:6). The language that Dewey uses to describe these situations is explicitly that of James's *Principles of Psychology*. He invites us to imagine him sitting at his typewriter. The point of his intentional focus moves about within a selected portion of a field, a context that itself exists within a wider environment, which in turn extends spatially farther than it is possible to say, and whose temporal aspects, his own habits and interests, extend both forward and backward in time. His focus is temporary; it is a single, shifting point, the movement of which helps to create its context. The spatiotemporal matrix in which it moves about is both vast and changing. Dewey chooses the words "world" and "environment" to designate the indefinitely extended spatiotemporal matrix in which experience is formed of focus and context.

But experience in this impoverished sense does not constitute *an* experience in the full and honorific sense of the word. This is so because such experiences have not been the focus of a specialized type of attention that Dewey calls "cognitional interest." He puts this somewhat differently in *Art as Experience*: "Things are experienced but not in such a way that they are composed into *an* experience. There is distraction and dispersion; what we observe and what we think, what we desire and what we get, are at odds with each other. We put our hands to the plow and turn back; we start and then we stop, not because the experience has reached the end for the sake of which it was initiated but because of extraneous interruptions or of inner lethargy" (LW10:42;AE:35).

Experience in this sense is only something "experienced." There is something "undergone," but there is no active knowing, because there is no significance. There is no "taking of some things as representative of other things" (MW10:322;EEL:4).

Such experiencings, which Dewey terms "affectional," "aesthetic," "social," and even "technological,"[6] do not require active responses so long as they remain unproblematic. They are simply undergone and enjoyed. They may have traits and elements that are isolable as the result of previous inquiries, but they themselves do not call for further inquiry.

But it is a fact of human life that such situations sometimes call for responses that cannot be simultaneously undertaken or that give rise to other incompatibilities. When such conditions arise, when a situation is tense and unresolved, and something is the matter, reflection or cognitional interest becomes its dominant trait.

In Dewey's analysis, "reflection" means not only a careful inspection of the traits of the problematic situation with an aim to its resolution, but also an actual *going outside* the immediate situation "to something else to get a leverage for understanding it" (MW10:327;EEL:12). There is a search for a *tool* with which to operate on the unsettled situation. The tool becomes a part of the active productive skill brought to bear on the situation. The purpose of the tool is to reorganize the experience in some way that will overcome its disparity, its incompatibility, or its inconsistency.

A tool is in this sense a theory, a proposal, a recommended method or course of action. It is only a proposal and not a solution per se because it must be tested against the problematic material for the sake of which it has been created or selected. Some tools are not appropriate to the settlement of a particular situation, but may be forced upon it in any case. Sometimes, for example, attempts are made to resolve existential difficulties by means of appeals to "authority, imitation, caprice and ignorance, prejudice and passion" (LW1:326;EN:353). In such cases, inquiry is not brought to a successful close, even though it may cease for a time because of frustration or indolence.

Tools may also be used in ways that are not primarily inquirential. They may, for example, take part in responses that are largely habitual in the sense of being routine or mechanical. Though the example is not Dewey's own, the repair of a light switch may serve to illustrate Dewey's point. A faulty light switch is a problematic situation that requires attention. To an experienced electrician, however, the use of the proper tools to effect its repair may be an experience that has been so often repeated that it is just a "technological" experience, in the trivial sense in which Dewey groups that experience with ones that are "affectional" and "social," but not in the sense in which he associates technology with inquiry.

The experience of repairing the switch hangs together by means of certain qualities, but those qualities are not the subject of inquiry. An electrician may carry on a spirited conversation about baseball with his assistant as he locates the trouble and repairs the switch. To someone not accustomed to such matters, however, what is habitually done by an experienced electrician may constitute a dangerous situation. It may call for reference to a home-repair manual or advice from friends who are more knowledgeable; a trip to the hardware store to purchase a circuit tester; a search for a mislaid screwdriver; the implementation of a plan of action that will render the circuit safe to work on; and perhaps even the reactivation of certain dormant motor skills, such as those associated with the use of a screwdriver or pliers.

Dewey says that the manner in which we judge the appropriateness of our chosen tools is by means of their concrete and overt application to the specific problematic situations for which they have been chosen. They do not stand apart from a situation, but enter into it. Tools are tested against a set of resistant circumstances, and the circumstances are tested against the tools. A screwdriver may be too large, judged in terms of the circumstances. The indicator light on a circuit tester may fail to come on, signifying either that the circuit has no electrical current or that the indicator light no longer functions and needs to be replaced. A circuit is checked by means of a circuit tester, and a circuit tester is checked by means of another circuit that is patently live and unproblematic. If the situation is resolved, the tool, the proposal, has performed satisfactorily with respect to the other circumstances. That particular process of inquiry ceases.

Knowing in the "honorific" sense of the term has been pro-duced, led to, as the result of inquiry. Productive skill has ceased to be active because it is no longer required. The unproblematic situation can now be enjoyed as a kind of consummation, as well as in terms of new extrinsic and intrinsic meanings to which it gives rise.

The simple scenario I have sketched illustrates another feature of Dewey's treatment of the role of tools in inquiry. He thought it unproductive and misleading to talk about the "essences" of tools, suggesting instead that they should be considered in functional terms. A particular object may be a tool in one situation and not in another. Something becomes a tool only when it is used to do some kind of work.

It is possible to isolate in the previous example several types and levels of tools, as well as several levels of functions performed. Plans of action at their various levels are tools, as is the hardware utilized in their realization. The problematic light switch may itself be a tool, as may the circuit tester used to probe it. The unproblematic circuit by which the circuit tester is itself tested may likewise become a tool, as may the fingers used to change the defective light in the circuit tester, and the various plans and subplans that direct the stages of the repair.

Dewey was by no means reluctant to count cases such as the successful repair of a light switch under the conditions I have just described as knowing in an honorific sense. Knowing that a circuit tester is not functioning properly is no less honorific than the resolution of a complex problem in crystallographic research or in the successful completion of a difficult mathematical problem, although its concerns are concentrated upon different materials, and its requirements and results are less precise. The consequences of resolving the electrical problem may be fewer, but they are not thereby less important than the consequences of the resolved mathematical problem. Failure to resolve the electrical problem may under certain circumstances be life-threatening.

The importance of this aspect of Dewey's account of technology— active productive inquiry—cannot be stressed too heavily. Productive inquiry is relative to an individual in a concrete situation. It is impossible to say absolutely of a particular situation, such as the repair of a light switch, that it does or does not require inquiry. Seen only from the standpoint of an accomplished goal, a task has been brought to completion: a light switch has been repaired. Seen from the standpoint of the total situation, however, an accomplished electrician has behaved according to well-established routine or a novice has engaged in an important learning experience, or what has transpired is something between these extremes.

III

I have already indicated that Dewey treated his critique of technology as more than simply an area of applied philosophy. His inquiry into the empirical features of technology provided him with the means to re-examine dominant themes within the history of philosophy and to utilize the results of that research to sharpen his reconstruction of technology. Several important consequences follow from Dewey's application of this tool-using—or, as Dewey terms it, "instrumentalist"—account of inquiry to traditional epistemological and metaphysical positions.

First, it no longer makes sense to speak of a distinction between the "real" and the "apparent" as philosophers have often done, that is, in wholesale or global terms. Plato, for example, spoke of the senses as yielding only apparent knowledge. His view was that it is the function of reason to establish contact with the "real." But what is real and what is apparent in Dewey's account are determined only with reference to specific inquiries mounted within the context of concrete situations. What is real on Dewey's account is whatever has effects; that is, whatever points beyond itself because it is meaningful or significant. Electrical current is thus prima facie no more or less real than a pair of pliers or the Pythagorean theorem. The issue is for Dewey one of actual significance in specific situations.

This in turn has further consequences for metaphysics as that discipline has been understood from the time of the Greeks to the time of the idealists, who were the dominant force within professional philosophy during the early portion of Dewey's career. Dewey's early work exhibits a rejection of Aristotelian essentialism, as well as a turn away from the Hegelian objective idealism he espoused during the first few years of his career. By the time of his middle period, in

Reconstruction in Philosophy, for example, Dewey's references to metaphysics were largely pejorative. He wrote disparagingly of the metaphysical systems of the Greeks and the scholastics because of their reliance on the supernatural. He criticized the metaphysical systems of modern rationalists such as Descartes, empiricists such as Hume, and objective idealists such as Hegel because their conclusions were not amenable to tests, or what he called experimental "checks and cues."

But in his later works Dewey wrote of metaphysics with greater approval. He used the term to designate a kind of taking into account the generic traits of the existential world in which we live, a world that includes not only the situations in which we "find" ourselves, but also the means and instruments that we utilize to alter these situations and accommodate ourselves to them.

Such taking into account, or criticism, is in Dewey's view a kind of inquiry, and hence a special type of production. What is produced is a kind of map of the province of criticism. Hence, metaphysics is for Dewey unproductive unless it is instrumental; that is, unless it produces something testable, as a map is testable. Wherever metaphysics is treated as an instrument rather than as a set of dogmas, Dewey thought that it involves a special type of production, a special type of technology.

Inquiry with respect to a specific electrical circuit (an example of technology in its quotidian sense), inquiry into the established and public features of electrical theory (an example of science), inquiry into inquiry (logic), and inquiry into the generic traits of experience (metaphysics)— each of these activities is for Dewey a form of pro-duction and con-struction, a form of leading to and drawing together. Each requires the use of instruments for its articulation and advancement, and each is dependent upon experimental checks and cues in order to generate new meanings and new significance.

Since active productive inquiry is everywhere tied either directly or genetically to the existential, it follows that the kind of "armchair" inquiry that has been a central feature of the history of philosophy, and that was practiced perhaps most conspicuously by Descartes, is from the instrumentalist viewpoint inconsequential in the literal sense of that word. Dewey thought that such inquiry had a fatal defect: it did not begin with real doubt, and so tended toward speculation about matters that were not a part of anyone's experience. Since there was no problem, no "resistance" against which to test proposed solutions, it was not possible, save by accident, to produce concrete, testable consequences.

Further (and this is a matter to which I shall return in more detail), Dewey's instrumentalist account of knowledge-getting cuts across the "inner-versus-outer" or "mind-versus-body" prejudices that have been part of metaphysics since the time of Plato. Screwdrivers, X-ray machines, and mathematical concepts such as the square root of -1 are, from the standpoint of Dewey's technologized theory of inquiry, the same: they are instruments that may be used to resolve problematic situations. For the purposes of inquiry, the distinction that Dewey thinks relevant is not between body and mind, or even between inner and outer, but between what is immanent and natural (and therefore significant and testable) and what is transcendent and supernatural (and therefore for which there are no checks or cues).

It should also be noted that Dewey's treatment of visual perception and visual metaphors is quite different from those of his predecessors. Descartes, for example, in rule 12 of the *Rules for the Direction of the Mind* treats vision as a passive conduit that is sensate only when being acted upon. (In his account, external nature is active; human perception, passive.) He extends this metaphor in the third of his *Meditations*, where he turns once again to the visual metaphors clarity and distinctness as criteria of truth. Sight operates for Descartes in a fashion that may be called "linear," insofar as it establishes a point-to-point conductance of information from its orifice to the common sense and to the mind. For Dewey, however, vision "handles" its objects; it is "nonlinear." It is not inert and passive, but active and exploratory. The image of vision that Dewey presents is not that of a ray entering the eye from an object, but rather that of a probing tool that moves and checks and interacts.

Sidney Hook understood this aspect of Dewey's instrumentalism, and he drew attention to it in *The Metaphysics of Pragmatism*. "We use our eyes as we do our hands—to grope, to pry, to scan, to escape danger, to signal to a friend," he wrote. "Sense activity, like all behavior generally, is not inertly receptive in the presence of stimuli or explosively active in their absence. It is *interactive*."[7] But Dewey was also aware, long before the notion became popularized by Marshall McLuhan in the 1960s, that even though the eye is active, the ear is even more so. "The connections of the ear with vital and out-going thought and emotion are immensely closer and more varied than those of the eye. Vision is a spectator; hearing is a participator" (LW2:371;PP:218–19). Dewey also anticipated in 1896 what was to become McLuhan's famous assertion that different matrices of technological artifacts establish distinctive "sense ratios." In his essay "The Reflex Arc Concept in Psychology," he argued that "as the ear activity has been evolved on account of the advantage gained by the whole organism, it must stand in the strictest histological and physiological connection with the eye, or hand, or leg, or whatever other organ has been the overt centre of action. It is absolutely impossible to think of the eye centre as monopolizing consciousness and the ear apparatus as wholly quiescent. What happens is a certain relative prominence and subsidence as between the various organs which maintain the organic equilibrium" (EW5:101).

IV

Dewey also warned against treating inquiry as subjective and, more specifically, against interpreting his instrumental account of it in such terms. "It had not occurred to me," he wrote in his preface to the 1916 *Essays*, "that the history by which human ignorance, error, dogma, and superstition had been transformed, even in its present degree of transformation, into knowledge was something which had gone on exclusively inside of men's heads, or in an inner consciousness. I thought of it as something going on in the world, in the observatory and the laboratory, and in the application of laboratory results to the control of human health, well-being, and progress" (MW10:361;EEL:66).

His characterization of the kinds of tools available to be brought to bear on problematic situations is consummately tactile, public, and observable. The list includes hands, feet, and apparatus and appliances of all kinds, as well as organic changes in the brain. He describes his instrumental tests as the activities that take place in "the public out-of-doors world of nature and human companionship" (MW10:361;EEL:67). Though the proposals of theoretical mathematicians are not as palpable as the heavy equipment developed to launch a spacecraft, they are subject to the same public demands of tests conducted within human communities.

In distinguishing between experience that is just undergone and experience into which inquiry has entered, Dewey was utilizing a distinction made by William James, but going beyond it. Following the distinction between types of knowing present in Greek, as well as in most Romance and Germanic languages, James had distinguished between "knowledge of acquaintance" (*noscere, kennen, conocer*) and "knowledge about" (*scire, wissen, saber*). His examples of the former are knowledge of the color blue when it is seen and knowledge of the flavor of a pear when it is tasted. Since this type of knowledge is primarily a matter of feeling, James suggested, it is not possible to describe the objects of this kind of knowledge as long as they remain in that state. "Knowledge about," on the other hand, is knowledge that is the result of thought and analysis. And the more analysis is undertaken, the more relations we are able to perceive and to develop, the more of this type of knowledge we have. But James also indicated that these two types of knowledge are relative to one another. "The same thought of a thing may be called knowledge-about it in comparison with a simpler thought, or acquaintance with it in comparison with a thought of it that is more articulate and explicit still."[8]

However, in 1890, when he published the *Principles*, James was still using the Aristotelian language of substance and accident: "The grammatical sentence expresses this. Its 'subject' stands for an object of acquaintance which, by the addition of the predicate, is to get something known about it."[9] James's account stands in stark contrast to Dewey's non-Aristotelian technologized or instrumental account of the proposition as he stated it in its mature form in his 1938 *Logic*:

> The traditional theory in both its empiricistic and rationalistic forms amounts to holding that all propositions are purely declaratory or enunciative of what antecedently exists or subsists, and that this declarative office is complete and final in itself. The position here taken holds, on the contrary, that declarative propositions, whether of facts or of conceptions (principles and laws) are intermediary means or instruments (respectively material and procedural) of effecting that controlled transformation of subject-matter which is the end-in-view (and final goal) of all declarative affirmations and negations . . . . All controlled inquiry and all institution of grounded assertion necessarily contains a *practical* factor; an activity of doing and making which reshapes antecedent existential material. (LW12:162;LTI:160)

Though there are superficial similarities in the two accounts, only in Dewey's is there an attention to the active productive skill that is capable of transforming a situation. Dewey's language is technological: there is no simple taking of this and putting it with that, but an active *reshaping* of "antecedent existential material," as a woodworker would reshape raw materials into a finished artifact.

Dewey argues that even in the case of knowledge by acquaintance there is evidence that considerable work has been done. He suggests that to call this type of knowledge "immediate apprehension" or "direct knowledge" is a mistake. It is evidence of prior activity of productive skill. It "represents a critical skill, a certainty of response which has accrued in consequence of reflection" (MW10:329;EEL:16) previously undertaken, or even perhaps found as an instinct or habit bequeathed by forebears.

Another way of distinguishing between these two senses of knowledge is to say that knowledge that is the outcome of properly controlled inquiry is richer in terms of its "meanings," its "significance," its "value." These terms are, however, ambiguous. A thing may have significance in terms of its function as a sign of something further, in which event its meaning or significance is said to be extrinsic. Or it may have meaning that is inherent in it, "a quality intrinsically characterizing the thing experienced and making it worth while" (MW10:330;EEL:18). When reflection is underway, extrinsic meaning, instrumentality, is primary. The meaning of the height of a column of mercury in a barometer, for example, points beyond itself. It serves as an instrument to indicate atmospheric conditions of a particular sort. Following reflection, however, meanings become intrinsic, that is, they lose their instrumental value. The primary meaning of the brightly polished brass barometer is then intrinsic as, say, an aesthetic object. Its meaning doesn't *do* anything; it just is.

Dewey cautions against attempting to compartmentalize these two kinds of meanings. There is a continual passing back and forth in

consciousness between them; each has some of the flavor of the other.
"Knowing as a business, inquiry and invention as enterprises, as
practical acts, become themselves charged with the meaning of what
they accomplish as *their* own immediate quality. There exists no
disjunction between aesthetic qualities which are final yet idle, and acts
which are practical or instrumental. The latter have their own delights
and sorrows" (MW10:330).

V

Interesting debates have emerged regarding the status of these two
kinds of experience and their relationship to each other within Dewey's
wider philosophy. In one camp there are those, such as Richard
Bernstein and Webster Hood, who read Dewey as a forerunner of
phenomenological analysis. According to this view, as Bernstein
articulates it, Dewey "consciously rejected the interpretation of
experience as primarily a knowledge-affair. There is more to experience
than knowing. Furthermore, knowing, as systematic inquiry, can be
properly described only when we appreciate its function within the larger
context of experience."[10]

Bernstein supports his thesis by quoting a passage from Dewey's
essay "The Need for a Recovery of Philosophy," published in 1917. "In
the orthodox view, experience is regarded primarily as a knowledge-
affair. But to eyes not looking through ancient spectacles, it assuredly
appears as an affair of the intercourse of a living being with its physical
and social environment" (MW 10:6).[11]

Bernstein's intent is clear. He is anxious to contrast Dewey with
those philosophers of the past, both empiricist and rationalist, who
made knowledge the paradigm for every experience. Bernstein thinks
that Dewey's emphasis was on experience as "lived." But while this is
an excellent starting point, I believe that it fails to take into account the
pervasiveness of what I have called "production" within all experience
that Dewey regards as vital. It fails to place sufficient emphasis on
Dewey's view that inquiry of one sort or another is present everywhere
in human experience at its best, and consequently that human
experience is evaluated by and grows as a result of the application of
skills and tools.

In the same paragraph from which Bernstein draws his quotation,
Dewey made it clear that his reference in that material was to
knowledge regarded as final and complete, what he also called
"epistemic" knowledge. It is to this kind of knowledge that he contrasts
knowledge that he elsewhere called "honorific" and that he here calls
"vital." In Dewey's view, "experience in its vital form is experimental, an
effort to change the given; it is characterized by projection, by reaching
forward into the unknown; connexion with a future is its salient trait."
Furthermore, "experience, taken free of the restrictions imposed by the

older concept, is full of inference. There is, apparently, no conscious experience without inference; reflection is native and constant" (MW10:6).

For his part, Webster Hood suggests that Dewey's instrumentalism was a kind of incomplete phenomenology, one that needs to be brought to fruition by recourse to an empiricism more thoroughgoing than Dewey's own. He proposes to "clarify and develop his ideas on technology from a phenomenological perspective, which . . . requires a more comprehensive empiricism than Dewey's instrumentalism permits." Hood suggests that "such an effort is quite in keeping with the central thrust of [Dewey's] philosophy, since, for Dewey, the goal of any philosophic investigation is one of elucidating and reconstructing the texture and significance of lived experience."[12] By "phenomenology" Hood understands "looking for and hopefully finding invariant or structural features in . . . experience."[13]

In the course of his phenomenological investigations Hood finds important "structural aspects" and "common patterns" beneath the surface of Dewey's treatment of technology: they include what he calls "technics as transactional mediators, organizers of perception, and platforms for experience."[14] Hood's common patterns not only offer considerable insight into technological experience, but also provide valuable tools for understanding Dewey's critique of such experience.

But how are such common patterns arrived at? Hood tells us that "we would want the product of inquiry to afford a new and decisive way of seeing technology, opening *new avenues* for reflection as well as effecting an intellectual transformation of the ways we *had seen* technology. There is an important distinction between seeing something new, according to tried and true categories, and a new way of seeing, *i.e.*, one in which our categories are transformed and replaced by the metamorphosis of our whole mental landscape."[15]

What Hood has in fact described in this passage is considerably more complex than "looking and finding"; in fact, the method he proposes fits well within the scope of what Dewey described as the pattern of instrumental inquiry. Insofar as Hood's phenomenological program with respect to technological experience is to be productive of knowledge that is valuable, it fits the instrumentalist pattern of inquiry developed by Dewey. It is not more or less empirical than Dewey's own method, since it falls well within the bounds of that method.

John J. McDermott has also contributed to this debate. McDermott's approach appears at first to be close to that of Bernstein and Hood. *The Structure of Experience* and *The Lived Experience* are the titles he chose for the two volumes of selections from Dewey's work that he edited and for which he wrote critical analyses. We could rightly conclude, he suggests,

that the search for the structure of experience *is* the lived experience. Thus for Dewey, in the most fundamental sense, philosophy deals with experience which is "had"—that is, undergone, lived. Yet, in functional terms, in this case the pedagogy of presentation, a difference does obtain between Dewey's writings on the meaning of experience and his writings on those specific clusterings of experiences which constitute problematic situations for man such that they elicit direction and possible resolution. Dewey's writings, then, on politics, the arts, society, education, and religion are not to be construed as merely applications of principles derived from his metaphysics. Rather, these writings should be seen as working from a change in venue, sensitized to the qualities of new data and new patterns of organization but nonetheless faithful to the experimental mode of inquiry, which runs consistently throughout all of his work. The "structure of experience" and "the lived experience" represent two contexts from which Dewey proceeds to articulate the nature of the human endeavor.[16]

McDermott's claim that there are two contexts from which Dewey operates is both undeniable and relevant. But it is equally clear that the one that is more purely aesthetic has been given meaning and is sharpened by the one that is more inquirentially productive. McDermott is not only aware of this fact, but also acknowledges it in his remarks on Dewey's reconstruction of the term "meaning." "The meaning *of* the world is inseparable from our *meaning* the world. Experience, therefore, is not headless, for it teems with relational leads, inferences, implications, comparisons, retrospections, directions, warnings, and so on."[17]

Meanings are for Dewey the artifacts of inquiry at one or more of its levels of complexity and precision, and whether they are at rest in experience that is aesthetic or whether they are undergoing active generative transformation in productive inquiry, meanings constitute what is important in human experience.

Ralph Sleeper is perhaps closer to McDermott's position than he realizes or is willing to admit, although the language he chooses to describe Dewey's position pays more heed to Dewey's interest in science and the philosophy of language than does McDermott's. For Sleeper, Dewey's vocabulary "is not phenomenological at all, but naturalistic. Accordingly, his approach to language is logical, rather than phenomenological. Dewey's phrase 'the logic of experience,' introduced in the 1903 *Essays*, is an indication that Dewey was already trying to work out a theory of language that would link it more closely with the vocabulary of natural science than with that of phenomenological discourse."[18]

In Sleeper's view, it was Dewey's task to show that his theory of inquiry, his logic, had its genesis in and was modeled on inquiry in experimental—that is to say, technological—science. Experimental science, in turn, was presented as continuous with existential inquiry of a more quotidian variety, from which it sprang and on which it in its turn was modeled.

VI

Another ongoing debate among Dewey's interpreters regards his position on the status of the objects of inquiry. Did he hold some variety of realism, namely that objects and events in the world exist independently of and prior to our knowledge of them? Or did he maintain some variety of idealism, that the world is somehow constituted by our knowledge of it?

It was one of Dewey's primary tasks in his 1916 Essays *to reject both realism and idealism.* Even though this point is a matter of considerable importance to understanding his larger account of inquiry, there is ample evidence that it has been almost universally misunderstood. Dewey has been interpreted as both a realist[19] and an idealist.[20] Yet if his 1916 *Essays* are read as a contribution to a critique of technology—that is, if Dewey regarded inquiry in its several levels of complexity and precision as levels of complexity and precision with respect to production, construction, and the choice and use of tools, as I suggest that he did—then Dewey was neither idealist nor realist. He instead set forth and developed a view that has a unique position between these extremes. At first he called that view "instrumentalism," later "experimentalism," and finally "technology."

An important clue to understanding Dewey's position in this matter can be found in the opening sentence of his introduction to the 1916 *Essays*: "The key to understanding the doctrine of the essays which are herewith reprinted lies in the passages regarding the temporal development of experience" (MW10:320;EEL:1).[21]

Most of Dewey's predecessors and contemporaries dealt with time by spatializing it in some way or else by treating it as discontinuous. Realists argued for an eternal present of irreducible objects such as "sense data" (or else the complete objects of the naive realists), and idealists reified the "history" of the working of "absolute" or "transempirical" thought. The former presented a metaphysics of a static "now"; the latter, a metaphysics of spirals and circles that tended to render time, in the sense that Dewey understood it—as a matter of events and an "affair of affairs"—unreal.

Dewey departed from both idealistic and realistic spatializations of time by "naturalizing" it. His inspiration and direction for this project were drawn from the functional psychology of William James and the evolutionary biology of Charles Darwin, as well as from the genetic psychology of his teacher G. Stanley Hall.[22] James likened consciousness to a stream or flow and drew attention to its two predominant features: its perches and its flights. Darwin offered what Dewey was to call a true Copernican revolution with respect to time: human life was made continuous in time with the rest of nature, and the idea of eternally fixed species gave way to the idea of temporal organisms caught up in the continual changes required of them in order that they might come to terms with their respective (and continually changing) environments. Hall argued, almost uniquely among American psychologists of his time, that the key to understanding the functioning adult organism is studying of the development of children.

Structure as reconstructed by Dewey became an enduring form of change; inquiry was characterized as linking past and future; and active productive skill can and does, according to his view, make a difference in the world. In Bertrand Helm's felicitous characterization of Dewey's insight, "form is seen as coherent process, and coherent process is seen as rhythmic endurance."[23] Though novel during Dewey's early period, this view came to be a familiar one to analytic philosophers during the 1960s, chiefly due to W. V. Quine's somewhat attenuated version of it as presented in his essay "Ontological Relativity."[24]

VII

The consequences for his analysis of realism and idealism of Dewey's novel account of time can perhaps be made more perspicuous by further consideration of the type of experience he took to be relatively antecedent to inquiry. Such experience is not of "primitive sense data," or sensory shapes, expanses, and colors, the entities beloved as epistemological starting points by many "realist" philosophers and psychologists. These "primitives" are already much more organized than the experiences of such data could be. Moreover, the experience of such data, when it serves any function at all in thinking, is the result of analysis of experience, not primitive in it.

A moment's reflection renders Dewey's point obvious: sensory expanses and colors as discrete objects of knowledge conclude thinking, rather than preceding or initiating it. This is to say, as Dewey does in chapters 2 and 3 of his 1938 *Logic*, that inquiry arises out of natural and cultural matrices *already formed*, situations already made definite and complex by the adaptation of organisms in their respective environments in such a way that those situations have already been rendered richer and more complex than are "sense data."

In his 1885 article "The Function of Cognition," and again in his formidable and momentous *Principles of Psychology* in 1890, William James had already sharply rejected as insufficiently empirical the view that thinking begins with pure sensations, or "qualia." It is not only the case, he argued, that no one ever had a simple sensation by itself,[25] but furthermore that such simple sensations couldn't exist, since "without context or environment . . . such a quality . . . would be indiscernible, and no sign could be given, no result altered."[26] Dewey implicitly accepts this account.

Dewey seems to say that there is a remarkable arrogance in the attitude of a philosopher or psychologist who believes that he or she can bracket millions of years of biological development from primitive to complex organisms, and hundreds of thousands of years of human cultural development, in order to go back to primitive sensations unqualified by the problems our nonhuman and human ancestors have struggled over and then bequeathed to us as solutions that form the very context in which we find ourselves in the world. The fact is that they have done work, and we are the better for it.

But neither are these nonreflective experiences the "determinations of thought pure and undefiled" (MW2:334;SLT:45;EEL:131), that is, the products of "absolute thought" held dear by many of the idealists of Dewey's early period. The idealist solution to the question of the nature of our nonreflective experiences and how we happen to find ourselves in the world in the ways that we do was that yes, thinking has already been done, but it has been the work of some absolute universal "thought," "mind," or "spirit" that "unconsciously to our reflection, builds up an organized world" (MW2:334;SLT:45;EEL:131)

Dewey rejected this family of views on two grounds. First, they involve complex and cumbersome metaphysical stances that are for the most part *ad hoc* to the solution of just this problem, and therefore expendable, given the less complex, more naturalistic account that he offers. In other words, he applies Ockham's razor—that is, Ockham's admonition that we should avoid multiplying entities beyond necessity. Second, he wonders why, on the idealist account, your and my inquiry should even be necessary. "How does it happen that the absolute . . . Thought does such a poor and bungling job that it requires a finite discursive activity to patch up its products?" (MW2:334;SLT:45;EEL:131). And if it be answered that the absolute is just working under the "limiting conditions of finitude, of a sensitive and temporal organism" (MW2:334;SLT:45;EEL:131), an even larger difficulty surfaces—namely, why would it constrain itself so by submitting itself to the difficulties, disturbing situations, and alien conditions that it would find in the thought activities of human beings?

These arguments were of course mounted against the views of the idealists who dominated much of late-nineteenth-century philosophy in America and whose influence was still strong at the time that Dewey published his 1903 *Studies*. Even though those views are not very fashionable among philosophers of our own time, and even though they had to a great extent gone out of fashion by the time of his 1916 *Essays*, Dewey's response to them still has relevance. Positions assumed by the idealists of Dewey's time are remarkably similar to some of those now held by members of various politically active fundamentalist religious groups. Contemporary assaults on the remnants of Dewey's educational programs provide an interesting example.[27] It is the view of many fundamentalist Christians that the context of experience in which we begin inquiry is just "given" us by a supernatural or transempirical deity. This view lays itself open to the same criticisms that Dewey advanced in 1903 against the idealists of his time.

It is significant that in 1903 Dewey's attack on idealism already was couched in technological terms. He was willing to admit that idealism has been a powerful source of insights into the activities of reflective thought. But its failure, he argued, was that it built a system that was nonnaturalistic and self-contained (as are most current fideistic systems), and that it ignored the "control of the environment in behalf of human progress and well being, the effort at control being stimulated by the needs, the defects, the troubles, which accrue when the environment coerces and suppresses man or when man endeavors in ignorance to override the environment" (MW10:333;EEL:22).[28]

This is tantamount to saying that idealism, in both its secular and religious forms, fails because it, unlike the application of productive intelligence, fails to take time temporally. Idealism was initially formulated to treat of the work of intelligence in our physical and social world, but this is precisely what it has failed to do because of its lack of concern with the concrete activities of men and women in specific situations, engaged in solving problems by instituting appropriate changes in real time. By just announcing that everything is rational (or, in its fundamentalist version, under the control of God), idealism effectively contends that productive skills—that is, the work of concrete, practical, temporal intelligence—is superfluous.[29]

Even though the antitechnological philosophical idealism popular during the early portion of Dewey's career is no longer widely held among professional philosophers, it has nevertheless taken a popular form in our own time. A favorite target of fundamentalists has been "secular humanism," which they condemn because of its view that appropriate control of human environments is a human task that must take place in evolving, continuous, nonteleologically defined time. Dewey was familiar with the views of idealists of many stripes, including religious fundamentalists. Contemporary versions of the positions they held during his lifetime would, I suggest, have surprised him not at all.[30]

None of this should be taken to say that there is *nothing* temporal in idealism. Idealism is in fact based upon a split between the *real* world of Absolute Thought and the sense world that is inferior to it. And the job of Absolute Thought, whether Platonic idealism or idealism of the Hegelian variety, is precisely to take the inferior and inarticulate, and to render it superior and articulate. So there are in some sense an earlier and a later in the thought of the Absolute. The failure of idealism, its lack of ability to generate an account of how human environments are appropriately controlled (an account of productive skills), lies in its placement of instrumentality outside the sphere within which human beings use instruments, or within that sphere only secondarily and contingently. Rather than encouraging human beings to undertake instrumental control of their environments, idealists depict human beings as instruments for "thought" in some absolute (usually religious) sense.[31] Idealistic time, like all forms of salvation history, is not so much time, but space.

Besides the ones advanced by realists and idealists, there are many other candidates for the nonreflective experiences that are antecedent to our inquiry—in fact, far too many to be discussed here. What are Dewey's own candidates? If they are neither bare sense data nor structures organized by some God or Absolute Thinker, what are they? Dewey offers three excellent examples: the quenching of thirst, the enjoyment of conversation with friends, and the delight of looking at a painting (MW10:320–21;EEL:2). What do these experiences have in common? We can neither ask nor answer this question while we are engaged in the experiences themselves. We may do so only when we pass beyond them to reflect upon them.

When we do so, we can see that even though our prereflective experiences are many and varied, what James called a "stream of thought," they nevertheless exhibit certain pervasive qualities. They hang together in certain ways. An evening with friends may consist of many factors; but I may say in retrospect that it was pleasant, stimulating, or perhaps even boring. It is an experience undergone. The qualities that color these experiences, rendering their diverse elements in some sense or another summable, are direct. They are not the immediate result of inquiry.

As I have already indicated, each has what Dewey calls "focus and context." "Movement about an axis persists, but what is in focus constantly changes. 'Consciousness,' in other words, is only a very small and shifting portion of experience" (MW10:323;EEL:6). Dewey says that he prefers the word "experience" for these situations because words such as "world" and "environment" leave out something that experience includes, namely "an actual focusing of the world at one point in a focus of immediate shining apparency" (MW10:324;EEL:7).

Each of Dewey's examples of nonreflective experience—quenching a thirst, enjoying friends, delighting in a painting—is an experience at rest, rather than one that is tense and problematic. Each is an experience of something valued for its intrinsic worth. Each is a *noncognitive* experience of the type that most of us have most of the time. In none of them is it the case that inquiry gives the experience its particular flavor.

But if these experiences involve intrinsic worth and are at rest, why reflect on them in any case? The occasion of inquiry into this largely undifferentiated body of experiences, which constitutes the bulk of what goes on in our quotidian lives, is that sometimes out of these multiple focuses there arise incompatible factors: in short, a problem. And because they demand or indicate courses of action that cannot be undertaken simultaneously, the meaning of the whole situation becomes uncertain. It is at this stage that inquiry attempts to locate the problem and devise a method of solving it.

Dewey suggests that the account of inquiry advanced by Greek philosophers and scientists got this far, but no farther. They were aware of problems, and they offered formulations or theories regarding their solutions. What was lacking in their approach, however, was the use of instruments and relevant tools to put their solutions into practice, that is, to try them out.

It is not that the Greeks did not have instruments and apparatus: the work of Greek artisans was not only competent, but also served as stimulus for the rise of inquiry during the Renaissance. The problem was that the social status of Greek artisans was inferior to that of scientists and "thinkers"; and their methods could not, therefore, *for reasons that were purely and unfortunately social* (and hence external to inquiry proper) be used as part of scientific inquiry. So the Greeks pursued a version of science in which instrumentation was no more than peripheral, as well as a variety of philosophical inquiry that lacked adequate tests. Greek scientists and philosophers failed to do what their artisans, businessmen, and practical people knew had to be done to solve problems: they failed to test their conclusions by means of overt actions. In short, they had not so much science as "the idea" of science: their science was not technological.

Dewey thus both expanded the purpose of inquiry and changed the locus of knowledge as each had been traditionally conceived. Inquiry and its artifact knowing were in his view not just things going on inside the cortex, but instead events with which the entire organism and its extensions are involved. "Hands and feet, apparatus and appliances of all kinds are as much a part of it as changes in the brain. Since these physical operations (including the cerebral events) and equipments are a part of thinking, thinking is mental, not because of a peculiar stuff which enters into it or of peculiar non-natural activities which constitute it, but because of what physical acts and appliances *do*: the distinctive purpose for which they are employed and the distinctive results which they accomplish" (MW10:328;EEL:14).

While there may be good grounds elsewhere for distinguishing extra-organic tools from those that are interorganic—a hammer from a "therefore," for example—such a distinction is not appropriate to Dewey's technologized theory of inquiry. Controlled thinking is technological insofar as it utilizes tools and instruments: some of those tools are conceptual; some, physical; some, the hardware that extends our limbs and senses. For the purposes of Dewey's theory of inquiry, tools of all types come into play; where they are distinguished into various kinds, such distinctions are made chiefly in terms of the various materials on which they operate and to which they are appropriate, and of the degree of precision required for the task at hand.

VIII

Once a matter is settled to the satisfaction of the initial problem, once knowing is produced, another situation is entered into that may be described as "nonreflective" insofar as it remains unproblematic. But such situations tend to mature and may themselves become unstable. Dewey's metaphor is a sexual one in which new "life" is created. In discourse meanings "copulate and breed new meanings" (LW1:152;EN:160). When problems and difficulties arise in such situations, the process begins again, and this pattern continues as long as the reflective human being continues to function.

This settlement of a problematic situation by means of formulating a procedure, and testing it by means of instruments of various sorts in the context of the actual situation, is quite different from what philosophers have traditionally called "knowledge" (and what Dewey called "epistemic knowledge") not only in terms of its location, but also in terms of its degree of finality. Dewey was aware of this disparity: he admitted that his work constituted an open rebellion against the long philosophical and religious tradition that identifies knowledge with final certainty.

Dewey addressed this problem in his Gifford Lectures, published in 1929 as *The Quest for Certainty*. He there argued that the quest for certainty arises out of the precarious natural situations in which human beings find themselves. Experienced perils give rise to the desire for effective control, but the intervention of productive skill has usually been overlooked as a means of such control because its effects are partial and because it requires continuing engagement with situations that become newly problematic as conditions change. In the place of technological inquiry men and women have put forward rites, religions, and philosophies of immutable Truth, Goodness, and Beauty as putative means of control.

Candidates for certain, once-for-all knowledge have included Hume's "impressions passively received, forced upon us whether we will or no" and Kant's "synthetic activity of the intellect" (LW4:18;QC:22). They have included Plato's perfect, eternal, and immutable forms, and Hegel's Absolute Spirit. But what is lacking in each case is "any element of practical activity that enters into the construction of the object known" (LW4:18;QC:22). Dewey thought that this is as true of idealism as it is of realism, of Kant's synthetic epistemology as of Hume's realistic one. "For according to them 'mind' constructs the known object not in any observable way, or by means of practical overt acts having a temporal quality, but by some occult internal operation" (LW4:19;QC:22–23).

Against these traditional philosophical views Dewey proposes a "Copernican" revolution. Its meaning would be that the world of our experience is a real world, but a world that is in need of transformation in order to render it more coherent and more secure. Knowing an experienced world is instrumental to rearranging it and giving it a form that is more useful to our purposes. But knowing in this sense is not something done apart from the world: it takes place experimentally inside experienced situations. The difference between knowing and

other existential interactions is, in Dewey's terms, "not between
something going on within nature as a part of itself and something else
taking place outside it, but is that between a regulated course of
changes and an uncontrolled one. In knowledge, causes become means
and effects become consequences, and thereby things have meanings
(LW4:235–36;QC:295–96).

If knowing is for Dewey no longer located only inside the cortex,
and if it is no longer a matter of once-for-all certainty, but of partial and
ongoing attempts to engage in the appropriate and effective control of
problematic situations, neither is it an affair that can be "coextensive
with experienced existence." Problematic situations do not occur
everywhere in existence, and so knowledge is limited in yet another way
(LW4:236;QC:296). Dewey tells us that knowledge "attends strictly to its
own business," and there are areas of existence which neither ask to
be known nor "ask leave from thought to exist" (LW4:236;QC:296).

It was Dewey's view that even what philosophers have called
"immediate knowledge," "simple apprehension," and "knowledge by
acquaintance" are not knowledge in its honorific sense, but rather what
he calls "critical skills," which are, to be sure, the result of reflective
inquiry undertaken in the past but which do not function logically in the
present.

Dewey preferred to reserve the terms "knowing" and "knowledge"
for what he called "the outcome of competent and controlled inquiry"
(LW12:15;LTI:8). But inquiry is specific to a particular situation. One of
the most enduring philosophical mistakes, he argued, is the attempt to
separate knowledge from the practice that gives rise to it in each
particular situation. Of course, he was willing to talk of knowledge in the
abstract as what is generalizable from numerous competent inquiries
(LW12:16;LTI:8). But accepting the term in this way, it must be recalled
that inquiry is a continuing process, that it is never completely settled.
"The 'settlement' of a particular situation by a particular inquiry is no
guarantee that *that* settled conclusion will always remain settled"
(LW12:16;LTI:8). In his 1938 *Logic* Dewey suggested that perhaps
"warranted assertion" should be substituted for "knowledge" so that
this traditional mistake could be avoided.

Whatever it is called, the settlement of problematic situations "aims
at clothing things and events with meaning—at understanding them"
(LW8:226;HWT:138). What are these meanings? I have already alluded
to Dewey's view that meanings do not "stay put": they vary from group
to group, from time to time, and from place to place. Even when they
are maximally standardized they operate only as a function of inquiry
and not in any absolute sense. More specifically, a meaning is a
*representative function of a physical existent that is a component in a
language* (LW12:52;LTI:46). But what does Dewey take to be the
meaning of "language"?

A brief comparison with the theory of language set out in the later works of Wittgenstein can prove helpful in answering this question since, ironically, Wittgenstein's work is now better known in America than is Dewey's. In his 1925 *Experience and Nature*—some four years before Wittgenstein returned to Cambridge to begin the re-examination of his *Tractatus* that would lead him to an eventual rejection of its treatment of language, eight years before the Wittgenstein lectures that became the *Blue Book* and the *Brown Book*, and eleven years before Wittgenstein began work on the *Philosophical Investigations*—John Dewey presented a view of language that had most of the elements that would later form the core of Wittgenstein's renowned and, it was said, revolutionary treatment of that subject. A detailed comparison of these two accounts of language would require a major departure from the task at hand; nevertheless, the following points should be made.

First, Dewey had from at least 1916 a well-worked-out theory of the social and cultural aspects of language use, and in 1934 he specifically argued that there could be no "private language." As I have already indicated, his term "conjoint activities," though it does not have the charm of Wittgenstein's phrase "language game," expresses essentially the same content.

Second, from 1916 on Dewey argued against a "picture theory" of language, the theory that sentences are literally "pictures of reality." Wittgenstein advanced the "picture theory" in his *Tractatus* in 1922, and he explicitly renounced it in the opening pages of the *Philosophical Investigations*.

Third, what Wittgenstein turned to in the 1930s, when he gave up the "picture theory," was precisely a form of instrumentalism. "Sieh den Satz als Instrument an, und seinen Sinn als seine Verwendung!" ("Look at the sentence as an instrument, and at its sense as its employment!") he shouts in section 421 of the *Philosophical Investigations*.[32]

Fourth, even in the *Tractatus* Wittgenstein is moving toward positions already worked out by Dewey. In 1893 Dewey wrote an article entitled "The Superstition of Necessity" (EW4:19–36), in which he argued that belief in existential necessity was a superstition. In 1922 Wittgenstein wrote, "Der Glaube an den Kausalnexus ist der Aberglaube" ("The belief in the causal nexus is a superstition") (5:1361).[33]

Richard Rorty also saw the similarities between Dewey's instrumentalism and the turn taken by Wittgenstein's later work, although his manner of expressing this insight would be anachronistic if taken literally. "I want to argue," he wrote, "that the later Wittgenstein belongs with Dewey as much as the earlier Wittgenstein belongs with Kant—that Dewey's debunking of traditional notions of philosophy, and his attempt to break down the distinctions between art and science . . . are a *natural outcome* of Wittgenstein's critique of the Cartesian tradition."[34]

Language was for Dewey both broader and richer than it was for his philosophical predecessors. As they had, he included both oral and written speech as examples of the use of language, but he also included "not only gestures but rites, ceremonies, monuments and the products of industrial and fine arts. A tool or machine, for example, is not simply a simple or complex physical object having its own physical properties and effects, but is also a mode of language. For it *says* something, to those who understand it, about operations of use and their consequences" (LW 12:52;LTI:46).

Existent objects within a language get their meanings "in and by conjoint community of functional use" (and not, for example, because they "picture" reality). But functional use is an ongoing project, as is the process of development of any tool in use. The elements of language, including tools, have "operational" force. They function as "a means of evoking different activities performed by different persons so as to produce consequences that are shared by all the participants in the conjoint undertaking" (LW12:54;LTI:48). Meanings as fixed elements of discourse may be, and most often are, the objects of experimentations. Logical universals are said by Dewey to "copulate and breed new meanings. There is nothing surprising in the fact that dialectic (or deduction, as it is termed by moderns) generates new objects; that, in Kantian language, it is 'synthetic,' instead of merely explicating what is already had. All discourse, oral or written, which is more than a routine unrolling of vocal habits, says things that surprise the one that says them, often indeed more than they surprise any one else" (LW1:152;EN:160).

In order to render this point perspicuous, it should be recalled that Dewey distinguished between meanings that are extrinsic and those that are intrinsic. As I have indicated, extrinsic meaning or instrumentality is a primary feature of inquiry. In the context of inquiry, a working barometer signifies something. It is a scientific instrument. But if it ceases to function in the context of inquiry—perhaps because it is broken, or perhaps because its owner does not require its services or does not know how to read it—its meaning may become intrinsic. It is then cherished as an object of beauty or as a bearer of sentimental value.

It is in this way that many objects that formerly served as tools become antiques, that is, objects in which intrinsic meanings predominate. Churns, oil lamps, and ceramic washstands that once functioned as hard-working instruments lose their functions when supermarkets, electric lights, and modern plumbing fixtures take their places. They may then become prized as examples of "craftsmanship" or because of sentimental attachment.

IX

What Dewey thought significant about inquiry, and what he thought discloses its technological character, is that *every reflective experience is*

instrumental to further production of meanings, that is, it is technological.
In fact, this is doubly so. Reflective experiences, including both inter-
and extra-organic tools, are instruments used to gain effective control of
a problematic situation (MW10:330;EEL:17), and so have practical force;
but they are also instruments that make for the "enrichment of the
immediate significance of subsequent experiences" (MW10:330;EEL:17).
In other words, we use tools, whether extra- or inter-organic, to do
things in order to settle difficulties. But in doing so, we more often than
not find that the control we have exercised gives us more than we
bargained for, that there come to be added intrinsic meanings that we
could not have anticipated, and that those intrinsic meanings may be the
occasion for the construction of further extrinsic meanings.

A perfect example of this double instrumentality of reflective
experience may be found in Jean Gimpel's account in *The Medieval
Machine* of the development of the mechanical time-telling clock. The
first mechanical clocks, he points out, "did not primarily tell time, but
rather were built to forecast the movements of the sun, the moon, and
the planets. Remarkably enough, the time-telling clock which dominates
our lives was only a by-product of the astronomical clock."[35] This is a
story of technological inquiry that solved a specific problem and got, in
the bargain, something else intrinsic to it that was to become expressive
of novel and momentous significance. The astronomical clock, that is,
had unintended meanings that were eventually to become instrumental
to further inquiry, inquiry that would ultimately produce the ability to
divide the day into uniform hours. The original solution is now
antiquated, and models of the celestial clocks reside in the Smithsonian
Institution and elsewhere. But the by-product set the stage for further
inquiry that led to the modern time-keeping practices that are the basis
of industrial societies.

The principal reason for calling inquiry technological, then, is that it
is the means of effective control of an environment that is not what we
wish it to be. Inquiry is in this way differentiated from other forms of
activity. It produces something new as a means of changing situations
that are not what we wish them to be.

It is distinguished from primitive magic and religion, for example,
since even though there are in those activities attempts at control, such
attempts are normally less instrumental than they are aesthetic,
commemorative, and decorative. With respect to magic, Dewey submits
that "it was not conscience that kept men loyal to cults and rites, and
faithful to tribal myths. So far as it was not routine, it was enjoyment of
the drama of life without the latter's liabilities that kept piety from decay
. . . . When rite and myth are spontaneous rehearsal of the impact and
career of practical needs and doings, they must also seem to have
practical force" (LW1:70;EN:68). But, he continues, "reflected upon, this
phase of experience manifests objects which are final. The attitude
involved in their appreciation is esthetic" (LW1:70;EN:68).

In other words, primitive magic and religious practices fail to be inquiry precisely when and because their interest is focused on intrinsic meanings as final and not as productive of further significance: extrinsic meanings or instrumentalities are merely coincidental to such practices. They therefore reverse the pattern of effective technological inquiry.

Dewey realized that because of the claims of those who have practiced magic, any comprehensive critique of technology is obliged to take those claims into account. He was aware that magic had a close kinship to technology, since in magic meanings that are primarily intrinsic can be converted to those that are instrumental. But such instrumental meanings often remain recondite from the viewpoint of the public and its officials because they regard the meanings of magic as purely intrinsic. In such cases, instrumental meanings of the magical practice are shared only within a limited group whose members do not participate, for one reason or another, in a larger community.

It is in this sense, for example, that Marcilio Ficino could write of natural (as opposed to supernatural) magic as the technique of coming to terms with four powers: the power of words, the power of music, the power of images, and the power of things. Each of these categories of objects and events has, Ficino suggested, both a public and a recondite life. The power of images, for example, has its public life in the meaning and beauty of the visual arts, and its hidden life in the figures and characters of the talisman. Ficino's account of magic is thoroughly instrumental, thus thoroughly technological: he indicated the use of qualities or powers of things, public and private, to effect changes in himself, a function he called "subjective magic," and in others, which he termed "transitive magic."[36]

It is also in this sense of technology that E. William Monter wrote of the numerous "cunning folk" in Tudor-Stuart England who practiced a kind of magic that mixed pharmacologically effective remedies with verbal and other rituals.[37] His suggestion is that their activities were "unofficial and even plainly illegal, but [that] they were not necessarily fraudulent." They were illegal because in the view of the religious establishment of the time they constituted "freelancing." But they were not necessarily fraudulent in terms of their effect: they constituted a technological use of medicinally effective flora and fauna. They utilized natural materials as tools to produce changes in problematic and undesirable situations so as to render them more satisfactory.

Inquiry may be contrasted not only with magic but also with poetry in terms of technology; that is, in terms of the application of productive skills to the management of effective control. Whereas magic often is an alternative to inquiry in terms of its tendency to take intrinsic meanings for extrinsic ones (or, in the case that Ficino describes, to assure the authorities that this is all that is being done), much poetry does not so much seek effective control of this environment as it does the production of alternative ones: parallel universes of imagination. "The poetic . . . condenses and abbreviates," Dewey writes, "thus giving words an energy of expansion that is almost explosive. A poem presents material so that it becomes a universe in itself, one, which, even when it is a miniature whole, is not embryonic any more than it is labored through argumentation. There is something self-enclosed and self-limiting in a poem, and this self-sufficiency is the reason, as well as the harmony and rhythm of sounds, why poetry is, next to music, the most hypnotic of the arts" (LW10:246;AE:241).

Poetry is doubly instrumental: it produces linguistic artifacts that exhibit intrinsic richness, and it produces new and alternative universes of feeling. But it is less instrumental than scientific inquiry (though not by that fact "inferior" to it) in that it is productive of worlds of intrinsic meanings that do not, as do scientific meanings, allow for maximum substitutivity.

X

Several objections might be advanced against Dewey's characterization of inquiry as a technological activity. First, it might be said that there has been an unwarranted lumping of tools that are extra-organic with those that are interorganic, or even of those that are mental with those that are physical. It is in this vein that some philosophers of technology and some who seek to understand technology from the viewpoints of the social sciences prefer to retain the term "technology" to denote the use of tools and methods that are exclusively extra-organic or, respectively, physical.

Second, it might be objected that terming Dewey's characterization of inquiry "technological" is reductive: that there is not so much a "lumping together" of different types of tools as there is a reduction of the function of many tools to the function of one specific type of tool, the extra-organic. Put another way, this objection would be that the functions of interorganic tools have been assimilated to the roles played by those that are extra-organic.

Both of these objections presume the existence of a sharp line between organism and environment, or between body and mind. But it is precisely against these dualisms that Dewey's arguments were so numerous and effective. Anticipating by years the work of Maurice Merleau-Ponty, for example, he argued that any line drawn between organism and environment will have to be drawn elsewhere than in terms of inquiry. For purposes of inquiry, the skin is not a very good indicator of where the organism stops and the environment begins. "There are things inside the body that are foreign to it, and there are things outside of it that belong to it *de jure*, if not *de facto* . . . . On the lower scale, air and food materials are such things; on the higher, tools, whether the pen of the writer or the anvil of the blacksmith, utensils and furnishings, property, friends and institutions—all the supports and

sustenances without which a civilized life cannot be" (LW10:64–
65;AE:58–59).

Dewey does not shy away from referring to bodily motor skills as
"equipment," that is, tools. "To know what to look for and how to see it
is an affair of readiness on the part of motor equipment"
(LW10:103;AE:98).

Neither does inquiry allow a line to be drawn between body and
mind. The title Dewey chose for chapter 7 of *Experience and Nature*,
"Nature, Life and Body-Mind," specifically refuses to allow that
traditional split. His Darwinian naturalism is evident in his argument that
in nonhuman animals, activity is "psycho-physical, but not 'mental,' that
is, not aware of meanings" (LW1:198;EN2:11). The emergence of mind
among human beings is but a higher degree of organization, in which
interaction with other organisms is effected through language, which he
calls the "tool of tools" (LW1:134;EN:140). "Body" in "body-mind" just
designates the aspects of an organism that are "continuous with the
rest of nature," whereas "mind" indicates "the characters and
consequences which are differential, indicative of features which emerge
when 'body' is engaged in a wider, more complex and interdependent
situation" (LW1:217;EN:232).

To identify the technological exclusively with the activities of the
physical body or with extra-organic implements is for Dewey sheerest
nonsense, just as it would be to identify inquiry exclusively with mental
or interorganic activities and structures. The simple reason for this is
that the two are continuous and, for practical purposes, the same.
Dewey put this matter quite precisely in *Experience and Nature*:

> Because meanings and essences are not states of mind, because they are
> as independent of immediate sensation and imagery as are physical things,
> and because nevertheless they are not physical things, it is assumed that
> they are a peculiar kind of thing, termed metaphysical, or "logical" in a style
> which separates logic from nature. But there are many other things which
> are neither physical nor psychical existences, and which are demonstrably
> dependent upon human association and interaction. Such things function
> moreover in liberating and regulating subsequent human intercourse; their
> essence is their contribution to making that intercourse more significant and
> more immediately rewarding. (LW1:153;EN:162)

Dewey's examples are technological ones: traffic regulations,
corporations, and franchises.

XI

What, then, is Dewey's definition of "technology"? Dewey provides no
single definition of the term. As I have already indicated, he uses the
word to characterize various activities. But in at least one important

sense technology can be said to be the appropriate transformation of a problematic situation, undertaken by means of the instrumentalities of inquiry, whatever form those instrumentalities may take.

To put this another way, inquiry is a technological activity because where inquiry takes place there is a shift from passive acquiescence toward the beginnings and endings of nature, its contingencies, to the active construction of artifacts to effect their control. Immediate use and enjoyment give way to the production of consequences. When human beings were content to just enjoy fire or to think of it as the gift of the gods, there was no inquiry, no technology, no effective control of it. But when they began to *make* fire, they began to institute a "method of procedure" (LW1:181;EN:193). When such a change occurs, mere enjoyment of fire and consideration of its "whatness" is supplanted by a technological concern with the "how" of its production and use.

In one of his rare outright definitions, Dewey defined inquiry in terms of such control: "*Inquiry is the controlled or directed transformation of an indeterminate situation into one that is so determinate in its constituent distinctions and relations as to convert the elements of the original situation into a unified whole*" (LW12:108; LTI:104–105; emphasis in original). Further, he specified that "'controlled or directed' in the above formula refers to the fact that inquiry is competent in any given case in the degree in which the operations involved in it actually do terminate in the establishment of an objectively unified existential situation" (LW12:109;LT:105).

In chapter 4 of *The Quest for Certainty*, in a passage that identifies technological activity as one of the most basic of human enterprises, Dewey characterized the search for effective control as "a revolution in the whole spirit of life, in the entire attitude taken toward whatever is found in existence" (LW4:80;QC:100). There, he argued that the objects of our senses are more properly interrogations than final answers and that such interrogations offer the only adequate means of transforming the constraints of nature into facilities for the improvement of human life. Nature becomes "something to be modified, to be intentionally controlled. It is material to act upon so as to transform it into new objects which better answer our needs. Nature as it exists at any particular time is a challenge, rather than a completion; it provides possible starting points and opportunities rather than final ends" (LW4:80–81;QC:100).

When this occurs, "there is a change from knowing as an esthetic enjoyment of the properties of nature regarded as a work of divine art, to knowing as a means of secular control—that is, a method of purposefully introducing changes which will alter the direction of the course of events. Nature as it exists at a given time is material for arts to be brought to bear upon it to reshape it, rather than already a finished work of art . . . . The attitude of control looks to the future, to production" (LW4:80–81;QC:100–101).

Yet another objection to Dewey's identification of inquiry as a form of technological activity and his characterization of both as effective control by means of instruments might be advanced. It might be argued that inquiry is not technology, but science—that is, that Dewey has taken the scientific method, not technological production, as a model for his depiction of the process of successful inquiry. A full discussion of this point will have to await a later chapter on Dewey's treatment of the relations between science and technology. But for now, it can be suggested that this objection both hits and misses its mark.

It is on target insofar as Dewey does in fact suggest that science has been his model for inquiry and that the theory of inquiry, or logic, is a study of scientific method. His 1938 *Logic* presents an experimental logic, one that is "in accord with actual scientific practice" (LW12:389;LTI:392). Further, he claims that the logical material he there presents represents "the conclusions of analysis of the logical conditions and implications of scientific method" (LW12:390;LTI:392).

But such a criticism fails to hit its mark, in the sense that Dewey clearly held that *science was a branch of technology*. In 1946 he generously attributed to his disciple C. E. Ayres priority with respect to an insight that had in fact been a part of his own work since at least 1916, that "science [is] a mode of technology" (PM:291n).

In *The Industrial Economy*, published the year that Dewey died, Ayres wrote that technology is "the sum of human skills . . . " as well as "the sum of human tools."[38] But skill is tool behavior, and it always has been. Ayres chose a case of the most abstract of scientific skill-uses, the work of the mathematician, to make his point. Even though mathematical thinking is often done in the absence of tangible tools, the mathematician nevertheless uses abstractions and symbols that are just as much tools as are hammers or microscopes. Like other, tangible tools, they have been constructed as instrumental to certain purposes. Also like tangible tools, if they fail to serve, they are discarded or improved.[39]

Ayres correctly saw that Dewey's instrumental logic is "the purest description of the technological function. Scientists call 'instruments' what artisans call 'tools'; but functionally the two are identical."[40]

XII

I have already alluded to Dewey's presentation of his view of the relationship between "abstract" and "concrete" tools during a discussion of the nature of "logical entities" in his address to the Philosophical Club at Columbia University in 1916. He there argued that the objects of logic—the things referred to by words such as "if," "or," and "the number 2"—are not physical properties of things that we just grasp in some type of "rational apprehension." They do not exist "mentally," nor do they exist in some metaphysical realm that is neither physical nor mental. Instead, they are just tools. Like crutches, skates, and pedals, they are just things that formerly existed (in some sense, perhaps as raw materials) in nature and that have been reshaped so that we can more efficiently control the performances of certain tasks.

The same may be said of points that do not have extension and instants that do not have duration. Rather than partaking of some shadowy metaphysical existence, they are clear indications of work that has been done and of work that is to be done in controlling the progress of some specific inference. Like other tools, they are derived not *by* inference, but *from* inference—that is, they are introduced in the course of inference in the same way that agricultural tools are introduced in the course of agricultural practice (MW10:93–95).

Once again Dewey used Ockham's razor: appeals to mental entities, metaphysical entities, or abstract properties of things can be dispensed with because they are unnecessary. Logical entities are tools that arise out of the techniques of control. The inquiry that scientists and logicians undertake is a tool-using activity and, therefore, even in its most abstract phases, a form of practical productive skill.

Harry T. Costello was present at Columbia during the time that Dewey was developing and presenting this view of tools.[41] He recalls a 1918 meeting of an "informal philosophy group" at the Faculty Club at Columbia University. It was Dewey's turn to read a paper after lunch that day, and the topic was "Logical Entities as Inventions." He presented logical entities not as eternal perfections, but as invented tools. Costello gives this first-person account of the occasion:

> They were as much manufactured as automobiles. I remember I wanted to know whether they were made out of nothing, and if he thought we could postulate them in any way we pleased. "No more than an automobile, and no less," he replied. Automobiles in those days were even more unruly than now, and had to contend with roads that were two grooves for the wheels and a groove for the horse, with continuous raised mounds of gravel between. You took your monkey wrench along, and "get out and get under" was a regular part of motoring. I said, "Cars are made of steel and rubber that have ways of their own, but what are logical entities made of?" "Not nothing," he said, "but the materials of experience, refined and tested for a special use"—I quote approximately. Professor Montague wanted to know whether a pile of grain did not have a mathematical volume of so many bushels before we thought about it? Dewey replied he would grant a certain cubic volume, but the "bushel" was invented by men—in fact, that was a very good example. Kant seems to be saying "what we *make* we know through and through," but that is not so.[42]

For Dewey, reflective thinking or inquiry starts as "an effort to get out of some trouble, actual or menacing" (MW10:333;EEL:23). But unlike magic or poetry, which are not primarily technological, even though they may use technological artifacts and function instrumentally in special circumstances, it "inventories what is there"; and it invents, projects, and brings to bear on a particular situation what does not theretofore exist as a part of it.

XIII

Dewey was aware that some of his critics accused him of being a closet idealist because of his view that the "processes of reflective inquiry play a part in shaping the objects" (MW10:338;EEL:30) of inquiry, that is, scientific knowledge. Dewey meets this claim head on, freely admitting that in his view intelligence is not "otiose." He is willing to admit to a charge of idealism, but only insofar as it is "idealistic to hold that objects of knowledge *in their capacity of distinctive objects of knowledge* are determined by intelligence" (MW10:338;EEL:30). But he lists several ways in which his view is *not* idealistic.

First, thought is defined by "function, by work done, by consequences effected" (MW10:338;EEL:31). His view does not postulate a power already at work, except that the closings of natural events become structural features of an environment and thus have continuing effects. This does not require a "thinking spirit" beyond the actual activities of individual human beings in communication with one another. Thinking is what some of the actual, naturally occurring things in the world do. It is not that they are constituted by thinking so much as that the problems of thought are set by *their* difficulties and goals.

Second, the effects of thinking are existential. Experimentation ends in actual, not just ideal, alteration of a problematic situation. (Moreover, it is not the thinker who is problematic, nor some "reality" separate from the thinker, but the very "situation" that comprises a reflective organism in transaction with an environment.)

But neither is his instrumental view of inquiry "realistic." Unlike realism, it holds that experimentation is necessary to knowledge. What he calls "analytical realism," on the other hand, holds that "even though [experimentation] were essential in *getting* knowledge (or in learning), it has nothing to do with knowledge itself, and hence nothing to do with the known object" (MW10:339;EEL:32).

His quarrel with the realists was that they, as Greek scientists and philosophers had been, seemed satisfied to accept the objects of knowledge as something to be "mirrored." Even when the scientist working in his laboratory brings to completion a long process of theorizing about, say, something to do with tin, rendering his results in the form of terms and propositions, he is not contemplating tin so much as describing a series of events that will happen under certain circumstances, when certain instrumentalities are put into effect with respect to the tin.

Dewey's account does have a "realistic" component, in the sense that he freely admits that "certain brute existences, detected or laid bare by thinking but in no way constituted out of thought or any mental process, set every problem for reflection and hence serve to test its otherwise merely speculative results" (MW10:341;EEL:35). Moreover, these are neither equivalent to the situations out of which inquiry starts nor to the point at which it rests.

Dewey gives an interesting technological example of what he means by this. He invites us to consider three things: (1) iron ore undisturbed in its natural place; (2) pig iron, which is bulk iron refined of the other things that naturally occur with it, and (3) manufactured steel articles, such as watch springs.

The iron ore may be compared to the antecedents, or the conditions that pre-exist a particular bit of thinking. The pig iron is like a datum or "immediate material" presented to thought (it might, for example, be the summative quality of an evening spent with friends). Finally, the watch spring can be likened to the thing that thinking strives for and the place where it rests. It is "the progress actually made in any thought-function; material which is organized by inquiry so far as inquiry has fulfilled its purpose" (MW2:317;SLT:24;EEL:104–5).

Now, just as a manufacturer keeps a stock of pig iron around for use in machine processes, so every mature person lives in an environment that consists of habits, of work previously done—what Dewey, continuing his extended technological metaphor, calls "extracted data." Not only are those extracted data the materials on which thinking operates, but they also are "ready-made tools of extraction" (MW10:341;EEL:35–36). I can remember, for example, that I experience pleasure, as a rule, when I spend an evening conversing with a particular circle of friends. Likewise, the pig iron can be used to make watch springs, but it can also be used as a tool of analysis to develop better smelting methods. The given quality of the evening with friends may either be the material on which my inquiry operates—comparing it, for example, to evenings with other friends or evenings spent alone—or it may operate as a tool for analysis. In this case, I may use it to pry open the heretofore indeterminate experience of the evening and to inquire into other of its aspects. In short, I may take what is just given and utilize it as a tool to analyze the very indeterminate experience from whence it arises as refined material.

The things of ordinary life—pets, autos, houses, and computers (as most of us interact with them)—are general; they speak many languages. Like the pig iron that can be made into a watch spring, a car fender, or a case for a computer, they can be made into many things, that is, they have many meanings. In terms of their complexity, they point in many directions. In terms of their unity, they run in a groove and point to whatever is most customary within a given lifestyle. It is in this sense that the objects of everyday life do not have "significance" in the same sense that scientific objects do. They are "neither the data of science nor the objects at which science arrives" (MW10:343;EEL:37).

Apart from setting up a distinction between what he will call "common sense" or "institutional" meanings on the one hand, and "scientific" meanings on the other, Dewey does something else very important by means of this analogy. By its use he invites us to consider what the things of our common experience are. What are the tables, chairs, and other ubiquitous things of our quotidian world? They are no more and no less than the things that controlled common-sense inquiry has found actually existent. There is no more reason to think that they exist independently of that context than to think that the pig iron really exists in the mountain. Something is "there" in some sense before analysis, but the question is "in what way?" It is certainly not there scientifically—that is, in the sense of knowledge—as a sign.

So when the things of our common experience function as signs, their sign qualities must arise from a reflective situation, and it is this sign function that finally allows them to function as evidence in scientific inquiry. Moreover, they cannot exist in the same purity and "external exclusiveness and internal homogeneity" outside the situation of inquiry as they do within it, any more than the pig iron that is used for manufacturing watch springs existed in that form inside the mountain.

Now, of course, it was not an easy matter to reduce the iron in the ore to the pig iron. It involved a complicated technology, but one that anyone now could master, given enough capital, interest, and education (MW10:345;EEL:41). In just the same way, it is by means of technology that the things of our "primary" experiences are purified and refined into data that is unambiguous and, hence, able to be used for further construction. The engineer who superintends the making of the watch springs is under no obligation to be interested in the history of the extraction of the ore from the mine, though his avocation might by chance be the history of mining or geology. And the user of logic, Dewey further suggests, is not really obligated to inquire into the conditions that led to that art form: it is the philosopher and the logician who do such work.

The central point of Dewey's extended mining analogy is that thinking, like other forms of industry, involves a process of extraction, refinement, and manufacturing. Thinking as pro-ductive and con-structive of objects of knowledge is a technological task.

XIV

I have said that Dewey was one of the first philosophers to have a coherent criticism of technology. This is so because he was one of the first philosophers to regard inquiry itself as a form of overt manufacture. The realist could not have such an account of technology: he or she thinks that the world is just out there ready to be discovered; that is, that what we "do" when we know the world is to "mirror" it as something already finished. For the realist, the pig iron already exists; we do not have to refine it.

But neither could the idealist have a proper account of technology, since for him or her the world is just constituted by thinking, and there does not seem to be evidence of any raw material except its own activity. He or she thinks it possible to make the pig iron whether there is iron ore or not.

Now insofar as what is given functions as "the immediate considerations from which controlled inference proceeds" (MW10:346;EEL:43), it ceases to be just "given" and begins its function as means and instrument. In this new role, what we formerly just "took" becomes a tool—something by means of which we know rather than something known (MW10:346;EEL:43). We know a cellular structure by a color stain, and we know by marks on a page what someone thinks to be so. To Dewey, it becomes crucial to recognize the "data" at this stage of inquiry for what they are—that is, it makes an enormous difference that we now call these things instruments rather than objects. This is so because if they remain objects, then change is in some sense unreal: we will tend to want to contemplate them, to make sure that we are "mirroring" them properly, rather than using them as tools to make changes in our environment.

Dewey's instrumentalist (technological) view of knowledge is for this reason "a behaviorist theory of thinking and knowing. It means that knowing is literally something which we do; that analysis is ultimately physical and active; that meanings in their logical quality are standpoints, attitudes, and methods of behaving toward facts, and that active experimentation is essential to verification" (MW10:367;EEL:331–32). Further, "a knowing as an act is instrumental to the resultant controlled and more significant situation: this does not imply anything about the intrinsic or the instrumental character of the consequent situation. That is whatever it may be in a given case" (MW10:367;EEL:332).[43]

For Dewey, the termination of the process of inquiry, its coming to rest as knowledge, is the securing of control. It is for this reason that we may term knowing a technological triumph.

As a matter of fact, most things suggest other things. The things that are suggested are not "there" in the sense that the things that do the suggesting are; otherwise, they would not need to be suggested. But suggestions tend to operate as stimuli with respect to human beings. For example, a fire that is merely suggested may cause greater reaction than an actual fire, one whose location we can determine or that we can determine to be under control.

Some suggestions are just that; a cloud may suggest a horse or a whale. But other suggestions are richer; they have what Dewey calls a significative or an indicative function. Thus smoke does more than just suggest fire; it indicates or signifies it.

Dewey argued that it is an important part of inquiry to gain clarity about what kind of suggestions are being made, since they can make a great difference in what we choose to do. This part of inquiry is what he calls experimental analysis or inspection, and it involves bodily movements and the use of tools and apparatus. Experimentation with respect to suggestions may lead to other suggestions that are more applicable to a situation, and its "physical" component is undertaken in order to "detect those elements which are the more reliable signs, indicators (evidence)" (MW10:350;EEL:49). When we treat suggestions in this way, we may be said to be *constituting meanings*.

For example, an objectionable smell in my tap water may suggest that it is unfit for use. I could leave the matter there and try to do without water, or seek another source of water, but both courses of action would generate their own further problems. More appropriate to the end that I have in view, however, I can utilize various chemicals in order to test the water, to analyze it. In doing so I find something more reliable, namely signs and indications. I put certain chemicals into a sample of the water and find that it turns a certain color that does not merely suggest, but signifies or indicates, the presence of sulfur. The chemical test constitutes a more reliable sign, and in fact it constitutes the meaning of the smell and provides the grounds for deciding whether I will continue to drink or bathe in the water.

It is helpful in experimentation to have as many meanings as possible to draw upon and to have them organized in such ways that they can be efficiently manipulated. This is why we prize former suggestions that have been turned into meanings. It is a great good that libraries contain information about what kind of chemicals are signs of sulfur in water. But some people hold these meanings so highly that they hypostatize them—that is, they turn them into fixed, completed essences, unalterable for all time.

Before Darwin, for example, nature was thought to comprise orders of fixed essences or "natural kinds." Dewey regarded this view as indicating a kind of laziness or what perhaps will turn out to be the same thing: a kind of pride, an exaggerated sense of the importance of investigations already carried out. To put this in the language of the medieval Aristotelians, the doctrine of fixed essences involves the construction of a realm of essences apart from existences. Dewey argued that meanings should be prized in use, not in contemplation, for to treat them as complete for all time, as finalities instead of tools, is to give them more than their due and to stifle inquiry. Experimentation functions for Dewey both as bridge and as checking mechanism between essences and existences.

If *data*, or what is existentially given (or taken), function in inquiry as signs that *indicate* other existences (smoke as a datum may indicate existent fire), *meanings* are signs that *imply* other meanings. Dewey uses another technological example to establish this point. A variety of wheels, cams, and rods can do a job that could not be done by any one of them separately or by all of them together in a heap on a workbench.

The same is true of terms related to one another. Bringing them together in certain ways generates something new and unexpected.[44] So the term "brother," for example, is something that results from a solution with respect to some prior situation, namely "brother of." As such, it has implications, such of "the brother of Prince Charles" or "the brother of Edward Kennedy." Both of these examples express a situation in which being a brother has implications: it "expresses an interaction of different terms from which something might happen" (MW10:353;EEL:54). But when it is taken out of the machinery of its context, the term "brother" no longer implies a relationship, but rather becomes a relative term: like a camshaft on a table, it remains lifeless until it is again "set to work in some other situation" (MW10:353;EEL:54).

Dewey thought that we stock these meanings as in a storeroom (this is a metaphor that Heidegger also used, in a somewhat different context), according to distinct arrangements so that they can be gotten and related more easily. But not all meanings are of equal use to a particular task, and "it is a work of art to select the proper qualities for doing the work. *This corresponds to the working over of raw material into an effective tool*" (MW10:354;EEL:55;emphasis added). Moreover, the meanings that are so stocked are not the finished products with respect to the projects at hand, even though they may be products that have been fabricated in the course of some earlier project. What is stocked is the raw material of the watch spring (the pig iron) or perhaps the spring itself, if we view it not in terms of a finished product but in terms of its future uses. It is an important technological art to know what kind of material to draw from the storeroom, for this is a stage in fabrication. Or it is like going to a storeroom in which a number of springs are shelved: the selection of the proper spring for the assembly of the watch is an ingredient in the art of its successful assembly.

Incidentally, this analogy gives a hint of the meaning of "proper" or "appropriate" in the context of inquiry. This matter will be of great importance later, when I shall discuss Dewey's criticism of valuation in the public spheres. But leaving the question somewhat inchoate for the moment, it is easy to see why the spring on the shelf will contribute as an instrument to the proper control of the assembly of the watch: it was made for that purpose, and if the design of the watch, what Dewey calls an "end-in-view," were to change, the spring would have to be redesigned. So there is no question about why the refined metal is the proper one for making the spring or, respectively, why the spring will fit. Each has been made to perform a task.

XV

The close analogy that Dewey develops between the production of metal artifacts and the production of the artifacts we call ideas serves to reinforce his remarks on what have been called the logical "connectives" (a term that reveals their technological or instrumental function; they function as do connecting rods in a machine), such as "and" and "therefore." Just as the logical connectives arise *from* inference and not *by* inference (MW10:94), so the materials and parts of the watch arise *from* the application of the arts of metalworking, not simply *by* them.

Dewey's target in this material was a position defended by Bertrand Russell in his book *Our Knowledge of the External World* (1914). Russell claimed that logical connectives represent knowledge that is "not obtained by inference but is primitive."[45] Since they must already exist if inference is to take place, Russell seems to say, and since inference does occur, they must be *a priori*—primitive to experience. Dewey confronts the urbane Englishman with the humble language of agriculture. He treats inference as if it were agricultural practice and the logical connectives as if they were agricultural tools. Neither type of tool, logical connective or agricultural tool, existed before the arts that introduced them in order to solve some concrete problem.

We do not measure the worth of a tool, whether it be logical or made of metal, by measuring how close it is to what it originally was. We examine what kind of work it will do, what kind of behavioral change it will generate. Dewey calls this change of behavior "an outdoor fact, an observably identifiable fact, something verifiable in the same way as are the existence and peculiarities of walking or skating, or hoeing a garden" (MW10:91). A steel plow has as a natural prototype a limb pulled from a tree. Its measure is not in terms of its natural origin, however, but in terms of the efficiency with which it does its work. In just the same way, mathematical relations are no more inventions of the mind than a telephone is an invention of the mind. "They fit nature because they are derived from natural conditions." Further, intelligence, or the process by which tools of all sorts are developed and brought to bear on indeterminate situations in order to exert effective control, is specifically defined in technological language: "Things naturally bulge, so to speak, and naturally alter. To seize upon these qualities, to develop them into keys for discovering the meanings of brute, isolated events, and to accomplish this effectively, to develop and order them till they become economical tools (and tools upon tools) for making an unknown and uncertain situation into a known and certain one, is the recorded triumph of human intelligence" (MW10:355;EEL:56–57).

Every instance of intelligent behavior has two important effects. In addition to the immediate organization and control of a definite outcome, it has an indirect effect: it initiates an intrinsic meaning that may be put in the storeroom to serve in some later inquiry for which it will be deemed appropriate. It may be that the meaning, like the watch spring, will have to be discarded or retooled in the event that the end-in-view (or the design of the watch) changes. But it may also be that the meaning will fit some situation that has not so far occurred and that when it is drawn from the storeroom, it will prove to be just what is required.

This matter troubled Costello in terms of Dewey's view of the use of tools in inquiry. He thought that Dewey was saying that tools are called upon to solve temporary difficulties, and that thinking was a kind of crisis management in which there is an attempt to keep things on a kind of even keel, to return something out of balance to its former state.

> Thought, for Dewey, was something called up to solve a temporary problem, as you might call the fire department to put out a fire. The main problem for him seemed to be to avoid so many false alarms and work hereafter only on real fires. When the fire was out you went back to the firehouse, and smoked a pipe and played cards and slept. But it seems to me that good thought goes beyond solving temporary difficulties. It is the development of culture itself, and if it broadens down from precedent to precedent, it does continue and broaden. I am not sure Dewey really meant to deny this—he said later that if he had it to do over, he would speak of the development of culture, rather than the adjustments of experience.[46]

But it should be obvious from the examples of iron ore, pig iron, and watch springs, which Dewey had already given in his 1916 *Essays*, that inquiry is not only not otiose (smoking, playing cards, and sleeping), but in solving problems it also finds that the firehouse to which it returns is quite different from the one that it left.

XVI

So far I have indicated some of the senses in which Dewey treated knowing as instrumental, and I have attempted to suggest what this means in terms of his implicit criticism of technology. Instrumentalism makes knowing a technological activity, a kind of pro-duction and con-struction at their most fundamental levels. It explains why there could be no proper account of technology either in traditional versions of realism, because of their view that our knowledge must conform to some external set of conditions, or in traditional forms of idealism, because of their view that our knowledge is in fact constituted in a coherent way by a supernatural or transempirical thinker, or else that it is subjectively determined without reference to objective checks and cues. Furthermore, instrumentalism renders science, as knowing that determines "meanings determined for possible use in remote and contingent situations" (LW 12:55;LTI:49), a special type of technology, and it renders theory a kind of practice.

While a full account of the relations between technology and science must await chapter 5, this seems to be the proper place to discuss Dewey's views regarding what he takes to be the two basic spheres of knowledge: the "institutional" and the "scientific."

In his 1908 essay "What Pragmatism Means by Practical," published as a review of William James's *Pragmatism* and included among his 1916 *Essays*, Dewey identified three loci of meanings: the meaning of an object, the meaning of an idea, and the meaning of truth.

The meaning of an object "signifies its *conceptual content or connotation*" (MW4:102;EEL:309;emphasis in original). Further, its "practical meaning" signifies "*the future responses which an object requires of us or commits us to*" (MW4:102;EEL:309;emphasis in original). The meaning of an idea, however, "resides in the existences which, as changed, it intends" (MW4:103;EEL:310). Putting each of these senses of meaning in the terms of the other, he submits that "while the meaning of an object is the changes it requires in our attitude, the meaning of an idea is the changes it, as our attitude, effects in objects" (MW4:103;EEL:310). Finally, once the meanings of the object and the idea (what are commonly called the denotative and connotative references of a term associated with the object and the idea) have been ascertained, it is possible to ask about the meaning of the "truth" of the matter. This he characterizes as the difference it would make to anyone if this, rather than something else, were the case. In other words, the truth of the matter is its value, its importance (MW4:103;EEL:311). All significant constellations of related meanings (that is, languages) share these factors. And meanings are only meanings in such contexts.

Beyond this, however, Dewey differentiates two important classes of languages. They correspond to two distinct ways of approaching technological matters. In the first, the domain of common sense and institutions, meanings are "determined respectively in fairly direct connection with action in situations that are present or near at hand" (LW 12:55;LTI:49). In the second, the domain of science, meanings are "determined for possible use in remote and contingent situations" (LW12:55;LTI:49). (The objectives of the inquiry may be remote, but by no means does the inquiry thereby become "useless.") Both of these meaning constellations or languages are instrumental, but they are so in different ways.

Common sense or institutional languages are somewhat haphazard. They are a function of group expectations, habits, and activities. Meanings in this constellation contain much that "is irrelevant and . . . exclude much that is required for intelligent control of activity," that is, the application of productive skills. Dewey calls these meanings "coarse" and suggests that they may be inconsistent with one another. In any complex society, for example, there will be words that mean different things in the context of religious, financial, or familial institutions. The American experience of diversity with respect to ethnic and cultural origins has sometimes tended to exponentially exacerbate such confusion.

Scientific languages stand in stark contrast to institutional

languages. Terms that enter scientific languages are subject to greater
strictures: they must demonstrate their specific relationships to other
elements within the language. This takes place in terms of inference that
is facilitated by the use of special types of signs and indications called
"symbols." It is not that symbols do not also function in institutional
language, but just that in science they are used more precisely. Dewey
uses the word "sign" to designate natural signification, in which an
actual existence points to or is evidence of something else existential,
as in the case of smoke being a sign of a fire. He uses the term
"symbol" to refer to artificial signification, in which signification depends
upon social use.

XVII

I conclude this chapter with a further word regarding Dewey's
reconstruction of the meanings of the terms "meaning" and
"technology." As I have indicated, he undertook this reconstruction in a
way that baffled many of his critics during his lifetime, but that in our
own post-Wittgensteinian period no longer seem quite so radical. With
respect to what he termed the "wider" branch of inquiry into inquiry, it
was his view that meanings may in some sense be "multiply
standardized"; that is, they may become habitual among a particular
group of language users in a way that is "institutional" or "ceremonial."
That the same word ("offering," for example) may be used quite
differently in the contexts of religious and financial activities seemed
obvious to him. Classical and medieval philosophers knew as much, and
exhibited great interest in the equivocal uses of words.

More specific to what he called the "narrower" branch of inquiry
into inquiry, however, it was Dewey's view that the meaning of a
proposition is not determined by or uniquely associated with its syntactic
structure, but by its function in inquiry. In science such standardization
is the result of relating meanings to one another in inference, and it is
this activity that provides the basis of the objectivity of science. Among
scientific meanings are those that have proved to be useful tools and
hence are largely safe from alteration, as well as those that are
periodically retooled in order to perform novel tasks as such tasks
emerge.

In any case, the meanings of words are for Dewey always
contextual; they do not have a unique correspondence to objects or
events. Years before Wittgenstein was to grasp and develop this point in
the first twenty paragraphs of his *Philosophical Investigations* (published
in 1953, the year after Dewey died), Dewey argued that "there is not
possible any such thing as a direct one-to-one correspondence of
names with existential objects; that words mean what they mean in
connection with conjoint activities that effect a common, or mutually
participated in, consequence" (LW12:59;LTI:53). Wittgenstein was later

to call these conjoint activities by their now-familiar names: "language games" and "forms of life."

Meanings may, then, differ within a particular time frame between one group and another, depending on interests and goals, and they tend to change over time within a group or for an individual as old conclusions cease to serve, thereby setting the stage for the development of new meanings.

The case is not different with respect to the meaning of the word "technology." It can truthfully be said that the purpose of this book is to explain the meanings of "technology" and its cognates and associated terms as Dewey used and reconstructed those terms. But if that task is to remain true to the spirit of Dewey's instrumental method, the meanings of technology must be patiently developed with sensitivity to the many contexts within which he utilized those terms. It may be said by way of preview, however, that Dewey variously writes of technology as the active use of productive skills; as the most satisfactory method of inquiry; as production within the fine, vernacular, and industrial arts; as what distinguished the scientific revolution of the century of Galileo from the science prior to it; as the general use of tools (including language, which he calls the tool of tools); as industry and commerce; as an essential ingredient in education; and as planning in the various forms in which it corresponds to specific human social and political arrangements. Moreover, as we shall see, this list is far from exhaustive.

The very names that Dewey gives to his method—"pragmatism" (a term he eschewed in his 1938 Logic for fear that it would be misunderstood), "experimentalism," and "instrumentalism"—connote technological production and construction. Technology, since its earliest manifestation, has been interdefined with the use of tools and instruments. And what is unique about scientific technology, or what is more frequently called simply "modern science," is its use of instrumentation in order to conduct orderly and productive experimentation.

Late in his career, in his 1946 book Problems of Men, Dewey unequivocally identified his instrumental method with technology. In an aside that provides a kind of key for understanding his lifelong struggle to articulate his method, he remarked, "It is probable that I might have avoided a considerable amount of misunderstanding if I had systematically used 'technology' instead of 'instrumentalism' in connection with the view I put forth regarding the distinctive quality of science as knowledge" (PM:291n).

This remark is all the more notable in view of Dewey's observation, expressed in his 1916 Essays, that science serves as a kind of "key to the control and development of other modes of practice" (MW8:81;EEL:439) and his emphasis in Art as Experience that "science is itself but a central art auxiliary to the generation and utilization of other arts" (LW10:33;AE:26).

It is in this sense that technology was a tool that Dewey used to show that the bulk of what had been treated in the history of philosophy as "the problem of knowledge" was nonsense. Such "problems," whether identified with the unreliability of the senses, the difficulties attaining "certainty," or the "difficulty of gaining access to 'other minds' " existed only because of a failure to employ the "resources of experimentation, all sorts of microscopic, telescopic, and registering apparatus" (MW8:63;EEL:412) to "straighten out" logic, to control inference. Costello was quite right when he suggested that it was part of the job of the fireman to be able to distinguish the false alarms from the real blazes.

Chapter Three: Productive Skills in the Arts

Art is a process of production in which natural
materials are re-shaped in a projection toward
consummatory fulfillment through regulation of trains
of events that occur in a less regulated way on lower
levels of nature. (LW1:8;EN:xix)

Even technological arts, in their sum total, do
something more than provide a number of separate
conveniences and facilities. They shape collective
occupations and thus determine direction of interest
and attention, and hence affect desire and purpose.
(LW10:347;AE:345)

I

In the preceding chapter I presented Dewey's theory of inquiry as an
account of the rhythms that permeate the interaction of human beings in
and with their various experiences. As William James and Charles Peirce
before him had done, Dewey isolated two types of experience: that
stable phase in which union with an environing situation is enjoyed; and
that motile phase in which loss of integration importunes, and recovery
of harmony and balance is actively sought.

But such an account indicates that experience at rest is also of
two types between which inquiry is active: the old repetition of
ceremony, tradition, institution, and the habitual; and the novelty of
freshly solved problems, newly pregnant situations, and enjoyed recent
successes. Experience alternates between the dully repetitious and the
recently enriched, both of which are stable. When what is customary
becomes enriched it is because of inquiry—or else by luck. And when
recent successes become stale, or when luck runs out, inquiry is often
called for. The medium of exchange between these differently stable
poles, their common coin, is the activity of the productive skill we call
inquiry.

Dewey's account of inquiry, his logic, concerns itself with the
means of reunification and reintegration that are sought when and for
whatever reason what is repetitious becomes unstable or unsuitable.

Such means are for Dewey characterizable as tools and as productive skills or techniques. On this reading, technology becomes a generic pattern identifiable as inquiry not only in its quotidian sense, but also in science, in logic, and in metaphysics.

Technology, however, should not be regarded as a fixed and finished method or as a set of such methods, applicable without transformation to the indefinite number of novel situations on which it is brought to bear. "Productive skill," even though wonderfully concrete in its original sense of *techne*, is not rich enough in connotations and significance to exhaust contemporary methods of logic and science, any more than primitive hammers and chisels are sufficient to all aspects of modern woodworking, or any more than bent tree limbs are adequate to modern agriculture.

Technology may thus be thought of as a family of methods and tools that evolves in response to the needs and goals that it is called upon to serve, and in response to the uses to which it is put. In this regard Dewey argued quite forcefully, for example, that major advances in productive skills had been achieved as a result of the expanded use of instrumentation that was an essential part of the rise of modern science and industry.

For Dewey, however, in contradistinction to Heidegger, there is no radical break between the productive skills that predated the rise of modern science and those that precipitated and attended it. Nowhere is his position on this matter laid out more clearly than in his works on aesthetic and artistic experience. For Dewey, productive skills that are prescientific and those that are scientific exist along a continuum of ever more complex and fruitful articulation of instrumentation in the broad sense of that term—including tools, methods, means, meanings, and even language, which he calls "the tool of tools."

Inquiry into inquiry, or logic, is for Dewey a genetic account—a history—of the expansion and improvement of productive skill; it is a history of advancements in technical precision, of augmentation of exact instrumentation, of enrichment of working hypotheses, and of the sloughing off of old problems and issues that improved instruments have demonstrated to be irrelevant or inconsequential.

II

In chapter 9 of *Experience and Nature*, published in 1925, and in *Art as Experience*, published in 1934, Dewey expanded his analysis of inquiry as productive skill to include a more specific treatment of the experiences of making and enjoying artifacts that are commonly identified as "artistic." But because inquiry is a productive skill, and because art and productive skill have both ancient and contemporary connections, his application of logic to the problems of production and enjoyment in the arts sheds further light on the nature and function of inquiry itself.

In his account of logic Dewey emphasized the problematic aspects of situations that fail to serve and therefore require inquirential activity. In his account of aesthetic enjoyment and artistic production Dewey pursued this same lead, but enlarged its scope. Situations mature and offer new possibilities for enjoyment; far from being the occasion of a sharp pain of perceived difficulty that initiates some types of inquiry, an aesthetic situation may call for decision between alternatives that are problematic because they are so nearly equally delightful.

One of Dewey's primary goals in this material was to argue that the traditional separation of the arts into those that are "fine" and those that are otherwise—whether they are called "useful," "practical," "industrial," or "vernacular"—results in an impoverishment of experience by obscuring the ways in which meanings can be expanded and developed. This he did by undertaking an extensive reconstruction of the terms "fine" and "useful." These terms, he suggested, are "adjectives which, when they are prefixed to 'art,' corrupt and destroy its intrinsic significance. For arts that are merely useful are not arts but routines; and arts that are merely final are not arts but passive amusements and distractions, different from other indulgent dissipations only in dependence upon a certain acquired refinement or 'cultivation' " (LW1:271); (EN:293).

It was Dewey's contention that what are commonly referred to as the "technical" arts—the arts that bring into existence shoes, automobiles, refrigerators and computers—are customarily and for the most part called "useful" in order to avoid consideration of their full range of consequences. To be useful in the honorific sense of the term is to fulfill need, and to do so by engagement in inquiry. Inquiry, here as elsewhere, is an attempt to satisfy characteristic human needs for increased appreciation and insight into a full range of the meanings and significances of things.

But he argues that when the art of producing automobiles is called a useful art, it is usually meant that a full consideration of the consequences of their production has been cut short. Inquiry into meanings has been foreshortened, and a problem has been isolated and then abandoned.

The same may be said of works of art that are called "fine," since that term is usually taken to mean "final." One of the principal ways in which "fine art" fails to be art is as it is egocentric. This occurs when an artist attempts to engage in self-expression that is isolated and without reference to the context out of which inquiry into materials arises. In such cases there is also, as a rule, scant consideration of the necessary means of communicating the results of inquiry. An attempt may have been made to avoid repetitiveness, but inquiry is thwarted because the artist ignored the constraints of originating contexts and the social character of outcomes. Theories that identify artistic production with the expression of the artist's emotion also fail on these grounds: they neglect the indispensible link between context and outcome.

Nevertheless, Dewey did not think that meaningful art is so because it is directed to an existing audience, or even that such communication must be the intent of the artist. On the contrary, it is not so much the artist who communicates as it is the object or event produced, an aesthetically rich and suggestive artifact doing *its* work. "Indifference to response of the immediate audience is a necessary trait of all artists that have something new to say. But they are animated by a deep conviction that since they can only say what they have to say, the trouble is not with their work but those who, having eyes, see not, and having ears, hear not. Communicability has nothing to do with popularity" (LW10:110;AE:104).

Artists may in fact fail to communicate if they are committed to a special message, and consequently not open to the means by which their materials may be expressed and expressive. Communication is the consequence, not the intention, of the work of art. Another way of putting this is that communication is the purpose, but not the motive, of the work of art.

In *The Metaphysics of Pragmatism*, Sidney Hook argued that the distinction between motive and purpose is central to an understanding of instrumentalism. The stated purpose of his remarks on this subject was to elucidate the instrumental nature of inquiry in its general sense; but since instrumentalism makes no distinction between inquiry in general and inquiry in one of its particular instances (except in terms of materials and tools), what he wrote can be fruitfully applied to inquiry that is artistic.

Since thinking (including the thinking with materials that is undertaken by the artist) "occurs in incomplete situations for the sake of integrating or unifying certain of their dissonant aspects, the movement and truth of thinking in any particular case cannot be completely intelligible without reference to the specific purpose it fulfills or subserves in its subject-matter."[1] Critics of this position fail to distinguish between "purposes" and "motives." For the instrumentalist, Hook suggests, purpose "is as different from motive as novelty is from surprise. Purposes are more objective than any motive can possibly be, for they are set in and can be inferred from the terms and relations of the subject-matter whose rips, tears and open seams thinking tries to sew up."[2]

The purpose of a bridge, for example, is to span a river. But this is quite different from the political and economic motives that may have led to its construction. And whereas motives may be forever private and at best the object of conjecture, purposes are objective. "Knowledge of purposes enables us to *test* intelligently and so distinguish between by-products and major results."[3]

Thus understood, purpose is natural as well as instrumental. Purposes pertain to the productive utilization of materials in order to serve natural functions. Structure becomes meaningful as it bears upon and pertains to those functions.

Once this distinction is understood, it becomes apparent that art that is commonly called "fine" fails to be meaningful whenever it is directed by motives of status or propaganda, rather than being the purposive result of inquiry into situations and materials. In such cases works of art become commodities associated with decoration that is superadded and gratuitous, with conspicuous display,[4] or with political goals that are extraneous to them. Whether such art is produced for the wealthy or, as in the case of what has been called "social realism," produced for the proletariat, there is an emphasis on final and fixed goals at the expense of honest and incisive inquiry into materials and of communication of results.

Dewey suggested that when production in the arts is subjugated to class interests, whether they be those of the upper classes or those of the lower, or to religious or political requirements, art returns to a position that it has historically outgrown (LW10:194;AE:19). Examples of this phenomenon are not difficult to find: Gainsborough's *Mr. and Mrs. Andrews* brings materials together to express nothing so much as the Andrewses' ownership of a large estate.[5] The neoclassical kitsch so beloved by Hitler and Mussolini, to say nothing of the bulk of American advertising, subsumes intelligent expression of materials to the exigencies of political and economic manipulation.[6] The history of religious painting and sculpture in the West is replete with examples of the perversion of materials to satisfy narrow ideological ends, as well as the defacing of images already produced so as to bring them into line with changed stances within those ideologies.[7]

III

Thus far, Dewey's critique of art is not unlike that of members of the Frankfurt School, in particular that of Max Horkheimer. Horkheimer's essay "Art and Mass Culture" constitutes a biting criticism of works of art that fail to live up to the potentialities of the media on which they draw, and in terms of which they operate, because of the imposition of political and economic ends that are extraneous to them. Horkheimer was particularly critical of the Donald Duck cartoons of Walt Disney and the entire Hollywood film "industry" in this regard. He viewed the American culture industry as a kind of pale shadow of another usurpation of aesthetic ends to extraneous considerations, at once more serious and more tragic, that he had left behind in Fascist Europe in the 1930s. His remarks on Dewey's instrumentalism were in that essay a remarkable departure from the criticism he articulated elsewhere of

Dewey's position as "mere" instrumentalism, a position he regarded as an unprincipled apologetic for American industry.

Horkheimer honored with the appellation "beautiful" the passage in *Art as Experience* in which Dewey explained that communication is the consequence, and not the intention, of the work of art.[8] But even though "the imaginary future audience has become questionable, because, once again, man within humanity is as solitary and abandoned as humanity within the infinite universe,"[9] Horkheimer held fast to the hope he found articulated in Dewey's work. The Fascist masses, he suggested, might turn out to be like the "catatonic patients who make known only at the end of their trance that nothing has escaped them."[10] He found support in Dewey's position, which he took to be that it is not entirely senseless for the artist "to continue speaking a language that is not easily understood."[11]

But Dewey went further to embrace a position that I believe Horkheimer would have found unacceptable. Art, in Dewey's view, may be legitimately and productively motivated by concerns that are proletarian, commercial, or religious. These interests may in fact mark "a new direction of attention and [involve] observation of materials previously passed over. . . . " (LW10:194;AE:190). In such cases they can "call into activity persons who were not moved to expression by former materials, and . . . disclose and thus help break down boundaries of which they were not previously aware" (LW10:194;AE:190). But in these cases, as well as others, works of art are still effectively judged only in terms of objective purposes fulfilled, and never by the recondite motivations that serve to initiate their construction.

To put this point more precisely, Horkheimer seemed to think Donald Duck cartoons and jazz unredeemable because they had been so exploited, whereas for Dewey they offered the occasion not only for aesthetic delight, but also for inquiry into the possibilities of aesthetic enrichment.

It was Dewey's view that all meaningful works of art are marked by some special interest or other, else they would have no point of origin, no context, no impetus. But here as elsewhere in inquiry, interests must be checked against one another, means against ends, and narrow interests against broader ones. Purity of heart, ideological correctness, adherence to laissez-faire economics, theological or moral rectitude—none of these motivations guarantees the successful bringing to completion of a work of art, either in terms of its production or in terms of its appreciation.

It seemed to Dewey ironic that art that has yielded to narrow interests at the expense of ones that are wider is often called "instrumental" art; that is, instrumental to the achievement or display of status or instrumental to political outcome. Dewey's own use of the term "instrumental" with reference to works of art is tied to his understanding of what is required for excellence in that field. Such excellence, he suggested, "occurs when activity is productive of an object that affords continuously renewed delight. This condition requires that the object be, with its successive consequences, indefinitely instrumental to *new* satisfying events. For otherwise the object is quickly exhausted and satiety sets in" (LW1:273–74); (EN:295).

He suggested that "a consummatory object that is not also instrumental turns in time to the dust and ashes of boredom. The 'eternal' quality of great art is its renewed instrumentality for further consummatory experiences (LW1:274;EN:296). This is as true of Disney's feature-length cartoon *Snow White* as it is of Picasso's *Le Demoiselles d'Avignon*; and it is as true of Oldenburg's *Clothespin* as it is of Duchamp's *Fountain*, of Frank Lloyd Wright's corporate headquarters for Johnson Wax, or of the "matchless precision" present in the "handles of scythes and the shafts of . . . axes" when they are well crafted.[12] As George Bourne put the matter, "the beauty of a tool is an unfailing sign that in the proper handling of it, technique is present."[13] According to Dewey's instrumentalism, we "handle" Oldenburg's *Clothespin* or Duchamp's *Fountain* in the same sense that we handle fine tools, provided that we possess the requisite techniques. Further, to handle is to do more than simply grasp: it is to manipulate.

IV

Dewey's contention that what are commonly referred to as the fine and the practical arts are not separable in terms of inquiry may perhaps be better understood in terms of his treatment of means and ends. It was his view that means are often confused with antecedents and that ends are often mistaken for what happens to be the last term of a sequence. When this happens, naturally occurring events have not only taken the place of, but have been taken for, art. Another way of putting this is that such a situation involves the acceptance of natural and uncontrolled experiences in lieu of those that are technically transformed; that is, those that are the results of the application of productive skills.

Mere antecedents or "causal" conditions on the one hand, and mere consequents or "effects" on the other, do not except by accident have a place in properly controlled inquiry. What marks them off from means and ends, respectively, is that means and ends are interdependent, and instrumental for one another and for a given process of inquiry.

Dewey steadfastly refused to place means in a position that is menial or subservient with respect to ends. To do so would be to make the traditional philosophical mistake of those who speak of a *summum bonum*, of final and unalterable goals against which all means are measured, or of transcendent or supernatural grounds of value. In aesthetic theory means have often been made secondary to "Beauty" or to "The Sublime."

In production that is fruitful, means and ends cooperate; they receive checks from one another;[14] they undergo alteration and accommodation with respect to one another; and their interaction is normative for inquiry. (This is a feature of Dewey's critique of technology that distinguishes his view from that of the straight-line instrumentalists, and this is a point that most of his critics have missed.) This is true in the case of painting, in which pigments, brushes, and technical skill interact with the product that is dependent upon them. It is true in the case of the baking of bread; flour, water, and the baker's art are the media by which the finished loaf organizes and articulates those elements. It is also true in the case of those social and political arrangements we call judicial systems, legislative bodies, and the forces that execute and enforce the laws. "An active process is strung out temporally, but there is a deposit at each stage and point entering cumulatively and constitutively into the outcome. A genuine instrumentality *for* is always an organ *of* an end. It confers continued efficacy upon the object in which it is embodied" (LW1:276); (EN:298).

Failure of artifacts to do their work—that is, to be meaningful, whether such objects are classified as "fine" or "industrial"—is a failure of properly conducted inquiry; it is a technological failure. One of the principal causes of failure of inquiry is neglect of the reciprocal connections among means and ends. Such connections may be well or poorly constructed. When they constitute a work of art, that is, an artifact *that works*, meanings are rich and productive of further meanings. When productive skill is lacking, when art fails, when connections among ends and means are thin or scant, meanings are impoverished and human experience is restricted.

Dewey repeatedly emphasized his view that failure of artifacts to do their work is not necessarily due to lack of productive skill on the part of the artist, but may be due to lack of such skill on the part of the person who is confronted with and called upon to take account of produced artifacts. This insight, which Horkheimer found in *Art as Experience* and which he thought of great value, was one that Dewey had in fact been articulating since the introduction to his 1916 *Essays in Experimental Logic*.

Productive skill is required on the parts of the mining engineer and smelter in order to effect the transformation of natural materials such as ores into artifacts that possess intrinsic as well as extrinsic meanings. Productive skill is required on the parts of individuals going about their quotidian business in order to effect the transformation of the raw and immediate materials of focus and context, enjoyment and routine use, into *an* experience that exhibits enlarged meaning and significance. And productive skill is required of those who appreciate and use art objects in order to effect the transformation and appropriation of those objects into sources of renewed delight and refined insight.

Aesthetic appreciation may in some sense be innate, in the sense that we inherit the results of productive work done by the organisms whose genetic material becomes our own. Babies would not learn to see or to develop their other senses if it were not for certain inherited structural and functional opportunities for experiencing delight. But if we are not to remain children, these opportunities must be developed in ways that involve the production of new skills and capacities. Each person is responsible for the extent to which he or she is capable of aesthetic enjoyment; production in this area of human experience is the counterpart of the productive capacities developed and exercised by those who produce those artifacts commonly referred to as artistic. Capacity to enjoy is also artifactual.

Dewey's insistence that from the standpoint of production and appreciation no meaningful distinction can be made between the "fine" and the "useful" arts is to this day a radical position, despite the fact that he was anticipated in this matter by Emerson and Whitman, and despite the fact that this view has gained some measure of acceptance by critics such as Herbert Read and John Kouwenhoven and by historians such as Lynn White. Nevertheless, there are still treatments of modern art that bifurcate "art" and "technology," as if art objects were not examples of productive skill and as if "technology" were somehow the enemy of "art." Dewey's response to this is that painting and shoemaking are just different kinds of technological production.

Dewey's views on this matter were unequivocal. "Technology," as he understood the term, cannot be the enemy of art. It *is* art. Where art is threatened it is not because of "technology," but because of the failure of activities of intelligent inquiry required for its production and because of the failure to apply the skills necessary for its appreciation.

V

The realization that technology *is* art does not lessen the need to ascertain the ways in which this is the case. It might be tempting to say that a painting utilizes technological means, such as commercially available pigments, and leave the matter at that. Or it might be tempting to say that a painting solves a technical problem and that it therefore involves the production of a solution, and nothing more. In Dewey's view, however, this is a very low level of analysis of the way that art products do their work.

The fact is that some art objects are identifiable as technological in a variety of ways. I offer four nonexhaustive examples: (1) art products may be the result of the extension and application of productive skill; (2) they may be representative of or even (as is the case of collages) contain other objects that are the result of productive skill; (3) they may utilize productive skill to criticize or comment upon the objects of productive skill that they represent or contain; and (4) they may utilize productive skill to comment upon the productive skill utilized in their own articulation.

Although examples abound, I shall mention just one. René Magritte's *The Treason of Images*, which contains the well-known representation of a pipe and its label "Ceci n'est pas une pipe," utilizes technologically refined media to construct an image. It contains a representation of a well-proportioned technological artifact, in this case a pipe. The pipe that Magritte chose was, however, not just *any* pipe, but the pipe that Le Corbusier had reproduced in 1923 in *Towards an Architecture* as a symbol of design that was plain and functional[15]—it was a modernist pipe. In addition, Magritte's painting works to convey a message about the role of symbolism in painting. As Robert Hughes has put it, "No painter had ever made the point that 'A painting is not what it represents' with such epigrammatic clarity before. Corbusier's pipe, as redone by Magritte, was the hole in the mirror of illusion, a passage into a quite different world where things lose their names or, keeping them, change their meanings. At one border, Magritte's field of action touched on philosophy; at the other, farce."[16]

Magritte's paintings are rich in meanings and significance: they afford continuing delight, and they are a fund of vectors that carry those who interact with them in directions that are at once disturbing and satisfying. But Dewey's examples of meaningful works of art are not restricted to what have been termed the "fine" arts. They include not only successful paintings, but also shoes, buildings, bread, jazz performances, and motion pictures. Humble objects such as buttons may have meanings that are indefinitely rich.

Lynn White has provided an example of this instrumentalist point that probably would have delighted Dewey:

Thirteenth century Europe invented the sonnet as a poetic form and the functional button as a means of making civilized life more nearly possible in boreal climes. Since most of us are educated in terms of traditional humanistic presuppositions, we value the sonnet but think that a button is just a button. It is doubtful whether the chilly northerner who invented the button could have invented the sonnet then being produced by his contemporaries in Sicily. It is equally doubtful whether the type of talent required to invent the rhythmic and phonic relationships of the sonnet-pattern is the type of talent needed to perceive the spatial relationships of button and buttonhole. For the button is not obvious until one has seen it, and perhaps not even then. The Chinese never adopted it: they got no further than to adapt the tie-cords of their costumes into elaborate loops to fit over cord-twisted knobs. When the Portuguese brought the button to Japan, the Japanese were delighted with it and took over not only the object itself but also its Portuguese name. Humanistic values, which have been cultivated historically by very specialized groups in quite exceptional circumstances, do not encompass sufficiently the observable human values. The billion or more mothers who, since the thirteenth century, have buttoned their children snugly against winter weather might perceive as much of spirituality in the button as in the sonnet and feel more personal gratitude to the inventor of the former than of the latter. And the historian, concerned not only with art forms but with population, public health, and what S. C. Gilfillan long ago identified as "the coldward course" of culture, must not slight either of these very different manifestations of what would seem to be very different types of creativity.[17]

White held the view that technological creativity was in no sense "unitary"; that is, that the same talents and propensities were required for the invention of blown glass as for the invention of the water mill. He suggested that the abilities required to produce those two great first-century B.C. inventions may be regarded as being as different as the abilities of Einstein and Picasso in our century. He thus rejected the view that *Homo* is *sapiens* because *Homo* is *faber*. "*Homo*," he pointedly remarked, "is also *ludens*, *orans*, and much else."[18]

Dewey also held this view, but in a somewhat different form. Technology is for Dewey, in one of its many senses, productive skill brought to bear by human beings on the project of *altering* their environments and *accommodating* themselves to those environments. Dewey calls these two activities, taken together, *adjustment* with respect to environing conditions and *transaction* with them (LW9:12;CF:15–16). Moreover, beyond the concrete activities that the adjustive and transactional project comprehends, technology may also be said to be that project itself. Nevertheless, not everything that human beings do involves adjustment to their environments, that is, not every human activity is technological. Dewey reminds us that there are regions of experience in which knowing has no business, and there are also regions of experience in which production is not active. Human beings engage in ceremony, routine, and commonplace activities; and they focus on delights that are immediate, in the relative sense in which Dewey used that term.

Nevertheless, technology has for Dewey significance that is singularly broad and inclusive. There has probably been no other critic of technology for whom ideas, knowing, and intelligent activity have functioned as technological artifacts in the broad sense given them in Dewey's view.

This position forms a potent linkage between Dewey's general theory of inquiry and his theory of the production and enjoyment of works of art. As I demonstrated in the previous chapter, ideas, knowing, and active engagement with experiential contexts are artifacts of inquiry in just as important a sense as are works of art that are made of canvas and paint, stone, metal, plastic, steel, or shoe leather. Dewey put this matter quite unambiguously: "The idea is, in short, art and a work of art. As a work of art, it directly liberates subsequent action and makes it more fruitful in a creation of more meanings and more perceptions"

(LW1:278;EN:301). For Dewey, buttons are no more or less technological artifacts—that is, no more or less works of art—than are sonnets, logical objects, or scientific theories. In each case, ends and means are bound up interactively and meaningfully if the artifact works.

VI

In an attempt to render more perspicuous Dewey's unconventional treatment of means and ends, and to distinguish his sense of "ends" from the fixed and final ends that played an important part in classical Greek and medieval philosophy, Dewey introduced the term "end-in-view."

If an analysis of human experience reveals anything, it is that "man is naturally more interested in consummations than he is in preparations; and that consummations have first to be hit upon spontaneously and accidentally—as the baby gets food and all of us are warmed by the sun—before they can be objects of foresight, invention and industry" (LW1:71;EN:69). "The history of man shows . . . that man takes his enjoyment neat, and at as short range as possible" (LW1:69;EN:67).

Such enjoyments, as long as they are immediate, are unknown and unknowable. They consist not of comparisons, contrasts, relationships, and coexistences, but of aesthetic enjoyment whose value is self-involved, self-sufficient, and final. Dewey thought that the Greek founders of philosophy made the mistake of taking these naturally occurring aesthetic enjoyments for the objects of knowledge. They tried to deploy knowledge in an area where it has no business, and they thought the work of nonhuman nature superior to the work of human intelligence.

The outcome of this error was the diremption of means and ends that has been a dominant feature of most of the history of philosophy. "In classic Greek thought, the perception of ends was simply an esthetic contemplation of the forms of objects in which natural processes were completed" (LW1:86;EN:86). For both Plato and Aristotle, there are naturally occurring ends for the sake of which other things exist, but that do not exist for the sake of any further end. It was in this sense that Greek thought was static rather than dynamic, and contemplative rather than experimental.

In the modern period of philosophy, during the two centuries that followed the work of Descartes, ends were treated as the creations of private and subjective selves attempting to articulate personal desire, or else as "finite copies of the fulfilled intentions of an infinite mind" (LW1:86;EN:86). The mistake of the moderns was precisely that of the Greeks: ends were taken as final and as radically different from those things that exist in order to bring them about and for their sake.

Dewey's own analysis of means and ends attempts to overcome this long-standing diremption. He thought that the Greeks were correct on at least one point: natural processes must have come to fruition before ends can be the object of inquiry. But on two important points his account differed from theirs. First, natural ends are not final in the sense of objects worthy of contemplation, but are, rather, the means of active regulation of further outcomes that are artificial or technological. Second, if natural ends are not considered as means for further inquiry but as ends in themselves, adaptive inquiry degenerates because it loses its sense of the connections among things and turns into metaphysical fancy (LW1:86;EN:86).

Dewey thought that in their assessment of these matters the moderns went to the opposite extreme. In their hands, natural terminations and boundaries were often taken as irrelevant to the formulation of objects of desire. "In empirical fact, [ends] are projections of possible consequences; they are ends-in-view. The in-viewness of ends is as much conditioned by antecedent natural conditions as is perception of *contemporary* objects external to the organism, trees and stones, or whatever" (LW1:86;EN:86). He thought that the moderns had missed the point that naturally occurring ends are the "platforms" from which it is possible to regard other things.[19]

For Dewey, all ends are ends-in-view—that is, "aims, things viewed after deliberation as worthy of attainment and as evocative of effort. They are formed from objects taken in their immediate and terminal qualities; objects once having occurred as endings, but which are not now in existence and which are not likely to come into existence save by an action which modifies surroundings" (LW1:88;EN:88). The work of realizing and appropriating natural ends, knowing them, removes them from the realm of immediate enjoyments, and allows assessment of their worthiness and usefulness as something to be strived for. Controlled inquiry generates a situation in which the better is separated from the worse and things that are meaningful (productive) are separated from those that lead nowhere. Ends-in-view thus have qualities that are relatively final and intrinsic, as well as those that are relatively extrinsic and instrumental to the development of further meanings that are only implicit in them: "The esthetic object may be useful and an useful one esthetic, or . . . immediacy and efficacy though distinguishable qualities are not disjoined existentially" (LW1:90;EN:90).

Typically, Dewey provides an example of this insight that is both straightforward and technologically familiar. When a person builds a house, he suggests, the end-in-view is the plan that *operates* with respect to selection of materials and their arrangement in construction. The end-in-view, far from being remote, is immanent at each stage of construction and constitutes the meaning of the materials used. Even when the house is complete, it is no final "end," since the decisions made at each stage continue to affect the ways in which the finished product can be lived in. Means and materials continue to render the finished house significant, and the house continues to provide significance for the means utilized. In the production of every successful artifact, which is to say in every stage of successful inquiry, means and ends so interpenetrate that they can be sorted out only in retrospect. "Every process of free art proves that the difference between means and end is analytic, formal, not material and chronologic" (LW1:280;EN:303). This is yet another of Dewey's many statements of the "philosophic fallacy."

VII

Dewey's treatment of ends and means provides him with the tools to sharpen two distinctions that were operative in the foregoing discussion: he distinguishes aesthetic enjoyment from artistic production and nature from the technological or artificial. Both aesthetic enjoyment and artistic production, he suggests, involve a perception of meanings. In experience that we call aesthetic, there is "appropriative enjoyment" of tendencies in things that have already been brought to some fruitful conclusion, whether by nature or by previous (technological) artistic endeavor. But aesthetic enjoyment is, at its best, nevertheless a result of the working of productive skill.

Appreciation, unlike simple delight, is not otiose but appropriative. Appreciation is delight informed by knowing in its honorific sense: as such, it is a species of controlled inquiry and thus a technological undertaking. Objects produced by artists do their work at a primitive level when they afford delight. But they work better when they interact with individuals who have prepared themselves to appreciate them. That preparation is itself a form of technological con-struction.

A very special type of developed appreciation is that of the scientist who has developed the skill required for the interaction with and transformation of some special class of natural events. The scientist must also be able to appreciate the scientific artifacts, including physical and conceptual tools, that have been developed by fellow scientists. There is an important sense in which scientific work is spurred by aesthetic delight that accompanies interaction with instrumentation: fast computers, X-ray machines, centrifuges, gleaming glassware, graphic displays from color plotters. Scientific work is no less stimulated by the aesthetic delight that arises from interaction with scientific colleagues, from the satisfaction consequent upon the publication of results, and from systems of national and international honors and awards. This is one of the reasons that Dewey calls science a special type of art.

But some objects and events to be appropriated and appreciated are richer and more suggestive than others, just as some individuals are better prepared than are others to appropriate them. Artistic production has been done, and the result is that the perceiver has been furnished with certain guides, directions, and clues that aid the work of appropriation. Artistic production seeks out, takes hold of, and further develops the possibilities of situations exhibited in natural or previously developed tendencies.

It is in this context that the intuition that "art imitates nature" comes alive. The production of objects that are aesthetically delightful and meaningful may, of course, involve models, renditions, or even tracings of natural objects. The photographs of Edward Weston and Ansel Adams, as well as the paintings of Georgia O'Keefe, provide numerous examples. And there is an enormous body of literature devoted to criticism of the ways in which films succeed or fail to be "art" insofar as they are "realistic."[20] But mimicry is only one of the many senses in which art imitates nature. In a richer and more general sense, art imitates nature because nature is fecund and productive, and brings forth consequences, and this is also what productive skill accomplishes. Art continues and brings to fruition what is only implicit or incipient in nature.[21]

The imitation of nature by means of the development and use of technology—productive skill—is, then, more than simple mimicry, though it may be that. It also involves imitation in the sense of continuing what nature has begun, but going natural processes one better. Productive skill takes the processes and events of nature, and further develops them for human use and enjoyment. It takes the beginnings and endings of nature, and transforms them into conditions and consequences. For Dewey, as for Aristotle, *techne* or productive skill is a primary term because it calls out the connections and interactions of human beings with and as a part of nature. But it also establishes the uniqueness of human beings within nature. Human beings do what nature does, not only because they are natural beings caught up in an existence that is natural as well as artificial, but also because they are fecund and productive in a way that nonhuman nature is able only to suggest, unable to bring to fruition without human intervention.

VIII

There is no room to doubt that the manner in which Dewey expressed himself in *Art as Experience* has led, and continues to lead, to considerable confusion. Stephen Pepper, who had already begun to write what he called "an exposition of the pragmatic esthetics"[22] two years before the appearance of *Art as Experience* in 1934, and who thought his own work "a prediction of what . . . a pragmatist of importance would write if he undertook to make a carefully considered and extended statement,"[23] was shocked by what he found there. He thought that Dewey had suffered a regrettable relapse into the "organic" or Hegelian idealism that characterized his work in the mid-1880s before his turn to instrumentalism.

Benedetto Croce, though he shared Pepper's assessment that

Dewey's work on aesthetics was a species of organic idealism, thought the situation anything but regrettable. He was elated by what he took to be Dewey's return to his intellectual roots, and he announced that the views expressed in *Art as Experience* were almost point for point his own, as they had been articulated in Croce's 1902 *Estetica*.

Dewey rejected both interpretations of his work. His reply to Croce was uncharacteristically acerbic. He not only did not concede ground to Croce, but also denied that they stood on ground that was common.[24] Apart from its combativeness, however, Dewey's two-page reply to Croce is of value because of its concise statement of the position articulated in *Art as Experience*.

First, Dewey repeated the claim that he had been making since even before the 1903 *Studies* (see MW2:313;SLT:19;EEL:98) that "knowing is an activity of human beings as *living* beings; that knowing represents a highly important concern of human life."[25] In other words, although knowing is the means of enriching human life and making it more meaningful, it is by no means the sole human activity.

Second, Dewey emphasized another point that he had been articulating since 1903: science, even though it is a significant activity, is not the paradigm of human experience. "If it be a legitimate question to ask which one of the two, science or art, owes the most to the other, I should be inclined to award the palm to art."[26] But "art" in this sentence does not mean the philosophy of art. Dewey claimed that he had learned little from "the *official* treatises on art composed by philosophers"[27] (among which he undoubtedly included Croce's) because they almost universally subordinated art to philosophy "instead of using philosophy as an incidental aid in appreciation of art in its own language."[28]

Finally, Dewey identified science as a "highly skilled technology."[29] Productive skills brought to bear on the problems of creating works of art and sharpening aesthetic appreciation are not only inclusive of the skills we call scientific, but also offer the key to understanding the "operation of human life AS life."[30]

Dewey, here as elsewhere, clearly stated his view that there are areas of human life that are not the business of cognitive knowledge. He argued that there are vast regions of aesthetic experience that will never be the object of transformation by intelligent inquiry or the application of productive skill. Life is rich in such experiences, even though some of them may not themselves be rich; there is never sufficient opportunity to pursue every lead, to assess and come to terms with every suggestion. But in this connection it is worth repeating John J. McDermott's felicitous paraphrase, which I quoted in the previous chapter:

> Experience . . . is not headless, for it teems with relational leads, inferences, implications, comparisons, retrospections, directions, warnings, and so on. The rhythm of *how* we experience is an aesthetic, having as its major

characteristic the relationship between anticipation and consummation, yet
having other perturbations, as mishap, loss, boredom, and listlessness . . .
the entire human endeavor should be an effort to apply the method of
creative intelligence in order to achieve optimum possibilities in the never-
ending moral struggle to harmonize the means-end relationship.[31]

What uniquely characterizes human experience is its taking of some
suggestions as potentially significant, its bringing them to fruition as
meaningful, and its enjoying of the superadded value that is the result of
productive activity. Humans do this daily, hourly, in each waking
moment. This basic activity comes in many shapes and sizes, as well as
in a multitude of levels of intensity and significance. These activities
overlap, and they compete for priority. Seen in these terms, the end of
human living is not practice, as some Marxists have indicated, or
contemplation, as Hannah Arendt has suggested, or even enjoyment, as
some aesthetes have thought. It is, rather, a cycle of production:
production of new significances, production of new feelings, production
of new means of enjoying, production of new techniques of production.
To be human is to be involved in production, to advance what nature
has given, to con-struct ourselves, to be technological.

    This, in sum, is what Dewey called "instrumentalism." In *Art as
Experience*, in the context of a denial that the aesthetic experience can
be defined as a mode of knowledge, he provided what is perhaps his
most precise definition of that term: "I have from time to time set forth a
conception of knowledge as being 'instrumental.' Strange meanings
have been imputed by critics to this conception. Its actual content is
simple: Knowledge is instrumental to the enrichment of immediate
experience through the control over action that it exercises"
(LW10:294;AE:290).

    Everything is here in this remark: immediate experience as just
undergone, controlled inquiry and *an* experience that is enjoyed as
enriched. This is also a definition of productive skill in active use.

IX

One of Dewey's insights that is often missed even by those who read
his work quite diligently is that the material of "aesthetic experience"
frequently grows on its own, quite apart from our conscious intent. It
can find expression only through concrete, productive activities, but by
that point it has already undergone enormous maturation and
development. One critic who understands this point quite well is Thomas
Alexander. "As *an* experience grows," he writes, "it reveals its material
and the possibilities of that material for being expressive and belonging
together. The material is gathered together as it becomes evident or
established in the work. The work is the process, the demanding

enactment binding creator and appreciators through the care for the subject matter."[32]

To recall an analogy that Dewey used in 1898 in his criticism of Huxley, experiences exhibit the same ambiguity that characterizes gardens: in one sense, one *grows* a garden; in an equally important sense, however, flowers and herbs just *grow*.[33] Even while a gardener tends planting beds with great care, exercising meticulous care to ensure that weeding is properly done and that appropriate amounts of water and fertilizer are applied, there is something going on over which he or she has little or no control. The plants are maturing. Genetic information, for which the gardener is in no way responsible, is expressing itself. Photosynthesis, which the gardener may understand in a way that is at best cursory, is taking place.

That human beings are able to undertake and even to effect control of problematic situations is in Dewey's critique of technology a natural event among other natural events. In the opening pages of *Art as Experience* Dewey calls upon yet another image to express this fact: the inhabitants of an island, because of their involvement in quotidian affairs, may tend to forget that what takes place for them, their successes and failures, occurs upon the peak of a great mountain, the bulk of which lies under the ocean unseen. The activities that dominate their narrow focus is supported by more than they know.

Dewey calls upon a passage from William James's great study of religious experience to illustrate his point. James suggested that the aim and focus of consciousness is generally something quite dim and inaccurate. At the same time, however, conscious processes exhibit an "organic ripening" that is aided by confederate subconscious forces that are active but behind the scenes. Too much conscious effort may actually interfere with the maturing appreciation of a set of circumstances. Hence, "when the new centre of energy has been subconsciously incubated so long as to be just ready to burst into flower, 'hands off' is the only word for us; it must burst forth unaided" (LW10:79;AE:72).[34]

The key to understanding this matter lies in the appreciation of two facts. The first is the fact that activities that are otherwise independent are undertaken by one and the same living creature. Below the level of conscious intention, there is the interplay of the results of projects undertaken independently and a coming to fruition of projects begun but not finished. But "when patience has done its perfect work, the man is taken possession of by the appropriate muse and speaks and sings as some god dictates" (LW10:79–80;AE:73).

Dewey makes clear his view that this is no less the case with respect to "thinkers," scientists, and technicians than it is with respect to "artists." In both cases there is "emotionalized imagination" at work on inchoate and unformed material. Materials encountered in a business office are, of course, different from those found in a painter's studio.

And the tools explicitly developed by each occupation in an attempt to effect the expression of its own pertinent materials are also different. But techniques of inquiry in these different fields are, in Dewey's view, not dissimilar. Both involve the coming to terms with tendencies in existential things, both natural and artificial. Both involve the creative manipulation of meanings in order to render articulate material that would otherwise continue to be unconnected and lifeless. In neither is expression a property of an artisan, an object, or a perceiver; it is what occurs in a situation in which materials are brought to fruition in such a way that communication is enhanced.

The second important fact is a larger one: activities that would otherwise be independent are undertaken by members of a community whose stock of tools and meanings is shared. For groups, however, just as for individuals, there are compartments of inchoate material, material that has not been fully expressed and that demands to be opened, explored, and developed. Dewey was nowhere clearer on this point than in his essay "Human Abode of Religious Function," which forms part of his 1934 Terry Lectures at Yale, published as *A Common Faith*. Dewey quotes C. E. Ayres: "Our industrial revolution began, as some historians say, with half a dozen technical improvements in the textile industry; and it took us a century to realize that anything of moment had happened to us, beyond the obvious improvement of spinning and weaving" (LW9:50;CF:75).[35] The important point that Ayres put his finger on is that the forces unleashed by scientific and industrial changes are anything but neutral. As McDermott has reminded us, situations are not headless—they teem with values. But while these forces have tended to mature and grow in certain ways, often quite independently of active human technical control, they should not therefore be thought of as the sharply defined historical "forces" approved of by historical determinists such as Marx (in certain of his writings). They are instead inchoate and confused, from the standpoint of human purpose. They present conflicting patterns, and exhibit arbitrary and inefficient outcomes. They are not what they can be. They are much like the beginnings and endings of nature. But they are also like the subconscious "centers of energy" of which James writes. Like the materials utilized by the individual artist working with paint or stone, they require a type of reorganization and restructuring that is best called artistic.

The means of expressing these centers of energy, these scientific and technological forces, is what Dewey calls "social intelligence." And social intelligence is for him a type of artistic production that is undertaken by an ensemble—by a public.

I shall return in chapter 7 to the role of various publics in expressing technological tendencies. I shall conclude this chapter with a brief remark concerning how the arts can be instrumental to their expression.

Science may be instrumental to such expression, but it is more often those forms of inquiry that are commonly termed "the arts" that perform this function. This is true for several reasons. First, the arts are a part of the quotidian life of the average person in a way that science is not. Decoration, ceremony, and ritual are not restricted to the life of human beings in the incomplex societies we label "primitive": they color virtually every area of the life of the most sophisticated member of the most complex industrial society. Second, as Dewey puts it, the sciences have to do with the significance of objects; the arts have to do with their expression. Science leads to an experience; art constitutes one (LW10:91;AD:85). The scientist may offer analysis of the contents of a grape harvest in terms of its sugar content, its acidity, and so on. But it is up to the vintner as artist to *express* that harvest in terms of a finished product. Third, the arts are cross-cultural in ways that science only aspires to be. International scientific convocations still depend upon natural languages within which their technical vocabularies are nested. Concerted efforts at translation must be made, and they meet with varying degrees of success. But international auto rallies, baseball tournaments, jazz and rock festivals, and industrial fairs cross cultural boundaries in ways that are truly marvelous. Their languages are more universal, more immediately apprehended than are the languages of scientific or literary events.

   This leads Dewey to conclude that education in the arts, the process by which we sharpen the processes of production and appreciation that interact to produce enriched aesthetic experience, is much more than simply conveying information. Art is not something that can be "brought to" industrial workers whose everyday surroundings are in all other ways artistically impoverished. Neither traveling museums nor public sculpture work as substitutes for thoughtful measures undertaken to improve the aesthetic qualities of a total environment.

   In this regard it was Dewey's view that the emphasis of the industrial arts must be removed from the domain where debits and credits are balanced; that it must instead be located in that area where final use and consumption are accepted as criteria of "valuation, decision and direction" (LW5:105;ION:135). Under such improved conditions, he suggested, education in the arts can become instruction in the arts of living. Education in the arts is, thus, for Dewey ultimately "a matter of communication and participation in values of life by means of the imagination, and works of art are the most intimate and energetic means of aiding individuals to share in the arts of living" (LW10:339;AE:336).

Chapter Four: From *Techne* to Technology:
Dewey's Reading of the History of
Technology

> To know, means that men have become willing to
> turn away from precious possessions; willing to let
> drop what they own, however precious, in behalf of a
> grasp of objects which they do not as yet own.
> Multiplied and secure ends depend upon letting go
> existent ends, reducing them to indicative and
> implying means. The great historic obstacle to
> science was unwillingness to make the surrender, lest
> moral, esthetic and religious objects suffer.
> (LW1:107;EN:110)

> When the appliances of a technology that had grown
> more deliberate were adopted in inquiry, and the lens,
> pendulum, magnetic needle, lever were used as tools
> of knowing, and their functions were treated as
> models to follow in interpreting physical phenomena,
> science ceased to be identified with appreciative
> contemplation of noble and ideal objects, was freed
> from subjection to esthetic perfections, and became
> an affair of time and history intelligently managed.
> (LW1:120;EN:125)

I

In his 1927 essay "Philosophy and Civilization," Dewey had much to
say about the construction of histories and their place in the broader
pattern of constructions we call "civilization." First, he suggested,
writers of histories are themselves caught up in history: they are among
the creators of its future as well as among the creatures of its past. The
historian may in fact be after truth; but in so doing he or she is even
more fundamentally after meaning, for "truths are but one class of
meanings, namely, those in which a claim to verifiability by their
consequences is an intrinsic part of their meaning" (LW3:4–5;PC:5).
Taking Dewey at his word, we should read his inquiry into the history of

the philosophy of technology not so much as a search for truth and falsity as an attempt to penetrate and enlarge meanings.

Because he rejected idealism, Dewey also rejected the claim that significance is coextensive with existence, that is, that values are the same as events. There is in fact a great expanse of existence that must remain without significance. The map is not, nor could it ever be, the territory. Although Dewey was the persistent enemy of dualisms of all sorts, he recognized in this matter one disparity that he thought irreducible: existence and meaning are not everywhere mappable one to one. Histories are never complete; they always reflect the interests of those who write them. The writing of history is more than the cataloging of facts; it is the bringing into existence of value where it had been lacking. "The characteristic life of man is itself the meaning of vast stretches of existences, and without it the latter have no value or significance" (LW3:5;PC:6).

II

There are many ways of approaching the history of technology. Some writers, including Lynn Thorndike, Lynn White, and Joseph Needham, have focused upon the invention and development of technological artifacts, and upon the consequences of those artifacts for daily life and for culture at large. For others the history of technology is economic history. For Karl Marx it was an account of the means of production and the types of social organizations that he thought were dependent upon those means. For John Kenneth Galbraith it was an account of the changing loci of economic power: first land, then capital, now information. Marshall McLuhan's history of technology was the history of types of communication systems and the diverse "sensory ratios" that accompanied them. Daniel Bell's sociological account of the history of technology turned on the extent and type of industrialization pervasive during what he took to be the stages of technological development. The history of technology written by José Ortega y Gasset was a study in philosophical anthropology. In his account, the technology associated with chance discoveries gave way in time to the static technology of the craftsman, and finally to the dynamic technology of the technician.

Despite their different perspectives, however, there is a startling consistency in these accounts of the history of technology. Each author articulates three stages: a remote past, an immediate past, and an immediate future. Some of these views distinguish within their remote past three further substages. In this regard Anthony Quinton has called our attention to some remarkable structural similarities between the history of technology given us by Marx and the one constructed by McLuhan.[1]

A somewhat oversimplified but not otherwise incorrect rehearsal of

Marx's views is the following one. For Marx, the first stage of technology may be simply termed "precapitalism." There, he found the primitive communism of the family and tribe doing their hunting and gathering, and engaging in primitive agricultural practices. As agricultural production became more advanced, and the crafts and trades were developed, slaves were required for the smooth operation of the technological system. The still more organized production of medieval Europe replaced the system of slaves with one that was feudal. The rise of the bourgeoisie, and their emphasis on the accumulation of capital and the exploitation of the worker, set the stage for Marx's second major period of technology, which we know as "capitalism." Finally, the internal contradictions of that system, in which the means of production are in the hands of the few to the disadvantage of the many, form the basis for a third distinct stage. Socialism is Marx's immediate future.

Though hardly known for its systematic features, the work of Marshall McLuhan nevertheless exhibits a strikingly similar structure. His remote past is oral-aural culture as it functioned before the invention of the printing press. His immediate past is "the Gutenberg era" of typographic human beings, with the individualism, nationalism, and linearity that McLuhan thought the printed word entailed. His immediate future is an electronic age in which there will be a return to oral-aural patterns of communication, but this time with the advantages of the visual stage, that is, with eyes wide open.

Like Marx's first technological stage, McLuhan's also exhibits three substages: strictly oral-aural cultures prior to the invention of printing, ideographic cultures of the Middle East and Orient, and the manuscript culture of the European Middle Ages.

Dewey's perspective is philosophical, so his history of technology is more than anything else a history of the philosophy of technology. This means that he was interested in the philosophical meanings of the history of technology; in the ways in which philosophers have understood the production and significance of artifacts of all types; and, even more generally, in the ways in which philosophers have treated all sorts of doing and making. It was Dewey's view that any given period of philosophy, including our own, can be understood and appreciated only as we grasp its cultural context. He was interested in the work of anthropologists, historians of science, and sociologists, among others; and he utilized their insights in his attempt to ascertain what is unique about our own time, as well as what present activities portend.

Like the histories advanced by Marx and McLuhan—indeed, like those of Bell, Galbraith, Ortega, and others—Dewey's history of the philosophy of technology has three stages. Given Dewey's philosophical roots, planted deep in the work of Hegel (and to a lesser extent in the work of Peirce, who was himself deeply influenced by Kant), this should not be surprising.

Dewey's first stage is that of the hunter. For the hunter, tools are almost nonexistent. The aesthetic and the instrumental are neither readily distinguished nor easily distinguishable. Means and ends interpenetrate, and there is little awareness of objects as such because they are thoroughly functionalized.

His second stage belonged to the Greeks. This stage in turn breaks down into three substages: (a) the fatalism of the culture of Homer and Hesiod, (b) the intellectual abstractions of Plato and Aristotle, and (c) the fideistic abstractions of their medieval heirs. The key to this period, however, is the philosophical work of the Athenian Greeks of the fourth century B.C. For both Plato and Aristotle, aesthetic contemplation precludes or renders inferior any serious interest in instrumentation. Means and ends are separated, and there is an abstraction and hypostatizing of ideas and events.

Finally, there is the scientific revolution of the sixteenth and seventeenth centuries: means and ends interpenetrate by alternation with one another, and objects and events are taken instrumentally as data for the development of further meanings and significance. Dewey suggested the possibility of a further development of this stage. If it were to occur, it would constitute yet another revolution. It would consist of the application of the methods of experimental science to a full range of human activities, including the social sciences.

Another way of reading Dewey's history of the philosophy of technology is to treat his remarks on hunting cultures as preliminary. This would make his first stage the one dominated by the Greeks. As I have indicated, this stage would in turn break down into three substages: the Hesiodic, the Platonic-Aristotelian, and the Medieval. Dewey's second stage would then be the scientific revolution of the age of Galileo, and his third stage would be the immediate future that offers the possibility of the application of the methods of scientific technology to every area of human valuation. This alternative description would have the interesting consequence of bringing Dewey's schema into line with those of the other historians of technology I have mentioned.

III

Despite the fact that Dewey was one of the last American philosophers to provide a comprehensive treatment of each of the traditional divisions of philosophical concern—for example, logic, ethics, aesthetics, and metaphysics—he thought philosophy in his time had been overly zealous in its attempts to build systems.[2] His general account of the history and philosophy of technology reflects this distrust of "history-as-system." It may even be correct to say that Dewey does not present a history of technology in a strict sense. What he does instead is apply the genetic method that he explicated perhaps most fully in his 1903 *Studies in Logical Theory* to the several dominant cultural attitudes toward instrumentation that he finds in his reading of the literature of history, psychology, anthropology, sociology, and philosophy. His interest thus focuses upon the incremental, though sometimes discontinuous, development of enriched instrumentality and capacity for appreciation. He argued that technological progress—by which he means human progress[3]—be measured in terms of the degree to which significance of artifacts is enriched. Such enrichment is the result of increased ability to substitute one thing for another, or one meaning for another, for the purpose of enhanced pro-duction and con-struction.

In "Interpretation of Savage Mind," first published in *Psychological Review* in 1902 and reprinted in *Philosophy and Civilization* in 1931, Dewey presented a fascinating interpretation of what he took to be a very early stage of technology. As Claude Lévi-Strauss would do some fifty years later, Dewey argued that "the psychical attitudes and traits of the savage are more than stages through which mind has passed, leaving them behind. They are outgrowths which have entered decisively into further evolution, and as such form an integral part of the framework of present mental organization" (MW2:39;PC:173).

There are several important elements at work in his account. First, his genetic method, which Peirce so sharply criticized in his review of the 1903 *Studies in Logical Theory*, is here conspicuous. Analysis is not sufficient to an understanding of structure and function, unless by "analysis" is meant a critical examination of the development of functions and their consequent structures through time and in their various contexts. As Dewey pointedly remarked in the introduction to his 1916 *Essays in Experimental Logic*, "Instead of telling about the nature of experience by means of a prior conception of individual man, I find it necessary to go to experience to find out what is meant by 'individual' and by 'man'; and also by 'the' " (MW10:363;EEL:69).

Second, despite his use of then-current anthropological terms "savage" and "primitive," Dewey refuses to regard the mental organization of the "savage" as exhibiting a different general functional pattern (Lévi-Strauss would later call this pattern a "structure") from that exhibited by human individuals in his own time and culture. It is possible to speculate about the debt Dewey owed to Hegel in this regard, since both recognize that developmental stages do not disappear but are "sublated" (Hegel's word is "*aufgehoben*,")—that is, they are taken up and preserved within a level of organization that is more complex than the preceding one.

Regardless of its pedigree, however, Dewey's idea is clear enough: human life, wherever it is found, exhibits certain characteristic traits, certain functions that have family resemblances. "We must recognize that mind has a pattern, a scheme of arrangement in its constituent elements, and that it is the business of a serious comparative psychology to exhibit these patterns, forms or types in detail" (MW2:41;PC:175). Recalling Dewey's discussion of "mind" from chapter 2, it should be obvious that what he means here is not the activity of an individual brain or even the activities of a group of brains, but a culture in which individuals are actively engaged in communication with one another. This is precisely the idea that Lévi-Strauss would later develop and popularize.

Considerable light is shed on the relation between Dewey and Lévi-Strauss in a remarkable essay by Edith Wyschogrod.[4] Wyschogrod is one of the few philosophers who has understood the centrality of technology in Dewey's larger philosophy. "Unable to abandon the methods of the particular sciences whose successes he believes are attested in their fruits and reluctant to give up the distinctively human cosmos," she writes, "Dewey turns for his model of inquiry to the world of doers. Shrewd and versatile, the everyday mechanics and artisans, inventors and craftsmen never lose sight of the needs and desires of human society."[5]

For Wyschogrod, the operative concept in the work of both Dewey and Lévi-Strauss is signified by the term *bricolage*, which Lévi-Strauss utilizes in his book *The Savage Mind*. "In its old sense the verb 'bricoler' applied to ball games and billiards, to hunting, shooting and riding. It was however always used with reference to some extraneous movement; a ball rebounding, a dog straying or a horse swerving from its direct course to avoid an obstacle. And in our own time the '*bricoleur*' is still someone who works with his hands and uses devious means compared to those of a craftsman."[6] Wyschogrod juxtaposes this passage with a remark by Dewey in *Experience and Nature*: "Acumen, shrewdness, inventiveness, accumulation and transmission of information are products of the necessity under which man labors to turn away from absorption in direct having and enjoying, so as to consider things in their active connections as means and as signs" (LW1:101;EN:103).

Dewey argued that "occupations" or "vocations" (general patterns of productive activity to which an individual is committed and which are for him or her the locus of meaning) determine "fundamental modes of activity," and thus that they "control the formation and use of habits" (MW2:41;PC:175). Habits in turn "furnish the working classifications and definitions of value; they control the desire processes. Moreover, they decide the sets of objects and relations that are important, and thereby provide the content or material of attention, and the qualities that are interestingly significant" (MW2:41–42;PC:176).

In other words, what individuals are inclined to select as important from the busy environment in which they find themselves, and the values or goals that they are capable of projecting and toward which they are willing to work, are specific activities of production that are conditioned by the larger pattern of production called an occupation. Perceptions, goals, and ideals will thus vary among hunters, shepherds, military types, traders, those engaged in crafts, and those involved in manufacture. What seems not to vary, however, is that there are occupations that condition habits, which in turn condition specific activities.

This is not a hard technological determinism of the type that Marx advanced in certain places in his work, paraphrased by Heilbroner as the view that "machines make history." Rather, it is a recognition of the fact that productive activities operate at different levels of generality, and that the more general, in the sense of more widely applicable, often encloses within itself less comprehensive tendencies to behave in certain ways. Moreover, these less general tendencies or habits determine individual responses. A more complete treatment of Dewey's and Marx's views with respect to technological determinism will follow in chapter 6.

In a footnote Dewey extends his metaphor of "occupations" into nonhuman nature, suggesting that biological genera are "occupational" classifications. "They connote different ways of getting a living with the different instrumentalities (organs) appropriate to them, and the different associative relations set up by them" (MW2:41n;PC:175n). This is more than a gratuitous remark. It underscores Dewey's use of biological models for what he calls "comparative psychology" and what is for us his sketch of the history of technology. But biological genera are ultimately for Dewey not so much structural as functional. Genera and species are not fixed essences but general patterns of organized activity—occupations. Moreover, this metaphor is itself a tool he uses to draw attention to the continuity between the portion of nature that is less well organized and nonhuman, and the better-organized part of nature constructed and inhabited by human beings.

IV

Dewey's example of primitive or low-level technology is that of the Australian aborigines. Perhaps the most significant thing about their lives is the environment with which they interact: it does not offer much natural resistance. It is not dangerous, and it offers sufficient food to sustain them as long as they are on the move. Their technology is thus very simple. It involves no cultivated plants, no domesticated animals (with the exception of the dingo dog), no beasts of burden, and no use or knowledge of metals.

Although there is tool use, such tools as there are remain simple and just those actually in use at the moment. They are not saved, stored, or improved upon, but found immediately at hand and discarded after use.

Also conspicuous in this type of technology is a concretely functional interpenetration of means and ends. Goals are short-term ones, concretely realizable in ways that are unambiguous. Things point beyond themselves only minimally. Such significance as exists is intense, pointed, and fleeting.

There are no intermediate appliances, no adjustment of means to remote ends, no postponements of satisfaction, no transfer of interest and attention over to a complex system of acts and objects. Want, effort, skill and satisfaction stand in the closest relations to one another. The ultimate aim and the urgent concern of the moment are identical; memory of the past and hope for the future meet and are lost in the stress of the present problem; tools, implements, weapons are not mechanical and objective means, but are part of the present activity, organic parts of personal skill and effort. The land is not a means to a result but an intimate and fused portion of life—a matter not of objective inspection and analysis, but of affectionate and sympathetic regard. The making of weapons is felt as a part of the exciting use of them. Plants and animals are not "things," but are factors in the display of energy and form the contents of most intense satisfactions. The "animism" of primitive mind is a necessary expression of the immediacy of relation existing between want, overt activity, that which affords satisfaction and the attained satisfaction itself. Only when things are treated simply as *means*, are marked off and held off against remote ends, do they become "objects." (MW2:43–44;PC:178)

Dewey was quick to point out that this manifestation of technology, though "primitive" enough when measured against its modern forms, does not indicate "stupidity or dullness or apathy" on the part of its practitioners. He found in the activities of the aboriginal hunters "highly specialized skills of sense, movement, ingenuity, strategy and combat" (MW2:45;PC:180).

A key word in Dewey's description of this type of technology is "drama." The hunt itself is a dramatic event, emotionally intensified because of its intimate connection with matters of life and death. The place of the successful hunter within his community—the admiration in which he is held, his consequent sexual successes, and the positions of authority accorded him—constitutes another level of drama that is no less intense for having only derivatively to do with the hunt. Moreover, aboriginal art, though it may sometimes involve drawing, is primarily dramatic and mimetic; it revives and celebrates the intense feelings that are part of the hunt.[7]

The dramatic identification of hunter and prey is but another aspect of this broader pattern. Animals are regarded as "co-partners in the life of the group. Why then should they not be represented as of close kin?" (MW2:49;PC:185).

In short, there is only minimal "objectification." In the passage just quoted, Dewey suggests that things become objects when they are treated as means for the attainment of remote ends. In chapter 4 of *Experience and Nature* he expands this suggestion by drawing attention to four characteristics of objects in their "scientific" sense.

First, whereas immediate things are transient (that is, they come and go), the spatiotemporal orders that we call objects are constant and therefore capable of mathematical formulation. "They present stability,

recurrence at its maximum, raised to the highest degree"
(LW1:115;EN:119). In order for there to be objects at all, work must
have been done: construction and production that have taken place in
the history of civilization provide a head start for any given individual. As
young children we are taught the history and value of successful
objectification. Individual artists—whether they be scientists, technicians,
those working in what are called the "fine" arts, or individuals involved
in their quotidian situations—then interact with culturally inculcated
patterns of objectification. Some of the novel objects they create
become in their turn part of the public store. At least in the domain of
human culture, there is a kind of Lamarckian evolution at work. Changes
in the individual—artifacts produced—are absorbed and built upon by
future generations.

Second, objects allow for the institution of substitutions.
Signification occurs when one thing, readily at hand, is used to stand for
something else that is momentarily, or even ultimately, beyond control.
Scientific technology is the maximal development of such significance.
"It is a system of exchange and mutual conversion carried to its limit.
The cognitive result is the homogeneous natural world of modern
science" (LW1:115;EN:119). But substitution is effective only because it
is public; this is the reason why Dewey calls such scientific meanings
"outdoor facts."

Third, objects allow for the possibility of control. In nature there are
only beginnings and endings. By objectification, the turning of things into
objects, it is possible to find the "right units" for the alteration of natural
processes to suit human ends. There is, of course, a danger in treating
the "right units" as independent and ultimate: this is Dewey's criticism
of those who hold to what he calls "orthodox empiricism" (MW10:19ff.),
among them Hume and Russell, as opposed to his own "empirical
empiricism."[8] Dewey thus once again emphasizes his rejection of both
subjectivism and objective realism. For the subjectivist, things cannot
fully become objects because there is no community in which they may
do so. For the objective realist, objects are primary and independent:
because they cannot be easily substituted for one another and thereby
transformed, objective realists are left with "association" as their
primary scientific category. But if association is interpreted with
sufficient richness to allow for the transformations necessary to science,
the objective realist has undercut his or her own position by rendering
objects much more malleable and permeable than objective realism
would allow them to be.

Fourth, only when objectification occurs—when a rich matrix of
objects as measuring and measurable, as signifying and signified, has
been developed—is it possible to speak of scientific laws and relations.
"These are the formulations of the regularities upon which intellectual
and other regulation of things as immediate apparitions depends"
(LW1:117;EN:121).

Because they do not care for objectification, the aborigines have neither science nor even the idea of science. They have a technology, but their use of tools is minimal. Such life is characterized by "immediacy of interest, attention and deed" (MW2:44;PC:178). But immediacy is not the same as sensuous indulgence. Dewey argues that the hunter has achieved a marvelous integration of the working of intellectual and practical skills with the dramatic play of emotion.

Dewey finds interesting the degree to which the language and emotions of the hunt pervade the lives of members of more technologically sophisticated societies. When nomadic hunting societies give way to those dependent on agricultural cultivation, tasks of material production are given over to women and slaves. The intelligence formerly required for the hunt becomes invested in activities of war. Of course, hunting itself is still a popular occupation among those industrialized men and women; but beyond that there is also the "transferred application of the hunting language to pursuit of truth, plot interest, business adventure and speculation, to all intense and active forms of amusement, to gambling and the 'sporting life' " (MW2:45;PC:180).

Dewey thus inverts the Victorian notion of technological progress, which was still a powerful force when this essay was published in 1902. Instead of looking among the "savages" to find possible rudimentary traces of the "superior" intelligence exhibited by industrial men and women, Dewey looks among the latter for vestiges of the particular intelligence of the former. It is his view that "the adjustment of habits to ends, through the medium of a problematic, doubtful, precarious situation, is the structural form upon which present intelligence and emotion are built. It remains the ground-pattern" (MW2:51). He thinks that a proper history of technology, which he here identifies as genetic psychology, would demonstrate how personal adjustments and habit formation in aboriginal people have become transformed into impersonal and objective tools by means of cooperation and the institutionalization of successful patterns of adaptation. This Dewey calls "the problem of the formation of mental patterns appropriate to agricultural, military, professional and technological and trade pursuits, and the reconstruction and overlaying of the original hunting schema" (MW2:51–52;PC:187).

V

Dewey thought that a significant change took place in Greek life between the time of Homer in the eighth or seventh century B.C. and that of Socrates and the Sophists some three hundred or four hundred years later. He saw in Homer and Hesiod "a gloomy temper of life," one in which "the sovereignty of fortune, largely ill-fortune, is prevalent" (LW1:103;EN:106).

Dewey's characterization of the culture of Hesiod could apply,

mutatis mutandis, to most of the prototechnological, religious,
agricultural cultures of the Greeks' Middle Eastern neighbors. It could
also apply to many cultures of our contemporary world. The activities of
the gods make or break human activities; try as one might, work as one
can, the ultimate avenue of control lies in attempts at "divination of the
intent of unseen powers and pious sacrifice" (LW1:103–4;EN:106).
Outcomes are a matter of fate, and fate is a matter of hope, not of
conscious control. Dewey quotes Hesiod: "Men favored by Hecate have
no need for knowledge, memory or effort to achieve success; she acts
alone without the assistance of her favorites."[9] Since he identified
technology with increased control of means and the enhanced
enjoyment of ends, Dewey thought that there was no significant
distinction to be made between types of fatalism. Whether fatalism
orients itself toward nature or toward the divine, there is a default from
intelligent control.

Dewey makes it clear that he thought this situation inferior to that
of the hunter. Despite his minimal use of instruments, the hunter was at
least free of a sense of impotence before the gods. His well-honed skills
were applied to the exercise of control within a situation, and it was this
exercise that was his source of delight. Dewey presents the hunter as
spirited, confident, and even joyful. In contrast, he presents the
superstitious agricultural cultures of the time of Hesiod as feckless,
riddled with doubts, and caught in a web of despair.

VI

By the time of the Sophists and Socrates, Dewey suggests, the Greeks
had undergone a change of mood. Perhaps taking their cue from the
increased successes of commercial ventures and production in the arts,
the Sophists taught that human beings could to a great extent control
their own futures.

Lynn White has drawn our attention to the connections between the
explosion of commerce in the Aegean in the fifth century B.C. and the
invention of coinage a century and a half or so before. But White has
also suggested that there is a connection between those commercial
events and the atomic theory of matter that was developed by the
Ionian philosophers during the same period. He thinks their idea that all
things could be reduced to one thing (whether air, fire, water, or
something else) "an intellectual novelty of the first order." But what
were the sources of this novelty? His suggestion is that "the
psychological roots of atomism would seem to be found in the saying of
Heraclitus of Ephesus that 'all things may be reduced to fire, and fire to
all things, just as all goods may be turned into gold and gold into all
goods.'[10] [Heraclitus] thought that he was just using a metaphor, but the
metaphor had been possible for only a century before he used it."[11]

Whether White's assessment turns out to be an accurate one is for our purposes irrelevant. What is important is that he provides an excellent example of the kind of reform that Dewey wished to see in philosophical historiography. Dewey took it as empirically obvious that tools and artifacts of all types have meanings, and that their meanings have commerce with other meanings. Even the most abstract philosophical meanings cannot remain aloof. To write the history of philosophy, or to *do* philosophy, as those enterprises have usually been undertaken, with proud ignorance of the cultural contexts with and within which ideas have commerce seemed to him a sure way to create false philosophical problems.

How does Dewey characterize the "stage" of technology manifested by the Greeks of the fourth century B.C.? If the hunter failed to objectify his world, the Greeks took the task of objectification so seriously that they overshot their mark. If the hunter had been caught up in a concrete functional interpenetration of means and ends, the Greeks not only focused upon aesthetic ends and abstracted them from the welter of experience, but also narrowed them beyond warrant by hypostatizing them as eternal objects of knowledge.

Greek artisans, like those of any age, lived in the midst of changing materials and conditions that it was their task to bring to successful fruition. The uncertainty of the grain of a piece of wood chosen to be utilized for the keel of a ship, the peculiarities of stone designated as material for a sculpture, the variable consistency of clay brought to the potter's shop for his use, the factors of Greek life and popular myth available as raw materials for dramatic rendition—these were elements of their variable and even, at times, precarious world.

To recall Dewey's remarks in *Art as Experience*, what differentiates crude art products from those that are refined is just the degree to which means and ends interpenetrate and cooperate, and the degree to which intrinsic meanings are enriched in the process. There were Greek sculptors and potters who were capable of bringing ends and means together into a consummatory product so rich and suggestive that we today make places of honor for their work in our museums and galleries. There were craftsmen whose shipbuilding techniques are still the object of admiration by engineers who are our contemporaries.

But the free Greeks, the Greeks who had the leisure for reflective *thinking*, exhibited an attitude toward such technological successes that was deeply contradictory. On the one hand, they regarded such production as "menial," literally as having to do with domestic affairs rather than those of public men. This was less so in the case of the dramatic arts because of their perceived links with life of the *polis*. But for the most part, and when not occupied with the tools and implements of battle, those who engaged in public affairs did not grapple with instruments and materials; they were proud to be "free" of involvement with, and knowledge of, the means of production.

On the other hand, aesthetic objects, once they were finished, received honored attention as objects of immediate enjoyment. "To the spectator," writes Dewey, "artistic objects are given; they need only to be envisaged; Greek reflection, carried on by a leisure class in the interest of liberalizing leisure, was preeminently that of the spectator, not that of the participator in processes of production" (LW1:78;EN:77–78).

To free or "liberal" Greeks the work of the artisan was not that of creating forms, but that of utilizing pre-existing ones, whether supernatural or natural, in a way that could never give them their full and final due. The artisans, because they were engaged with the vagaries of materials and conditions, were caught up in a world of change and uncertainty. Theirs was a world where true knowledge of forms could not penetrate, and where such forms as were operative were pale shadows of perfect and eternal ones. And because they were concerned with instrumentalities or means, they were thought incapable of a full measure of the immediate delight that accompanies knowledge of ends.

Because they demeaned the work of the artisan, Greek thinkers failed to see that technological work and technological artifacts can be *transformative* rather than simply *additive*. "It was a consolidation, effected by nature, of particular natural occurrences into actualization of the forms of such things as are thus and so usually, now and then, upon the whole, but not necessarily and always. Experience was adequate and final for this kind of thing because it was as much their culminating actualization as rational thought was the actualization of the forms of things that are what they are necessarily" (LW1:178;EN:189).

Dewey did not fault the Greek thinkers for their absorption in immediately enjoyed ends. He thought it wonderful that some things are immediately enjoyed, that they speak for themselves; and he thought it wonderful that the "Greek thinkers heard their voice" (LW1:76;EN:74). He did, however, think that there was something tragically ironic in their treatment of artists. Not only did they appropriate the work of the artist as a model for their intellectualized accounts of nature, supernature and social engineering; but also, at the same time, they demeaned the work of the artist as of secondary importance in the context of their grand cosmologies. They also sought to subject artistic production to censorship by those they regarded as the truest practitioners of their relocated and refined *techne*, the statesmen.

Greek thinkers were absorbed in the aesthetic side of the arts, but they took the productive side of the arts as the model for their philosophy and their idea of science. Therein lay their confusion. If they had been content to speak as artists, room might have been left for the development of science. Instead, they developed only the *idea* of science, and this because of their distaste for the real contingencies associated with instruments of measurement and production. As Dewey reminds us in his remarks on the century of Galileo, the idea of science floats on a sea of ideas. Science, as the knowing of things as significant, has its basis in the technological and the experimental; it takes instrumentation seriously as the means to its ends and as the means to the development of further ends.

It was not that the Greek thinkers were not "empirical." Dewey thought that "no philosopher can get away from experience even if he wants to. The most fantastic views ever entertained by superstitious people had some basis in experienced fact; they can be explained by one who knows enough about them and about the conditions under which they were formed" (LW1:36;EN:30). Dewey thought that philosophers have tended to be less superstitious than other people, to be sure. It is not so much that they have been fanciful, but "that they have failed to note the empirical needs that generate their problems, and have failed to return the refined products back to the context of actual experience, there to receive their check, inherit their full content of meaning, and give illumination and guidance in the immediate perplexities which originally occasioned reflection" (LW1:36–37;EN:31).

For Plato, the function of the work of the artist was not to introduce the delights of sensory artifacts, but to educate away from them and toward a pure intellectual perception of timeless forms (LW10:295ff.;AE:291ff.). His dialectic turns out to be a one-way street. Both technological artifacts and the work of the artisan are emptied of their meaning: they are "de-meaned." Technological function and product are reassigned. The True Artisan, the demiurge, and the True Artifacts, the forms, are for Plato outside time and space, apart from the contingencies of even the most refined experience.

Homer had used the term "form," or "*eidos*," as a synonym for "shape," or "what one sees." "Eidetic," as an image able to be recalled almost photographically, carries a similar sense in contemporary English. The Pre-Socratics continued the Homeric use. By the time of Herodotus, however, the term had been specified to signify "characteristic property" or "type." Thucydides utilized the term in the even more abstract sense of "constitutive nature." For Plato, however, the forms exist separately. They are the transcendent realities that are the causes of what is available to the senses (*aistheta*). "In an elaborate metaphor, pervasive in Plato, the *aistheton* is said to be a copy . . . of its eternal model (*paradeigma*), the *eidos*. This act of artistic creation . . . is the work of a supreme craftsman," the *demiourgos*.[12]

It seemed obvious to Dewey that the model for Plato's theory of forms was the activity and product of the human craftsman, and that his metaphysics was little more than relocated—indeed, *mislocated*— technology. He suggested that Plato was motivated by his perception that the artisans do not involve themselves sufficiently with forms, working as they do in a world of changing matter. "Plato was so troubled by the consequences of this ignorance of form on the part of all who live in the world of practice, industrial and political, that he elaborated a plan by which their activities might be regulated by those who, above labor and entanglement in change and practice, provide in laws forms to shape the habits of those who work'' (LW1:78–79;EN:78).

It was Dewey's contention, then, that Plato's eagerness to apotheosize aesthetic ends had the consequence of deprecating and demeaning the free play of inquiry into materials and conditions that is necessary to a full spectrum of human interaction with environing situations. The result was not just a perversion of technology, but (what may be for Dewey the same thing) a stunting of the growth of science and social inquiry as well. *The Republic* richly, and sadly, documents the results for social thought in general, even more specifically for democracy, of this turn against productive experience. It is there that Plato arrogates all meaningful technical skills to the totalitarian social engineer.

As far as science is concerned, Dewey argued that Plato's abhorrence of the mutability inherent in the tasks and materials of technology led to a science of ''contemplation''; that is, a putative science that could never be a true science because it eschewed existential details. Dewey warned that when inquiry is focused in the sphere of the transcendently telic, whether that inquiry concerns itself with materials and artifacts, conceptual models of nature, or the ways in which social organization takes place, such inquiry will fail to be instrumental, that is, scientific.

No less acute was Dewey's critique of Aristotle. Plato invested the productive activities and artifacts of the artisan outside nature, or if inside nature, surely in the hands of those above the fray because they had been trained to contemplate the supernatural. Aristotle attempted to escape this Platonic dualism ''by putting nature above art, and endowing nature with skilled purpose that for the most part achieves ends or completions. Thus the role of the human artisan whether in industry or politics became relatively negligible, and the miscarriages of human art a matter of relative insignificance'' (LW1:79;EN:78).

The four Aristotelian causes are obviously borrowed from the work of the artisans. The efficient, formal, material, and final causes of nature are those of ''an artist that works from within instead of from without'' (LW1:79;LW1:78). If the artisan has an idea that is articulated in stone, so must nature have forms and designs that it imposes on material potentialities.

But for Dewey, a cause is not merely an antecedent. It is instead ''that antecedent which if manipulated regulates the occurrence of the consequent'' (LW1:91;EN:92). Nor does cause possess higher metaphysical importance than effect, as Aristotle thought. Cause and effect exist on the same ontological level. Each is an element in the historical explanation of a situation, and each has certain aesthetic qualities. Moreover, ''since existence is historic it can be known or understood only as each portion is distinguished and related. For knowledge 'cause' and 'effect' alike have a partial and truncated being. It is as much a part of the real being of atoms that they give rise in time, under increasing complication of relationships, to qualities of blue and sweet, pain and beauty, as that they have at a cross-section of time extension, mass, or weight" (LW1:91;EN:92).

Dewey thought it quite remarkable that "Aristotle could draw his account of the four fundamental affairs of nature from analysis of the procedure of [the] artisan, with no suspicion that he was thereby subjecting his metaphysics to an anthropomorphic rendering of nature; setting up the cumulative deposit of individual variations of insight and skill as the measure of nature" (LW1:166–67;EN:176).

Dewey faults Aristotle no less than Plato for his bias in favor of the certain and invariant. "His whole theory of forms and ends is a theory of the superiority in Being of rounded-out fixities. His physics is a fixation of ranks or grades of necessity and contingency so sorted that necessity measures dignity and equals degree of reality, while contingency and change measure degrees of deficiency of Being" (LW1:47–48;EN:43).

In this connection Dewey thought it quite remarkable that Aristotle treated quantity as one of the accidents of substance—"that is, as something which can vary within limits (set by the inherent essence and measure, *logos*) of a thing without affecting its nature" (LW4:74;QC:92). He thought this further proof of the "essentially artistic character possessed for Greek science by the object of knowledge" (LW4:74;QC:92).

In the hands of Plato and Aristotle concrete technology became abstract metaphysics and contingent production became invariant theory. Dewey chides both philosophers, despite their preoccupation with aesthetic matters, for having limited themselves in that very domain: "Since they were thinkers, aiming at truth or knowledge, they put art on a lower plane than science; and the only enjoyment they found worth serious attention was that of objects of thought. In consequence they formulated a doctrine in which the esthetic and the rational are confused on principle, and they bequeathed the confusion as an intellectual tradition to their successors" (LW1:76;EN:74–75).

What, in sum, is Dewey's assessment of Greek attitudes toward technology? First, the actual work of Greek artisans and artists was much more transformative of techniques and materials than was understood by the Greek thinkers. Greek philosophy was primarily additive.

Second, the activity of the craftsman was plundered for models from which to build intellectualist cosmologies and social theories. Plato relocated the work of the artist in supernature; Aristotle, in nonhuman nature. But the translation of the models from one domain to another was defective because it failed to reflect the concreteness of the activity of the craftsman.

Third, the activities of the craftsmen were consciously demeaned by both Plato and Aristotle. Plato has the practitioner of statecraft exercising censorship over the products of the craftsman. Aristotle places the sciences of production at the bottom of his hierarchy of knowledge, beneath those that are theoretical and those that are practical.

Fourth, the long tradition of dualism with respect to body and mind, theory and practice, nature and supernature, inherited by Western philosophy from Plato and Aristotle, is a direct result of their mislocation of technology.

Fifth, Plato and Aristotle did not just invent this inversion of values; it was not "arbitrary speculation." "What the philosophers [were] responsible for [was] a peculiar one-sided interpretation of . . . empirical facts, an interpretation, however, which [had] its roots in features, although less admirable ones, of Greek culture" (LW1:80;EN:79).

Finally, Greek philosophers failed to understand the nature and function of objects as they would later be understood by experimental science. Objects are constant and capable of mathematical formulation; they allow for substitutions; they provide the possibility of technological control; they are the basis for the formulation of scientific laws and relations. But only if objects are viewed as "events *with* meanings" (LW1:240;EN:259), not as fixed and finished entities, is experimental science possible. To a certain extent, Greek artists treated objects in this way; were this not true, we would not honor their buildings, their sculpture, their ceramics, and their drama. What Greek science and philosophy failed to do was learn from their practitioners of *techne*. Dewey thought it proper and even laudable that Plato and Aristotle borrowed from the fine and practical arts for their idealized theories. But they should not, after having borrowed, rejected the sources of their insight. Dewey thought that this rejection indicated a lack of piety that cut them off from "the poetic and religious character of their own constructions, and established in the classic Western philosophic tradition the notions that immediate grasp and incorporation of objects is knowledge; that things are placed in graded reality in accordance with their capacity to afford a cultivated mind such a grasp or beholding; and that the order of reality in Being is coincident with a predetermined rank of Ends" (LW1:90;EN:91).

VII

Even if the attitudes of Plato and Aristotle toward *techne* were unjustifiably reductionistic, making social control the highest and only true human technical achievement and making all human making inferior to the making of nature and supernature, Dewey suggested, those attitudes nevertheless represented an unquestionable advance over the fatalism of their ancestors and their neighboring cultures. Even if they

failed to develop experimental science, they at least had the idea that
"arts based on knowledge cooperate with nature and render it
amenable to human happiness" (LW1:104;EN:107). This assessment
was a more accurate portrayal of the work of Aristotle than that of
Plato.

Even if the Greeks showed little gratitude to the artists from whom
they borrowed their patterns and models, we should not, Dewey
suggested, demonstrate similar ingratitude toward them. For it was as a
result of their work that it could finally be said that "the gods recede
into twilight. Divination has a powerful competitor. Worship becomes
moral. Medicine, war, and the crafts desert the temple and the altar of
the patron-god of the guild, as inventions, tools, techniques of action
and works multiply" (LW1:104;EN:107).

Dewey thought it a shame that the progress they had made was
not continued and further advanced. He suggested that from the late
Roman empire until the Renaissance there was a regrettable retreat
from active involvement with experimental inquiry. Philosophy during this
period changed from "a supreme art into a way of access to the
supernatural" (LW1:104).

This period was not one about which Dewey had a great deal to
say. In chapter 4 of *The Quest for Certainty*, however, he briefly
characterized it. It was a time of deeply entrenched dualisms. "Art" and
"science" were virtually synonymous terms, and were opposed to all
things "mechanical." As had been the case with the Greeks, knowledge
was placed above doing and making. Dewey once again turned to the
language of means and ends to describe its defects. "Grammar and
rhetoric, for example, in dealing with speech, the interpretation of
literature and the arts of persuasion, were higher than blacksmithing and
carpentry. The mechanical arts dealt with things which were merely
means; the liberal arts dealt with affairs that were ends, things having a
final and intrinsic worth" (LW 4:60;QC:74).

It should not be surprising, therefore, that the practical and
industrial arts were not regarded as a source of innovation, nor were
they so in fact. "Apprentices literally 'learned by doing,' and 'doing' was
routine repetition and imitation of the acts of others, until personal skill
was acquired" (LW4:60;QC:74).

Two important points should be made about Dewey's brief remarks
on this period of the philosophy of technology. First, despite arguments
more recently advanced to the effect that there were periodic bursts of
an attitude that could in some sense be called "empirical," and despite
recent studies of technical innovations made by now-anonymous
craftsmen, the period is nevertheless still generally understood
substantially as Dewey depicts it. Dominant social, political, and
theological conditions were such as to systematically stifle tendencies
toward the development of scientific experimentation and to thwart
technological innovation. Where technological advances were made, it

was in spite of, not because of, the reigning intellectual climate. Technology was during this period primarily a matter of the doing (practice) of prescribed tasks. There was little concern with the making (production) of new methods.

This was a period that Ortega y Gasset described as dominated by "technology of the craftsman," and which he depicts in terms that are quite close to Dewey's own characterization of it:

> At [this] stage of technology everybody knows shoemaking to be a skill peculiar to certain men. It can be greater or smaller and suffer slight variations as do natural skills, running for instance, or swimming or, better still, the flying of a bird, the charging of a bull. That means shoemaking is now recognized as exclusively human and not natural, i.e., animal; but it is still looked upon as a gift granted and fixed once and for all. Since it is something exclusively human it is extra-natural, but since it is something fixed and limited, a definite fund not admitting of substantial amplification, it partakes of nature; and thus technology belongs to the nature of man. As man finds himself equipped with the unexchangeable system of his bodily movements, so he finds himself equipped with the fixed system of the "arts."[13]

Second, Dewey thought that attitudes dominant during this period were of more than purely historical interest; he thought that they were still quite virulent even in his own lifetime. The distinction between the "learned professions" and the occupations of the shop and factory, the distinction between the use of the intellect and the use of the hands, the distinction between the delights of the mind and the temptations of the body—each of these distinctions is an important, though infelicitous, constituent of our contemporary life. Dewey thought that philosophies that seek to maintain these entrenched disparities have had, and continue to have, a threefold advantage over those that he regards as more progressive. First, they have an enormous institutional advantage. They have behind them "the multitude of imaginative and emotional associations and appeals that cluster about any tradition which has for long centuries been embodied in a dominant institution; they continue to influence, unconsciously, the minds of those who no longer give intellectual assent to the tenets on which the tradition intellectually rests" (LW4:62;QC:77). William James wrote of habit as a great "flywheel" of society. Dewey generalizes this view to include cultural institutions.

Second, they have a psychological advantage. They address and reinforce the typical human distaste for the precarious and unstable. They offer the hope and prospect of a world in which prized goods are eternally safe in a higher realm, where moth and rust do not corrupt. They play upon fear of loss, and upon the weariness that follows frustrated effort or dull and monotonous toil.

Third, they capitalize on a certain cultural schizophrenia. The things and activities that most occupy men and women are thought by them to be incapable of honorific formulation. And the things to which they do give their allegiance are usually beliefs that are no longer connected to their quotidian lives. Dewey thought it a scandal that "conditions and forces that dominate in actual fact the modern world have not attained any coherent intellectual expression of themselves" (LW4:62;QC:77).

As Dewey characterized it, then, the period between the Greeks and the Renaissance was one in which there was a default from attempts at technological control, and a corresponding turn to the supernatural and transcendent as sources of goals and ideals. For Plato the supernatural had at least been associated with intellectual insight; for the medievals the supernatural had to do with the publicly acknowledged absurdities of faith. Dewey borrowed a phrase from Gilbert Murray to describe the dominant attitude of this period. It could in his view be characterized as a "failure of nerve" (LW1:104;EN:107).

VIII

Dewey argued that a necessary condition for the rise of modern science was its increased attention to and utilization of instrumentation. The Greeks were empirical in their own way, but Galileo and Newton went beyond observation and "experience" to experimentation. Dewey isolated experimentation as "the indispensible instrument of modern scientific knowing," and defined it as "the art of conducting a sequence of observations in which natural conditions are intentionally altered and controlled in ways which will disclose, discover, natural subject-matters which would not otherwise have been noted" (LW1:339).

Put simply, it was Dewey's contention that empirical science remained at the level of intellectual abstraction until it began to be technological, until it began to take seriously the production and use of tools and artifacts for the purpose of enlarging the significance of objects and events.

It was Dewey's unique insight that in the *actual productive activities* of modern science, as opposed to much of its account of itself and the accounts that philosophers have given of it, the Aristotelian hierarchy of the sciences was inverted. In the work of Aristotle, the theoretical sciences were awarded primacy. Immediately subordinate to them were the practical sciences. The productive sciences were subordinate to the other two, on the lowest rung. This was a hierarchy of certainty: *theoreia* was said to treat of what is always or for the most part the case, *praxis* to deal with the choice of relative goods, and *poiesis* with how to make things out of contingent matter.

For modern science, however, theory became a tool of practice and practice a means to the production of new effects. Theory no longer had to do with final certainty but instead, as working hypothesis, with the tentative and unresolved. To know was to be prepared to act, and action was for the sake of producing further novel meanings. Modern science turned from "the past toward the future, from precedents to consequences; from isolation to continuity; from laws imposed upon particulars to connections through which particulars became interchangeable parts of a whole ever-extending its spatio-temporal range" (LW1:339).

Dewey argued that the Greeks in effect distinguished "activity" from "action" but that modern science was interested only in the second of these categories, having treated the first as empty. By "activity" Aristotle had meant "rational and necessary knowledge . . . treated . . . as an ultimate, self-sufficient and self-enclosed form of self-originated and self-conducted activity" (LW4:14–15;QC:17–18). Knowing was thus separated from doing and making. In its actual procedures, modern science treated action as something directed by knowledge, as something directed toward production of novelty. Whereas the end of Aristotelian science was the activity of knowledge for its own sake, the goal of modern science was technological control by means of production: "the securer, freer and more widely shared embodiment of values in experience by means of that active control of objects which knowledge alone makes possible" (LW4:30;QC:37).

Modern science was above all the recognition of the importance of productive skills—technologies—and the adoption of their methods, which Dewey called "manipulation and reduction" (LW1:108;EN:112). Dewey turned once again in *Experience and Nature* to the metaphor of ores and metals that he developed in his *Essays* to explain his use of these terms. The uses to which ores may be put, before they are reduced and refined, are very limited. In case it possesses the appropriate qualities, iron ore may be enjoyed aesthetically. It may also serve certain restricted instrumental purposes; a chunk of it may serve as a weapon against game or an enemy.

But once it is reduced, refined, the range of its possible uses expands. It becomes more manipulable in the sense that it has enlarged possibilities with respect to the reduction of other things. An iron tool, reduced and refined from iron ore, may serve to reduce and refine a piece of wood. It may be used to turn the wood into an object of aesthetic delight, such as a ceremonial mask, or into a tool to be utilized in the manipulation of yet other objects, such as a bowl or a plow (LW1:109;EN:112).

Reduction and manipulation have, of course, been important aspects of human making from the very beginning. But during the sixteenth century there was a great change of attitude toward these processes. They began to be taken seriously as productive of knowledge, not just as productive of objects of aesthetic enjoyment. Knowledge itself began to be treated as an artifact, as something that calls for further reduction and manipulation.

Dewey illustrated this great change of attitude by means of brief analyses of the work of two innovators: Galileo and Newton. Galileo's great contribution "consisted precisely in the abolition of qualities as traits of scientific objects *as such*" (LW4:76;QC:94). Galileo's experiments with falling bodies dropped off the tower at Pisa decisively undercut the Aristotelian notion of levity and gravity as qualitatively *inhering* in objects, as just "aesthetic" qualities of objects.

What Dewey seems to have in mind is the following. The "ontological square" laid out by Aristotle in the *Categories* presented individual qualitative accidents as *inhering in*, but not *said of*, individual objects. "This particular white" (the white of Socrates) *inheres* in Socrates, but is not *said of* Socrates. Classes of individual accidents were then *said of*, but were not *inherent in*, those objects. "White," as qualitative genus, was said of Socrates ("Socrates is white"), but because of its universality, it did not inhere in Socrates. Individual objects were thus said by Aristotle to have intrinsic qualitative differences, such as their own individual gravity or their own individual levity. Though generalizable as classes of gravity or levity, Aristotle's substance-accident ontology laid the basis for treating such classes of individual accidents as to some extent heterogeneous, since their individuals could never be in more than one object. Individual accidents were treated simply as individual, and intrinsic, qualities. They were self-contained, or aesthetic, entities, even though they were capable of "sticking to" or "inhering in" substances.

The revolution initiated by Galileo, according to Dewey, consisted in the overthrow, implicitly if not explicitly, of the Aristotelian substance-accident model. Instead of accepting the gravity of objects as "this gravity" and "that gravity," and so on, collectible into a species or class called "gravity," he demonstrated that the motion of bodies was due to a common property, one that was homogeneous. Objects were treated as resistant to forces that tended to set them in motion, as well as resistant to forces that tended to alter their motion once they were underway. This homogeneous property was given the name "inertia." When taken together with Newton's experiments with balls rolling down smooth inclined planes, Dewey argues, the work of Galileo was "absolutely fatal to the traditional conception that all bodies in motion come naturally to rest because of their own intrinsic tendency to fulfill an inherent nature" (LW4:78;EN:96). A single homogeneous property was put in the place of multiple heterogeneous qualities.

Inertia is thus in Dewey's account a technological artifact. Its development is treated by Dewey in the same way that he treats the development of logical objects and "crutches, skates and pedals" in his 1916 lecture to the Columbia Philosophy Club. It arose not *by* inquiry, but *from* inquiry. It was instrumental to the reduction and manipulation of objects and events in a way that secured new meanings.

From these experiments it was a short step to the abolition of the idea of difference in kind between qualities in different parts of space. "All that counted for science became mechanical properties formulated in mathematical terms:—the significance of mathematical formulation marking the possibility of complete equivalence or homogeneity of translation of different phenomena into one another's terms" (LW4:78;EN:97).

There were of course enormous "spiritual" ramifications of this view. The Aristotelian view had been that an external force is necessary to maintain a body in motion that is not just "internal" or "natural" to it. If this was no longer the case, then what of the unmoved mover, which by the time of Galileo had long since been identified with the Christian God? I shall return to these matters in chapter 7.

More germane to our point here, however, is the role that instrumentation of all types played in this scientific revolution. Lenses, smooth inclined planes, and hundreds of other tools begin to take their place in active experimentation, the active manipulation of outcomes. It was not better theory alone that brought about the modern scientific revolution, but also a fundamental change in the ways in which tools were perceived and utilized. One of the most important of these changes was to regard theory itself as a tool, as instrumental.

Putting this somewhat differently, one could say that the new tools of modern science included the very qualities of objects that Aristotle had thought inherent in them, but that were now taken in a different way. In his 1938 Logic Dewey described this difference. In a manner reminiscent of Peirce's discussion of his own categories—quality, fact, and law (to use one of his designations of them)—Dewey distinguished among "qualities," "characteristic traits," and "properties."

Qualities are the objects of particular observations. They are as they are, and do not point beyond themselves. They are thus quite similar to the individuals of the category "quality" in Aristotle's system. To say that they are heterogeneous, however, is already to say too much. Taken as qualities, they just are, like the pervasive quality of an evening with friends. Dewey did not wish to deny that we sometimes take qualities as complete in and of themselves. Our quotidian lives are filled with aesthetic experiences that are pursued no further. Sometimes a poem does not mean, but just is.

But sometimes qualities are significant; they point beyond themselves. When this occurs, Dewey calls them "characteristic traits." Characteristic traits are those things that enable a "reasonably safe" inference to be made as to the occurrence of other qualities under certain conditions. They point beyond themselves by doing the work of distinguishing, isolating a descriptive characteristic of a kind. They are effective in reduction and refinement.

But what was at first taken as a quality, then as a characteristic trait, may become a property "when it is determined by negative as well as positive instances to be a constant dependable sign of other conjoined characteristics. It then *belongs* inherently to all cases of the kind'' (LW12:292;LTI:292).

Dewey's example is litmus paper placed in a chemical solution. The proposition "this turns litmus paper red" in and of itself simply reports an isolated observation. Without something further, it is insignificant. But a quality can become a characteristic trait, a tool, under the proper circumstances. Generalizing about the traits of other samples of the chemical solution in question, and about the traits of other pieces of litmus paper, a "reasonably safe inference" can be made about their interaction. Finally, "testing by negative as well as positive instances," we may say that any acid will turn any piece of litmus paper red. We have passed beyond qualities and traits to properties as dependable signs.

As in the simple case I provided in chapter 2 of the repair of the light switch, various objects in a chemistry lab function as instruments for one another. The litmus may be taken as instrumental to ascertaining the significance of the chemical substance in question. Acid may be taken as instrumental to ascertaining the significance of the type of paper in question. Paper that does not react to a chemical solution may not be litmus paper, or its own chemical properties may be depleted. Or perhaps the paper is fresh litmus paper, but the pH of the solution is neutral.

In each case, litmus paper and chemical solution no longer function as Aristotelian objects. They instead function as *data*. "Just what did the new experimental method do to the qualitative objects of ordinary experience? . . . I think our answer, stated in technical terms, will be that it *substitutes data for objects*" (LW4:79;QC:98–99). Whereas Greek science worked with objects such as rocks, trees, and stars, treating them as ontologically finished, experimental science concerns itself with what is manipulable and transformable. Such *data* point to the future: they become "subject-matter for *further* interpretation; something to be thought about. *Objects* are finalities; they are complete, finished; they call for thought only in the way of definition, classification, logical arrangement, subsumption in syllogisms, etc. But data signify 'material to serve'; they are indications, evidence, signs, clues to and of something still to be reached; they are intermediate, not ultimate; means, not finalities" (LW4:79–80;QC:98–99).

For Dewey, to be a datum is to function in a special way with respect to the control of the subject matter of a particular area of inquiry. Data allow us to fix a problem in a way such that a possible solution is indicated. Data provide evidence that is instrumental to testing a proposed solution (LW12:127;LTI:124).

To put this somewhat differently, what formerly was thought to be the object of knowledge became the starting point for problems. Objects were no longer thought of as stable, finished, and static, but problematic, perplexing, and provocative of new agenda. For the experimental scientist, objects ceased to be the locus of aesthetic contemplation and instead became instruments, tools for the effective control of human situations.

Recurring once more to Dewey's remarks in *Experience and Nature*, objects as understood by the scientist are constant and capable of mathematical formulation; they allow for substitution; they allow for the possibility of control; and they allow for scientific laws and relations. They are thus quite different from objects that are taken aesthetically. The experimental scientist may treat laboratory objects aesthetically, deriving pleasure from their colors, textures, and shapes. There are also certain aesthetic delights that accompany well-executed experiments. But though these experiences may be a spur to further scientific work, as aesthetic they do not point beyond themselves to the possibilities of further significance.

This point has been a source of deep misunderstanding among many of Dewey's critics. C. J. Ducasse, for one, thought Dewey's instrumentalism quite strange:

> The life of man, or rather of intelligent man, that is to say of man as he supposedly ought to be, is in effect depicted by [instrumentalism] as a life of toolmaking, all the tools made (whether physical or psychological) being themselves essentially tools for toolmaking. In a life of that sort there is no such thing as tool-using except for the making of other tools; and the only satisfactions acknowledged are those arising from the process of toolmaking itself, or from the perception of the utility of some tool for toolmaking. Immediate satisfactions are paradoxically said to be "their own excuses for being just because they are charged with an office."
>
> Such a life would indeed avoid the "dust and ashes of boredom" to which Professor Dewey says that a consummatory object which is not also instrumental turns in time; but it would bring to replace it a characteristic evil of its own,—the fatigue and weariness which no less surely result in time from the ever renewed stimulation of the ever instrumental; and the ingrained restlessness and incapacity for contemplation,—all to widespread to-day,— which insistence on somehow turning everything into a means, produces.[14]

Ducasse was partially correct in his assessment that instrumentalism turns everything into a tool. But this is true only insofar as it involves that "distinctive quality of science as knowledge"[15] that Dewey calls "technology." What Ducasse has described in this passage is precisely the ceaseless, perhaps even restless, activity of experimental science. What he has failed to grasp is what Dewey clearly and repeatedly argued: experiences that we call scientific have their own delights, their own aesthetic pleasures; and inquiry does not, and cannot, penetrate to every area of experience.

Since we must deal with quotidian objects, we have but two choices. The path taken by the Greeks led to treating objects as ends in themselves and the loci of aesthetic delights, knowledge being taken as aesthetic. Modern science takes the other path. It treats objects and their characteristic properties as instruments for discovery and for the development of further instrumentalities. Knowledge, far from being the object of aesthetic contemplation, becomes instrumental for further experience: instrumental for further aesthetic experience, and instrumental for the development of wider and deeper knowing.

IX

What about the immediate future? First, Dewey thought that philosophy had an essential role to play in the bringing to fruition of the next stage of the history of technology. His view was that philosophy was far from being at a dead end, as some since his time have suggested. (Some have even accused Dewey of holding this view, but it is doubtful that they have taken note of what Dewey wrote in chapter 10 of *Experience and Nature*.)

Philosophy is for Dewey "inherently criticism, having its distinctive position among various modes of criticism in its generality; a criticism of criticisms, as it were. Criticism is discriminating judgment, careful appraisal, and judgment is appropriately termed criticism wherever the subject-matter of discrimination concerns goods or values" (LW1:298;EN:322). Dewey characterized the function of philosophy in terms that are precisely those he used in his characterization of technology: its function involves increased regulation and control, enhancement of security and freedom, and avoidance of misdirection and waste (LW1:302;EN:327).

In this connection Dewey wrote of philosophy as "a messenger, a liaison officer, making reciprocally intelligible voices speaking provincial tongues, and thereby enlarging as well as rectifying the meanings with which they are charged" (LW1:306;EN:332).

Second, the next stage of technology, if it occurs, will involve increased interpenetration of science, morals, and aesthetic appreciation. Philosophy, because of its generality, has the task of showing the way to avoidance of the naturalistic fallacy—i.e., the view that there are "some objects or some properties of objects which carry their own adequate credentials upon their face" (LW1:303;EN:327–28). He calls this attitude a "snare and delusion of the whole historic tradition regarding knowledge, infecting alike sensational and rational schools, objective realisms and introspective idealisms" (LW1:303;EN:328). Its antidote is the bringing together of "inner" and "outer" means of control, the releasing of "cooped-up" thought by involving it with instrumentation of all sorts, and the alignment of thought with the "other arts that shape objects by informing things with meanings" (LW1:319;EN:346). The next stage of technology will be one in which traditionally rigid distinctions between hardware and software will give way to a new interdefinability between the two.

Third, the next stage of technology is by no means inevitable. It is not unthinkable that our generation should exhibit the "failure of nerve" that characterized the period from the late Roman empire to the Renaissance. Nor is it impossible that our generation should be the last of humankind, whether for reasons natural or artificial. Though he was an historicist in the sense I have already explained in connection with his genetic accounts, Dewey rejected historical determinism. A key element in his account of technology is that it involves individual and corporate responsibility for pro-duction of the future.

There are both positive and negative sides to this view. Absolute control of environing conditions is impossible. The domain of meaning is not, and cannot be, coextensive with the domain of experience. There is always an experiencable but unknowable residue. Moreover, a disaster, either natural or artificial, could terminate human life. On the positive side, however, Dewey thought that it would constitute great progress if human beings would begin to think of themselves as responsible for their own individual and corporate futures. In chapters 6 and 7 I shall return to these themes and address them more specifically.

Chapter Five: Theory, Practice, and Production

> There is no ground whatever upon which a logical line
> can be drawn between the operations and techniques
> of experimentation in the natural sciences and the
> same operations and techniques employed for
> distinctively practical ends. Nothing so fatal to science
> can be imagined as elimination of experimentation,
> and experimentation is a form of doing and making.
> Application of conceptions and hypotheses to
> existential matters through the medium of doing and
> making is an intrinsic constituent of scientific method.
> (LW12:434–35;LTI:439).

> The reason why we are on a higher imaginative level
> is not because we have finer imagination, but
> because we have better instruments. In science, the
> most important thing that has happened during the
> last forty years is the advance in instrumental design
> . . . . A fresh instrument serves the same purpose as
> foreign travel; it shows things in unusual
> combinations. The gain is more than a mere addition;
> it is a transformation.—Alfred North Whitehead[1]

> Indeed, it may be said that the distinction between
> science and other technologies is not intrinsic. It is
> dependent upon cultural conditions that are extrinsic
> to both science and industry. Were it not for the
> influence exerted by these conditions, the difference
> between them would be conventional to the point of
> being verbal. (PM:292)

I

In the previous chapter I indicated that Dewey turned Aristotle's order of
theoretical, practical, and productive knowing on its head. Like Plato
before him, Aristotle treated theoretical knowing as superior to practical
and productive knowing. Because of its ties to certainty, because its
object was said to be what is always or for the most part the case,
Aristotle regarded theory as having a share in what is divine. Practice
was said to be its inferior because of its involvement with choice among

relative goods. Production was said to be inferior to both theory and practice because it is the making of things out of contingent matter. Dewey's brief account of the scientific revolution of the seventeenth and eighteenth centuries included his contention that in its actual practice, though not everywhere in its account of itself, modern science inverted this hierarchy.

It is now time to examine this issue in a more detailed way. In this chapter I shall look at the Greek view in more detail, since that perspective continues to be influential even in our own culture, long after actual practices of scientific technology have rendered it obsolete. Then I shall examine Dewey's views of the relation of theory to practice and production, doing and making, and his account of the relation of technology to science. As a means to understanding his account of experimental science, I shall examine Dewey's treatment of cause and effect, necessity, and scientific law.

II

Like those of most other words, the roots of the word "theory" are quite concrete. Even before the use of its cognate "*theoros*" to designate the activities of the spectator at a game, that term was used as a name for envoys sent to oracles or to the religious festivals of sister Greek city-states (at which games were invariably staged).[2] Since both oracles and festivals were deeply tied to religious practice, and since the term "*theoros*" has obvious connections to "*theos*," or "god," there was from its beginnings something of the divine called out by the word. The Latin term "*contemplatio*," normally used to translate "*theoria*," had its root in "*templum*," a place of observation and prophecy. *Theoria* is thus a kind of wonder, a kind of observation of something divine.

The term "*praxis*" also has roots that are concrete. The first person singular "*prasso*" ("I manage" or "I accomplish") indicates the concrete performance of some activity based upon the deliberate choice of a free citizen.[3] Political activity, business, and even athletic performance seem to have been included among "practical" activities. But the activities of *praxis* included for the Greeks neither *theoria* nor the productive activities of the craftsman. The term utilized to refer to productive activities, whether those of the shipbuilder or the poet, was "*poiesis*" or "*techne*."

In his *Metaphysics*,[4] Aristotle uses these three terms—*theoria*, *praxis*, and *poiesis*—and their cognates to refer to three ways of knowing (*episteme*). The context of his discussion in both passages is the manner in which the principles or causes of things come to be known. Each of these sciences attempts to get the "what" as it is "in some class of things and tries to prove the other truths, whether loosely or accurately."[5]

Not only in the *Metaphysics* but elsewhere in Aristotle's work where he discusses these matters, most notably in the *Nichomachean Ethics,* the order of importance attributed to these three ways of knowing is clear either explicitly or from context. Theoretical knowing is superior to practical knowing, and practical knowing is in its turn superior to the kind of knowing that is involved in production. Hannah Arendt has claimed that in the *Metaphysics* Aristotle places productive knowing above practical knowing,[6] but the texts she cites simply do not support her claim. Perhaps Aristotle's most explicit ranking of doing and making is in his *Magna Moralia,* where doing is associated with wisdom and making with contrivance: "in the processes of doing there is no other end beyond the doing . . . . Wisdom, then, is concerned with doing and things done, but art with making and things made; for it is in things made rather than in things done that artistic contrivance is displayed."[7]

That Greek social organization reflected this ranking of theory, practice, and production is apparent. Ways of knowing were identified as ways of life. Because of the obligations of Greek citizenship, the doing of political life required freedom from the necessity of earning a living. That the artisans were involved in making in order to earn a living, and so had little to do with political life, is equally clear.

What Aristotle argued was that *theoria*, or contemplation, was an extension of practical political activity. "The argument of the philosophers consisted in saying that all positive aspects of politics— that it was an activity relatively free from fatigue, an activity entailing independence and leisure, and thus a free activity—were found in contemplation as well, and that they were found in contemplation in a significantly superior way."[8] The message of Aristotle and Plato was addressed to the free citizen; by engaging in contemplation, he could develop what was most divine in himself.

Besides *theoria, praxis*, and *poiesis*, one more way of life among the Greeks should be mentioned. At the very bottom of the social structure, then as now, were laborers. "*Ponos,*" a term that was applied to activities within this sphere of life, meant "not only hard labor and toil but also, and by no means incidentally, distress, suffering, and even sickness."[9]

That Greek history, drama, and philosophy were written by those who viewed society from the top down is indicated by the apparent absence of the idea that *techne* or productive activity could serve to make those whose lot was *ponos* less distressing. Nor did the Greeks seem to have the view that the natural or mathematical sciences could serve such a function.

Dewey thought that the Greeks' characterization of *theoria* as the highest form of knowledge was one of the principal reasons why they failed to develop experimental science. He argued that the Greeks excluded inquiry—by which he meant productive resolution of existential difficulty—from the scope of logic. The Aristotelian syllogism was, in his view, not so much a matter of inferring or reasoning as it was an "immediate apprehension or vision of the relations of inclusion and exclusion that belong to real wholes in Nature" (LW12:93;LTI:88).

Since logic was treated as a means of maneuvering oneself into position to get a better *view* of things that were already complete in themselves, as in the case of a trip to a museum, there was consequently no remaining room for a logic of discovery. Form and species were treated as views of wholes. Dewey accused the Greeks of holding the position that the weakness of mortal flesh robbed reflective inquiries of their logical importance. They viewed knowledge as grasp and possession brought about by intuition (LW12:93;LTI:88).

The central problem of Greek logic and "science" was, in Dewey's view, that it failed to relate theory and practice. It failed to adopt as a part of its procedure what was being done right under its very nose: it ignored as inferior the actual technical production that was a part of everyday Greek life. It "disregarded instrumentalities and procedures of productive workers" (LW12:99;LTI:94).

III

In his early essay "Moral Theory and Practice," published in 1891, Dewey worked out a view of theory and practice, the broad features of which he continued to hold throughout his career. Once understood, this essay provides considerable insight into Dewey's treatment of the subject not only in *Experience and Nature*, but in the 1938 *Logic* as well.

The problem that concerned Dewey in this material was what he took to be the incompatibility of two main approaches to ethics. On one side, there were those who argued that moral theory is the attempt to find a philosophical basis or foundation for moral activity, and that such foundations are something beyond moral activity itself. On the other side, there were the "cookbook" ethicists, who argued that moral theory was a collection of rules or precepts, perhaps like the Ten Commandments, and that moral practice was the scrupulous but atheoretical execution of their minutest details.

One of the striking things about the way in which Dewey lays out this problem is its close parallel to what is normally said about science and technology. Science is often said to be the search for foundations, the search for something beyond the products of science itself. And technology is often said to proceed by cookbook type rules; that is, rules just generalized from whatever has happened to work and then meticulously applied "by the book."

What characterized Dewey's strategy throughout his career, as C. Wright Mills reminded us, was his attempt to think across hitherto isolated fields. Mills puts the matter succinctly:

Observation of Dewey's bibliography shows that there are many articles which, without violating their content, could have been entitled "X *and* Y" . . . . He does not merely "relate" topics. He does not simply shift the meanings and shapes of two opinions so that he can "live" with both, as tends to be the rather patent case with much of William James. Dewey takes a point of sight and builds a conceptual structure within which he can grasp both the points which were being argued over; this structure is different from either of the conflicting or isolated doctrines which it "combines." It is Deweyan.[10]

I argued at considerable length in chapter 2 that this was precisely Dewey's strategy for dealing with the conflicting claims of realism and idealism. He adopted neither position, but was able to get a purchase on the insights of both by developing a third position, which he called instrumentalism. I have also argued that the central concepts of instrumentalism were pro-duction and con-struction, literally a leading to and a standing with that reflect Dewey's preoccupation with inference that is warrantable within a community of inquiry. Production and construction, terms that are utilized extensively in technological fields, were carefully chosen and extensively utilized by Dewey to articulate his instrumentalist position. Dewey consistently argued that human beings build their world by building the meanings of their world. His metaphors, from the early essays in the 1890s to those published almost sixty years later, were technological ones.

Dewey writes of ethics in this essay as if it were a species of engineering. As I have indicated, this is also a metaphor that Dewey uses in his discussions of inquiry; of aesthetics and artistic production; of the writing of history; and of logic, or inquiry into inquiry.

Moral theory is for Dewey identical with moral insight, and moral insight is the recognition of relationships. By itself, this statement could be a somewhat oversimplified gloss on Aristotle's *Nichomachean Ethics*. But Dewey follows this claim with one that Aristotle would have rejected as conflating *episteme theoretike, episteme praktike*, and *poiesis*—that is, theoretical knowledge, practical knowledge, and production. Ethical insight, he continues, comes by the same kind of intelligence "that measures dry-goods, drives nails, sells wheat, and invents the telephone . . . .There is nothing more divine or transcendental in resolving how to save my degraded neighbor than in the resolving of a problem in algebra" (EW3:95).

Dewey thus refuses to divorce theory from practice. Insofar as it is successful, each is productive. Theory and practice are in his view only different phases of a stretch of intelligent inquiry, theory being the "ideal act" and practice the "executed insight."

Some have contended against this view that one does not need a theory of locomotion to be able to walk and so, by analogy, that one does not need a theory of ethics in order to be able to act ethically. Dewey's response to this objection is to differentiate among levels of theory, that is, levels of ideal acts. Whereas a theory of locomotion may indeed not be necessary for walking, a knowledge of walking is precisely what is called for. Those who pair theories of locomotion with the activity we call walking have simply cast their net too wide. Theories of (insight into relationships involved with) locomotion include theories of walking, but the converse is not the case. A specialist in locomotor diseases needs both a theory of locomotion and a theory of walking, but children who begin to learn to walk do so in the absence of theories of locomotion.

Theories, then, are just ideas about what is to be done, and they function at various levels of abstraction with respect to existential matters. This is a matter that Dewey would develop extensively in his 1938 *Logic*. What is to be done must be carefully determined with respect to the proper level of abstraction called for, that is, with specificity to a problem at hand. Further, ideas about what is to be done are nested, those that are more specific in those that are more general.

Another way of putting this is that there are no theories in general, no theories that are groundless. Of course, imagination and fancy are capable of making connections that have little or nothing to do with existential situations. That human beings engage in such practices is often a source of great aesthetic delight (although it may also be a source of great evil). But flights of fancy and inventions of the imagination are not theories. A theory in a particular case is simply ''a thorough-going analysis of it'' (EW3:98). Analyses are broader or narrower as specific problematic cases are broader or narrower. The alternative to theory as ''thorough-going analysis'' is not practice, but sentimentality, instinct, authority, laziness, stupidity, or, perhaps more positively, flight of fancy. That there is practice that relies on such substitutes for thoroughgoing analysis, however, is a notorious fact.

Here, as elsewhere, Dewey argues that there are no differences between moral theories and those utilized by the physical sciences except in terms of the material they address. Theories—hypotheses—in both fields are expressible in the form of the conditional: ''if this, then that.'' Further, hypotheses do not deal with individuals, but with conditions. The hypothesis we call the theory of gravitation, for example, says, as Dewey puts it: ''I have nothing to do with your concrete falling stone, but I can tell you this, that it is a law of falling bodies that, etc. You must make your own allowances in applying this universal formula to the special case.'' (EW3:98).

The claim that a hypothesis in the physical sciences or in ethics is the final word, that absolute scientific or ethical foundations can be laid to cover all facts, and that particular cases do not call for particular applications of hypotheses, is what Dewey calls a mutilation of the facts.

But there is also a mutilation involved in claiming that moral activities are possible in the absence of moral hypotheses or theories.

The alternative to hypotheses as a basis for action is impulses. Actions based on impulse may serve; but if they are able to do so, it is only a matter of luck.

What this means for Dewey is that neither moral theories nor scientific theories are the kinds of things that can exist in books. Both types of theories are only "in the mind" of some agent.

It is not hard to see why some of Dewey's critics accused him of subjectivism. To write of theories as only existing "in the mind" was tantamount to waving a red flag. However, in his 1938 *Logic*, and even in his logical works of 1903 and 1916, Dewey expressly rejected subjectivism. In the 1938 *Logic* Dewey wrote of theories in terms of "ways" of acting, not in terms of something in the mind of an agent. And what his critics during his early period almost universally missed was his view that mind is an objective way of interacting with found existential situations by means of the construction of instruments for its use; he never treated mind as something private or subjective.

This is a point he made explicit in his essay "The Present Position in Logical Theory" (EW3:125–141), also published in 1891. In that essay he argued against two subjectivist positions. The first was one advanced in many of the standard logic texts of that time, that "logic is concerned only with the way in which the mind thinks, and has nothing to do with the particular objects thought about."[11] Dewey's objection to this view was that it made forms of thought independent of subject matter, not something dictated by facts.

The second view of logic that Dewey found unacceptably subjective was a similar one. He thought that the "transcendental" logic of Kant, Kant's view that *a priori* forms are found in pure thought and imposed upon data, also did violence to the facts. Opposed to these views, he took the road indicated by Hegel, that "relations of thought are . . . . the typical forms of meaning which the subject-matter takes in its various progressive stages of being understood" (EW3:137). He thought that one of the major differences between Kant and Hegel was that the former held the untenable view that the *a priori* was subjective, whereas for the latter the *a priori*, insofar as there was such a thing, was just "experience itself in its skeleton, in the main features of its framework" (EW3:137).

Dewey's logic is, thus, from the 1890s both antipsychologistic and instrumentalist. As I shall show in the remainder of this chapter, the mature treatment of theory and practice that he was to work out on the 1938 *Logic* was already there in seed form as early as 1891.

The objectivity of theories lies for Dewey, even in this early essay, in the fact that they are *tools*. Dewey returns to his technological metaphor: "Like every analysis, it [the analysis of moral activity] requires that the one making it be in possession of certain working tools. I cannot resolve this practical situation which faces me by merely looking at it. I must attack it with such instruments of analysis as I have at hand. *What we call moral rules are precisely such tools of analysis"* (EW3:100;emphasis in original).

Dewey's example is the Golden Rule. Like any other tool, it gives no knowledge in and of itself concerning what should be done with it. But as a tool of analysis, it is like a finely constructed axe: it "helps me hew straight and fine in clearing out this jungle of relations of practice" (EW3:101).

Modifying his metaphor somewhat, Dewey claims that moral rules (hypotheses) and scientific hypotheses are like another kind of tool: a nautical almanac. They are aids to navigation, but they do not tell us where to sail. Then, in a sweeping technological metaphor, Dewey writes: "In the supreme art of life the tools must be less mechanical; more depends upon the skill of the artist in their manipulation, but they are none the less useful. Our mastery of a required case of action would be slow and wavering if we had to forge anew our weapons of attack in each instance. The temptation to fall back on the impulse or accident of the moment would be well-nigh irresistible. And so it is well we have our rules at hand, but well only if we have them for *use*" (EW3:101).

In order to be useful, as opposed to burdensome, tools must be utilized within, as well as be continually reassessed by, the work of active intelligence. Insofar as is possible, they must continually be re-newed; that is, re-produced and re-constructed.

Both theory and practice should be thought of as products and as productive. In a remark that calls to mind James's remarks on the "perches" and "flights" of thought, Dewey invites us to imagine a scene in which an individual is confronted with a situation which requires resolution. The busy life of such a situation consists of needs, relations, habits, and cultural institutions. The application of intelligence to and within the situation requires the cutting of a cross section through it, an arresting of its movement. The abstracted cross section is examined for possibilities, for conceivable outcomes. Intelligence then "removes its brake, its abstracting hold, and the scene moves on" (EW3:109).

In this extended image, theory is the tool that cuts the cross section, but the cross section also serves as a tool—a theory—for further deliberation. Both the prior theory and the cross section to which it gives rise are abstract when compared to the buzzing situation. Theory is what allows us to stop the action. Practice then consists in the activities brought to bear on the actualization of insights gained during the abstractive moment. Theory is thus related to practice as insight to action. Together, they constitute two phases of intelligent behavior. And both involve production of novel consequences.

IV

Dewey expanded this analysis of theory and practice in his 1915 essay "The Logic of Judgments of Practice," and applied it to his examination of the relation of science to technology. In this essay he characterized science as a specialized mode of practice, a position that he maintained and continued to sharpen for the next three decades.

He invites us to consider two types of materials: wood that is used to construct a boat and the "natural existences" that are used in scientific inquiry, that is, in going from the unknown to the known. Boat construction is the giving of certain special shapes to wood; the process is called manufacture. By analogy, science is the giving of certain special shapes to its material, natural existences. This process is no less a form of manufacture than is the one we call shipbuilding.

The same may be said of language. "It may fairly be said that speech is a manufactured article: it consists of natural ebullitions of sound which have been shaped for the sake of being effective instrumentalities of a purpose" (MW8:66). The irregularities of speech attest to the difficulties involved in its manufacture, undertaken as it has been amid stresses of all sorts and with minimal planning or control. Written language was the result of finer techniques of manufacture than those used to produce spoken language.[12] The manufacture of written language had a finer material with which to work, and was undertaken with greater planning and precision. But the fundamental activity in each case is manufacture.

The quality of manufacture can be measured in terms of the type of use to which raw or intermediate materials are put. They may serve as prototypes, as in the case of a dugout canoe that is modeled on the log that is the material for its construction. Alternatively, original or intermediate materials may be treated as a limit, imposing certain restrictions that indicate a much richer domain, namely the domain of *possible* improvements according to selected uses.

It is in this sense that what Dewey calls "logical traits" are both manufactured articles and so constructed that they will be useful means for further manufacture. "Logical traits are just features of original existences as they have been worked over for use in inference, as the traits of manufactured articles are qualities of crude materials modified for specific purposes" (MW8:67). Like other types of manufactured articles, logical traits neither exist subjectively in some immaterial mental state nor existed prior to their manufacture. To attribute to them ontological pre-existence is to commit the error that Dewey repeatedly refers to as "the philosophic fallacy": the taking of something consequent upon inquiry as if it were antecedent to it.

Once again Dewey assesses the claims of two opposing camps and develops from their insights a third position. Logical traits are neither purely theoretical, in the sense that one school takes theories to be ungrounded, nor are they purely practical, in the sense that another school takes them to be a part of rote, that is, unconsidered practice. They are products; and production is for Dewey everywhen and everywhere a matter of purpose—something to be done.

It is not necessary to have an ontology to recognize the fact that human beings undertake acts of inference. Dewey's view of this matter stands in radical opposition to that of Quine, for example, that "one's ontology is basic to the conceptual scheme by which he interprets all experiences, even the most commonplace ones."[13] For Dewey, inference is a hard fact, like walking, chewing, or jumping. It is simply a fact that human beings use some things as signs, indications, and evidence that allow the procession from something given to something lacking or desired. We do not infer inference; we observe it as we do other types of behavior. It is not a part of a "conceptual scheme," but a matter of direct observation.

Inferential behavior allows us to make certain preparations. It renders us capable of success and failure to an extent not possible in its absence. It allows us to treat something that is lacking as continuous with things that are available. It takes time and deliberate action seriously; and it brings truth and falsity, hence heightened precariousness, into the world. Inference is the taking of a chance: it is behaving as if something *were* the case that is not yet, but that might be made to be so.

This is not the truth and falsity of the correspondence theory of truth, according to which propositions either correctly or incorrectly mirror states of affairs. Once Dewey's understanding of the nature of propositions is grasped—namely, that they are constructions of certain proposals for behavior from the raw materials of data—then the view that " 'snow is white' if and only if snow is white" appears either trivial or absurd. To say that a proposition corresponds to a state of affairs would be like saying that a boat corresponds to the wood chosen for its construction. Truth and falsity are for Dewey ultimately the ways in which we speak about the relation between what is proposed *to be* done and the way in which what *is* done turns out.

Inference involves technique. It is a form of art, that is, of production. *Homo* is not for Dewey so much *sapiens* as *faber*. Far from being naturally endowed with rational faculties, human beings must manufacture the tools of inference as they go along. Dewey's remarks on this subject are at times quite caustic. His observation is that human beings have improved their inferential skills slowly and grudgingly, preferring to act on the basis of irrelevant impulse or outworn habit wherever and whenever possible.

Scientific advances are technological advances: they are advances in the uses of tools in order to improve and test inferences. From simple behavioral responses such as moving the head, shading the eyes, turning objects over, and taking them to a different light (MW8:73), to more complex operations such as those that involve the use of prisms, lenses, and other devices, scientific knowing is an affair of testing by means of tools. Science is a technique of manufacture and of making sure that what we have manufactured serves our purposes. Dewey contends that the taking of the results of scientific inquiry as "something naturally or psychologically given is a monstrous superstition" (MW8:73). It is a case of the philosophic fallacy.

That scientific discriminations produce unmistakable signs is not itself a sign that isolation of a thing of scientific scrutiny has occurred, let alone that it was there as an independent object *before* scientific discrimination. Scientific discrimination does not impoverish relations, but extends them. Its presence is a sign that relationships to other things have been produced and specified with greater precision. What Dewey calls "dependable data for inference" does not exist in isolation but as a part of a whole, larger than it would be in the absence of scientific inquiry.

The arts of scientific inference are social in at least two important senses. First, they form a body of legends that are a part of a social group. The difference between the response of the aborigine and that of the average member of a technologically advanced society to a solar eclipse is not a difference in intelligence, but a difference in received legends and customs. Second, scientific instruction is itself a form of art or production that takes place in a social setting. The difficulty for scientific education is that assimilation of the legends—the body of scientific products—is customarily confused with mastery of the art of scientific inference. Reference to what is known is then taken for the activity that produces the knowing.

Because inference is a productive activity, new entities are created. Dewey calls these new entities "meanings." A meaning is an idea, a thing suggested. Meanings may be experimented with in their own right because they are detached from the immediate situation. They are manipulable. "They can be brought into relation with one another, quite irrespective of the things which originally suggested them. Without such free play reflective inquiry is mockery, and control of inference an impossibility" (MW8:76–77).

Dewey illustrates this point with the example of an astronomer who thinks that a point of light suggests a comet. In the absence of manufacture and manipulation of the ideal things called meanings, the astronomer would be reduced either to immediately taking the perceived light as a comet or rejecting it entirely. Meanings allow controlled inference to proceed because they call out other meanings. Meanings, unlike tangible objects, have implications. They are "possible" or "hypothetical" objects, and are related and relatable to other objects of their type.

Dewey warns, however, that if we forget how we get meanings and how they function—that is, that they are produced within controlled inference and that they allow for more facile manipulation within it—we fall into the traditional philosophical dualisms: "existence and essence, particular and universal, thing and idea, ordinary life and science" (MW8:78).[14]

Meanings are what are manipulated in scientific inquiry. They are its tools. They are the "specially adapted entities" (MW8:79) that science produces and utilizes to pursue its industry. Men and women of science handle these meanings, or what Dewey also calls "things-of-inference," just as the artisan does his or her tools. It is in this sense that meanings are more than "just" thoughts. They are things and tools: as such they are manipulable, and as such they yield knowledge and methods of knowledge. "When one considers the importance of the enterprise of knowledge, it is not surprising that appropriate tools have been devised for carrying it on, and that these tools have no prototypes in pre-existent materials. They are real objects, but they are just the real objects which they are and not some other objects" (MW8:78).

V

It should by now be obvious that the points of departure of Aristotle and Dewey with respect to their treatments of the relation between technology and science are inversions of each other. Aristotle looked at human productive activity from the top down, moving from the contemplation of the divine and immutable to the chancy and precarious manipulation of materials undertaken by the artisan. The human artisan was for Aristotle a faulty version of the grand artisan called nature and, beyond that, of what he took to be divine.

For Dewey, however, the perspective is reversed. He started with everyday making and built up to the ideal entities he called meanings. Meanings are not given independently of inquiry, but are tools that develop as inquiry is enlarged. Science is not contemplation of meanings, but active generation and manipulation of them.

Whereas Aristotle's point of departure has for the most part been read as ontological, a cataloging of the kinds of things there are, and his goal read as the putting of things into their proper categories, Dewey's point of departure was pragmatic. He began with inquiry and insisted that whatever grading and sorting needs to be done is required—and, indeed, meaningful—only in the context of inquiry. Another way of putting this is that Aristotle was interested in what kinds of things there are, whereas Dewey was interested in what is to be done, and consequently in what tools and products are required for the doing of it.

This is the basis of Dewey's claim that "controlled inference is science, and science is, accordingly, a highly specialized industry. *It is such a specialized mode of practice that it does not appear to be a mode of practice at all*" (MW8:78;emphasis added).

In an Aristotelian world view, to claim that science is a specialized form of practice is to deprecate an activity regarded as divine. For the experimentalist, however, it is nothing of the sort. By identifying scientific activity as practical, Dewey means nothing more than that science involves experimentation, and that experimentation relies on whatever tools are at hand or can be produced to attain a desired outcome. Dewey regarded the experimental use of tools and instruments as the key to the advancement of branches of inquiry in which it has not been fully applied.

This claim, and ones like it, were taken by some of Dewey's critics to indicate that he held to a form of scientism. If by "scientism" it is meant that the methods of experimentation have proved so successful in the domains in which they have been developed and applied that they *ought* to be utilized and further developed in areas where they have not been tried, the term is applicable to Dewey's instrumentalist program.

But "scientism" is often used in a pejorative sense to indicate opposition to those who would treat "spiritual" matters as if they were subject to the same kind of methods of inquiry utilized in the "material" sciences. It was Dewey's contention that the term "spiritual" has often been used to denote areas of human activity in which vested interest, ossified habit, or untutored impulse have reigned in lieu of the application of carefully controlled inquiry. Dewey treated this matter extensively in 1934 in *A Common Faith*, to which I shall turn in chapter 7.

Dewey argues that the industry of science advances only insofar as it successfully employs a mode of practice called theorizing. Theory is a kind of practice that enriches possibilities and opens up new aims, or ends-in-view. When ends are regarded as fixed and finished, as they were by Aristotle, inquiry becomes stagnant and scientific advancement ceases. Dewey offers this as one of the principal reasons why the Greeks failed to develop an experimental science.

The development and use of theories create standpoints that are impersonal, detached from any particular personal interest or involvement, and open to checks and counterchecks from the members of a community for whom those theories are meaningful. This does not mean, as some have claimed, that theories are "disinterested." Because theories are detached from one particular interest, they are applicable to many different types of interests. Because they are abstracted from a particular situation, theories are applicable to many concrete practical situations. Dewey calls the relation between theory and practice paradoxical: "Theory is with respect to all other modes of practice the most practical of all things, and the more impartial and impersonal it is, the more truly practical it is" (MW8:82). This remark stands in stark contrast to a comment once made by C. S. Peirce, that science operates in a realm that is the most "useless" of all types of inquiry.[15]

Theories not only arise out of other, less abstract modes of practice, but they also must return to them in order to inform them and as a check on their own meaningfulness. Theories that do not do this, flights of theoretical specialty, minimize the checks and cues that correct error and render inference dependable.

VI

An important part of Dewey's treatment of scientific theories is his reconstruction of what have traditionally been called the principles of "cause and effect" and "necessity." In his essay "The Superstition of Necessity," published in *The Monist* in 1893, Dewey argued that the doctrine of necessity is an old idea that long since ceased to be useful and is now just a hindrance. Using one of his favorite metaphors, he compared the doctrine to a tool, in this case an old crutch that is no longer needed. At one time it compensated for a certain debility, but now it impedes what it once facilitated. What was a support is now carried about as a burden.

Dewey's main point in this material is that the term "necessity" concerns matters that are logical, not matters that are existential. More specifically, this means that necessity resides in judgments, not in facts; that necessity indicates the degree to which successful passage has been made from "unconnected judgments" to a "more comprehensive synthesis"; and finally, that necessity is no longer needed once it has succeeded in unifying these disparate elements. Looking backward at unconnected judgments, necessity means that a synthesis is required. Looking forward to the organized and integrated subject matter of the new comprehensive judgment, necessity has no meaning whatsoever.

The analysis that Dewey makes of the doctrine of necessity is part of his philosophy of science. Science, he continually argued, does not have to do with what *must* be so, but simply what *is* so. But we can talk about what *is* so in two ways. First, we can talk about a whole fact, and following that, of the parts which it comprises. In doing this we are talking about a whole fact already had and the factors into which it may be analyzed. Second, we can begin with parts and talk of the roles they play in making a whole fact. But this is not a matter of the parts *causing* the whole fact, but of *making it up*, synthesizing it.

Following the suggestions made by William James as part of his call for a radical form of empiricism, Dewey's claim is that analysis and synthesis are relative to one another and to a stipulated end, that that end itself undergoes changes as a result of the means utilized toward its attainment, and that analytical elements neither ontologically nor logically precede the whole facts from which they are abstracted.

The problem with the doctrine of necessity, Dewey argues, its fallacy, is that it "consists in transforming the determinate in the sense of the wholly defined, into the determined in the sense of something externally made to be what it is" (EW4:21). He sees in this characterization of inquiry three distinct stages. First, inquiry begins with pieces in an attempt to make a whole, what Dewey calls a "real fact." But second, even after the whole begins to come into focus *as a whole*, there is still some retention of the idea that there are independent pieces, and there is usually some attempt to relate them by ties that are called "necessary connections." In the final stage, the whole fact is apprehended as a unity, and it is seen that what were formerly taken as individual pieces are not individuals at all: there is consequently no need of "necessary" ties. They can be dispensed with.

"We learn (but only at the end) that instead of discovering and then connecting together a number of separate realities, we have been engaged in the progressive definition of one fact" (EW4:21). That fact is the result of intelligent constructive activity and reflects some particular interest or sought-after result.

Necessity is thus doubly dispensable. As a doctrine, it is a relic of the history of logic and is no longer needed. Utilized in particular inquiries, it renders itself obsolete when its role is fully understood. To use a simile later made famous by Wittgenstein, necessity is like a ladder that is climbed and then pulled up from above.

Dewey illustrates his view with an example of a "savage" who comes by means of controlled inquiry to a more complete knowledge of the relation of the cycle of the sun to his emerging needs to control agricultural production. At first there is the simple apprehension of pieces that are taken as individual facts. There is a sun in the sky today. There also was a sun in the sky yesterday. The sun yesterday and the sun today have incompatible qualities: they exist on different days. They are therefore taken to be different objects. But at some point, possibly because of the need for intelligent control of agricultural practice, there comes to be a growing recognition of similarities in objects once thought disparate. Before the new fact, however, before the new whole that might be called "solar regularity" can come fully to consciousness, there is an intermediate stage. There is a "passage-way" from the two suns as isolated to the unity of solar regularity, "denying the former but not admitting the latter." This passage-way is "necessity or determinism" (EW4:25). "The wall of partition between the two separate 'objects' cannot be broken at one attack; they have to be worn away by the attrition arising from their slow movement into one another. It is the 'necessary' influence which one exerts upon the other that finally rubs away the separateness and leaves them revealed as elements of one unified whole. This done, the determining influence has gone too" (EW4:25–26).

The doctrine of necessity arises, then, because some fragment or piece of a whole is taken as a whole, rather than as something "under constant process of definition, of 'production' " (EW4:28). An actual fact, a whole, is mutilated by selecting some piece that reflects some need or end. That piece is then taken for the whole, and the other parts of the whole from which it is wrenched are called "accidental" to it. But when needs change, when there is a need to see the fragment in relation to the whole, some device is needed to justify that reintegration. That device is what has been called "necessity." "Necessity is a device by which we both conceal from ourselves the unreal character of what we have called real, and also get rid of the practical evil consequences of hypostatizing a fragment into an independent whole" (EW4:29).

Put somewhat differently, the difference between necessity and contingency reflects the difference between looking backward to what is already had and forward to what is required. Seen in broader perspective, however, the necessary and the contingent are just correlative aspects of a larger fact. Inquiry is a process of "filling in" this larger fact, determining *its* significance. When the full significance of the larger fact is satisfactorily determined—that is, satisfactorily with respect to some concrete inquirential situation—then talk of contingency and necessity is no longer appropriate. Instead, there is talk of what *is*.

VII

Dewey suggests that once this feature of inquiry is grasped—that the doctrine of necessity advanced in his time (and, alas, in ours) is a superstition—the traditional doctrine of cause and effect also comes into focus. Traditionally, an effect has been taken as clear and present, and its cause as something that must be sought for. In addition, philosophers have often occupied themselves with frustrating attempts to find a "principle of causation" that is the linking force between cause and effect.

In his 1938 *Logic*, Dewey argued that the term "causal law" is a figure of speech. Its use involves metonymy, the taking of something for something else: in this case, it is the taking of the "consequences of execution of its function" (LW12:440;LTI:445) for what is in fact its own content. Dewey pointed out that such metonymic usage is a familiar feature of quotidian life. An iron rod is called a lever in view of its function. An arrangement of wood and metal is called a hammer on the basis of the ways in which it may be used. Common-sense views of levers and hammers, however, following Aristotle, tend to designate such instruments in terms of some inherent "power" or quality of the particular things. With respect to use, however, as opposed to description, even common sense treats instruments in terms of their actual and possible interactions with other things, that is, their functions.

In his treatment of this topic, as he did generally, Dewey undertook a massive undercutting of received views. His radical proposal is that cause and effect are not ontological categories, but logical and instrumental ones. The two notions represent abstractions from a whole fact; they are phases of it that are logically abstracted from it. They are not distinct entities in the existential or ontological sense.

More than thirty years after the publication of "The Superstition of Necessity" in *Experience and Nature*, Dewey developed this proposal at length. Insofar as things are connected with one another, "in efficiency, productivity, furthering, hindering, generating, destroying" (LW1:73;EN:72), they are a manifestation not of nature as enjoyed, of its aesthetic phases, but of nature as it enters into the technical activities of human beings. The intervention of labor into naturally enjoyed things is the only means by which human beings determine what such things will do to other things. This, Dewey claims, is "the only way in which a tool or an obstacle can be defined" (LW1:73;EN:72).

Philosophers have expended great effort in their attempts to ground and sanctify the principle of causation elsewhere than within human technical activities. Realists have treated the regularities of nature as forces that can be known more or less well, but that are discovered as existing prior to inquiry rather than constructed in it. Some idealists have located causation within the dialectical intercourse of ideal categories, for which human labor figures as nothing more than a concrete realization of "absolute consciousness" in one of its multiple phases. Other idealists have turned solipsistic, some admitting no one, some only God, into the domain of their ideas. Some indeterminists have argued that there is a concrete power called the will that exists as part of the human self, but functionally distinct from it. Thus hypostatized, the will is said to be the unconditioned cause of certain effects.

Dewey's approach to this set of problems, as by now might be expected, was genetic. He located the origin of the idea of the principle of causation, insofar as it may be usefully employed as an instrument in inquiry, in the activities of the artisan. "The first thinker who proclaimed that every event is effect of something and cause of something else, that every particular existence is both conditioned and condition, merely put into words the procedure of the workman, converting a mode of practice into a formula" (LW1:73–74;EN:72). What sequences there are in nature cannot be known except by human technical activity, and the paradigm of that activity is the work of the craftsman. "Industrial arts are the type-forms of experience that bring to light the sequential connections of things with one another" (LW1:74;EN:72).

A careful analysis of Aristotle's doctrine of fourfold causation, in Dewey's view, constitutes a confirmation of this account. Aristotle freely and patently borrowed his notion of efficient, final, formal, and material causes from the work of the artisan. Moreover, the difference between efficient causation and final causation was based on a fact of Greek social organization: it is the distinction between the master who utters an order and the servant who executes the command.

It cannot be emphasized too often that for Dewey, it is a mistake to think that principles of causality are unconditionally operative in nature. Instead, nature exhibits sequences that consist of beginnings and endings. In nature, endings no more occur "for the sake of" beginnings than "a mountain exists for the sake of the peak which is its end" (LW1:84;EN:84). In Dewey's view, those who hold a mechanistic view of nature, or the view that there are events called causes that have the power to generate certain events called effects, commit the same fallacy as those who hold a teleological view of nature, or the view that ends bring about their own antecedents. "Both isolate an event from the history in which it belongs and in which it has its character. Both make a factitiously isolated position in a temporal order a mark of true reality, one theory selecting initial place and the other final place. But in fact causality is another name for the sequential order itself; and since this is an order of a history having a beginning and end, there is nothing more absurd than setting causality over against either initiation or finality" (LW1:84–85;EN:84).

That cause and effect are not existentially distinct, however, and that they are not found as such outside the activities of inquiry does not mean that they are not instruments that may have value within inquiry. When viewed as part of practical judgments—that is, when oriented toward future action—they become translated into means and ends of productive activities.

The agent of translation is technical operation itself. When they are put to use with an eye to prospective action, causes cease to function as instruments of analysis and become instead beginnings or antecedents that can be manipulated in order to regulate inquiry and produce desired outcomes. There is, however, a cheap and commonplace form of pragmatism that usually intervenes in the explication of such matters. From the recognition that if antecedents can be managed, consequents will take care of themselves, it concludes that "causes" are ontologically superior to "effects" (LW1:91;EN:91–92).

Technically informed pragmatism, however, emphasizes the technical management of events rather than their ontological classification. To be sure, distinctions are important tools in inquiry. But distinctions between degrees of "reality" constitute a diversion from the task of effective technical control. Effective technical control is based on knowledge of conditions, especially of temporal order. But temporal order is no more just given as a natural quality than is cause or effect; it is constructed through technical activities, through relating, defining, "dating, placing and describing" (LW1:92;EN:93).

> The effect is the end, the practical outcome, which interests us; the search for causes is but the search for the means which would produce the result. We call it "means and end" when we set up a result to be reached in the future and set ourselves upon finding the causes which put the desired end in our hands; we call it "cause and effect" when the "result" is given, and the search for means is a regressive one. In either case the separation of one side from the other, of cause from effect, of means from end, has the same origin: a partial and vague idea of the whole fact, together with the habit of taking this part (because of its superior practical importance) for a whole, for a fact. (EW4:36)

For instrumentalism, it is not distinctions between categories or orders of reality that allow technical control, but distinctions between modes of experiencing. This is a major difference between the long and dominant Aristotelian essentialist tradition and Dewey's instrumentalist version of pragmatism. But modes of experiencing are dependent upon attitudes and dispositions: "The manner of . . . happening is found to be affected by the habits of an organic individual" (LW1:182;EN:193).

Dewey provides two examples of how modes of experiencing allow technical control. In the first, he points out that it is possible to experience the sun, the moon, and the stars in ways that are emotional and imaginative—in ways that are productive of myth. But a far different way of experiencing them is consequent upon the reflective production of significance we call experimental science. Both myth and science are modes of experiencing, but one is clearly more *significant*; it allows for the greater interconnection and substitution of signs, which is the basis of greater technical control.

More appropriate to the analysis of the claims of technological determinists, which will be undertaken in the next chapter, is a second example, which Dewey takes from the theory of political economy. It is possible to approach that subject by means of certain economic categories or essences. The study of the rents, profits, surplus value, and wages in Marx's *Capital* is one such example. It is also possible to study political economy in terms of specific economic systems, noting their particular similarities and differences. Both of these approaches generate a rich matrix of categories and ontological pigeonholes that extend existing taxonomies.

If effective control is sought, however, another way of experiencing economic situations must be undertaken. A study of "incentives, desires, fatigue, monotony, habit, waste-motions, insecurity, prestige, team work, fashion, [and] *esprit de corps*" (LW1:182;EN:194) allows specification of matters that are *within* control and suggests possible means of effecting such control. It is not that this method does not use categories and taxonomies, or that it does not sort things into kinds. It is, rather, that its classifications are made on the basis of aims to be accomplished, rather than on the basis of attempts to find "correct" or essential structures, or even on the basis of assumptions that there must be "natural" kinds.

Structures are, in Dewey's view, just "constancy of means, of things used for consequences, not of things taken by themselves or absolutely" (LW1:64–65;EN:62–63). A structure is "what makes construction possible and cannot be discovered or defined except in some realized construction, construction being, of course, an evident order of changes" (LW1:65;EN:63). When structures are divorced from the means of their construction and posited as things in and of themselves, according to Dewey, the door is opened to gratuitous metaphysical entities and misleading hypostatizing of all sorts. Dewey thought that this mistake was both ubiquitous in the history of philosophy and devastating in terms of its consequences. He called it

"*the* philosophic fallacy" and characterized it more than once as the
"conversion of eventual functions into antecedent existence"
(LW1:389;EN:194;emphasis in original).

In each of these alternative approaches, the essentialist or
structural and the instrumental, the objective facts are the same. From
the standpoint of the facts, it does not matter which method of analysis
we select. What differs from one mode of experience to the next is the
extent to which desired ends can be regulated, the extent to which
technically informed production is made possible. We get "a new
leverage . . . when we can convert description of ready-made events
and dialectical relation of ready-made notions into an account of a way
of occurrence. For a perceived mode of becoming is always ready to be
translated into a *method* of production and direction" (LW1:183;EN:194).

VIII

These matters occupied Dewey throughout his long career. They
received their most extensive development, however, in his 1938 *Logic*.
There, Dewey once again took up the relation of theory to practice, the
doctrine of cause and effect and the "superstition" of necessity, but this
time his treatment was much more powerful because it involved a
technical account of judgments, propositions, and terms of logic, and of
the method of science.

One of the great problems of philosophical accounts of science
could, in his view, be described as the difficulty of bringing the notion of
uniformity of sequence, a matter usually taken to be existential, under
the same tent with causal necessity or unconditionality, a nonexistential
matter. A piece of iron placed in water oxidizes. This is true time after
time, in an unrelenting and uniform sequence. There has, however, been
a tendency among philosophers and scientists alike to speak of iron's
oxidizing in water in terms that are much stronger than that of a uniform
sequence, or what Hume called "constant conjunction." Oxidation of
iron in water is treated as causally necessary or, as one standard
account puts it, as an "objectively based physical necessity."[16]

Since the time of Aristotle it has been acknowledged that necessity
has to do in at least one of its senses with nonexistential propositions,
such as those that are universal and affirmative, of the form "All S is
P"; and those that are universal and negative, of the form "No S is P."
It has also been recognized that particular propositions—including those
that are affirmative, having the form "Some S is P"; and those that are
negative, having the form "Some S is not P"—concern matters that are
existential. They have to do neither with the universal nor the necessary,
but just with what is.

The problem, then, as it has usually been put is that science has to
deal both with existential matters, particular observations reportable in
the forms "Some S is P" or "Some S is not P," and with universal

propositions that take the form of general laws, such as "All S is P" or "No S is P." But what is the bridge from a particular observation to a universal law, or from the law to the observation? A favorite candidate for this bridge has been physical or existential "necessity."[17]

As Dewey indicated in "The Superstition of Necessity," this was not for him a productive or appropriate solution. His unique suggestion regarding this difficulty was to differentiate two types of generalizations: those that are generic and those that are universal. This distinction in turn rests on a second one: the distinction between propositions that are particular and those that are singular.

Particular propositions are those that are the most rudimentary in terms of their existential function. "They are propositions which qualify a singular, *this*, by a quality proceeding from an operation performed by means of a sense organ—for example, 'This is sour, or soft, or red, etc.' " (LW12:289;LTI:289). The qualities in question are objects of particular observations. Particular propositions are, thus, those that suggest something definite occurring uniquely at a particular place and time. A change has occurred in a particular situation.

Particular propositions share their grammatical or linguistic form with what Dewey calls "singular" propositions. Dewey's example of an ambiguous locution which can be interpreted as either particular or singular is "This is sweet." Taken as particular, this proposition indicates a "strictly limited local and temporal occurrence of the quality in question" (LW12:290;LTI:290). Taken as a singular proposition, "this" is determined to be one of a kind. In this case "the sweet quality is no longer simply a change which has occurred; it is a sign of a conjoined set of consequences that will occur when certain interactions take place" (LW12:290;LTI:291).

Particular propositions express the presence of qualities as discriminated from a sensory field. Singular propositions, however, are quite different: they note the conditions under which such qualities occur, and what Dewey calls the "involvement," within inquiry, of recurring operations on the part of the inquirer such that despite other variations of circumstance, the presence of one thing is a sign of the presence of some other thing.

Something more needs to be said about these "recurring operations," for they are the piers on which the bridge between existential and general propositions is built. The proposition "This is a flash of lightning" following a particular event clearly does not indicate recurrence in the sense of the reappearance of an individual event, one that has appeared before and has continued to exist during a given interval of time. Each individual flash of lightning is unique and unrepeatable. Recurrence in this case is instead something *constructed* in and for inquiry. It is "practically synonymous with identification of the flash as *one of a kind*" (LW12:247;LTI:248). "Identification" in this usage indicates a *way* of making something into something else. To put this another way, it is the *use* of something as a sign to signify some further thing.

Dewey argues that this is the same problem that the "savage" has with respect to the determination of whether different suns on different days are the same sun. Existentially, there is the discrimination from the perceptual field of one sun one day, the discrimination from a different perceptual field of another sun another day.

This leads Dewey to identify the problem of the existence of enduring objects with the problem of the existence of kinds, such as "a flash of lightning" in the example just given. "The only conclusion which can be drawn for logical theory from these considerations is that the problem of the sameness of the singular object is of the same logical nature as the problem of kinds. Both are products of the continuity of experiential inquiry. Both involve mediating comparisons yielding exclusions and agreements and neither is a truth or datum given antecedent to inquiry" (LW12:248;LTI:249). In short, both enduring objects and kinds are products, technological artifacts, constructed or manufactured in the course of inquiry. "*The determination that a singular is an enduring object is all one with the determination that it is one of a kind*" (LW12:248;LTI:250;emphasis in original).

The key to understanding the full intent of this remark is the two occurrences within it of the term "determination." "Determination" is a common noun that covers many types of activities or operations. An operation, unlike a single datum, a unique discriminated quality, is a *way* of acting; unlike the quality, it may recur. One form of determination, one way of acting, is *discrimination*. "Discrimination occurs because of consequences of agreement and difference—because agreements and exclusions are instituted by recurring operations in the experiential continuum" (LW12:250;LTI:251).

IX

Dewey thus offers a novel solution to a difficulty that had been at the heart of traditional problem of "universals" since the time of Plato. That problem, succinctly stated, was how to account for the similarities between objects or between their qualities, so that those similarities could provide the basis for universal propositions.

Realists posited forms or models over and above singular entities in which those entities "shared" or "participated." Platonic realism located the forms outside time and space, whereas Aristotelian realism located them in the individual things themselves.

Nominalists tended to deny the existence of similarities and to treat talk of them as nothing more than linguistic conventions. In other words, their view was that there are no real similarities, only names that are applied to different things for the sake of convenience.

Conceptualists held a compromise position. They argued that

singular things may be grouped together into classes on the basis of certain of their natural properties. The classes themselves were said to be conceptual, formed when the mind puts together things that naturally go together, but may not in fact be together in the same place at the same time. These mentally constructed classes then serve as sorting bins for single things. Most conceptualists treated these conceptual classes or kinds as things in their own right, capable of having certain properties of their own. Conceptual things were, however, said to belong to a different order of being than the things that provided their foundations. In late-medieval logic and ontology, such concepts were said by some logicians to have "rational" existence, existence as *ens rationis*, as opposed to the real being of concrete sensory objects.

Dewey's novel solution of this traditional problem was to relocate generality. Realists located generality in existent things: for Platonists, those things were supernatural; for Aristotelians, they were natural. Nominalists denied generality altogether, except in the sense of purely conventional groupings and the names conventionally applied to such groupings. Conceptualists located the *grounds* for generality in things, but maintained that the activity of the human intellect is required to construct the classes into which they are sorted on the basis of their naturally occurring essential properties.[18] Dewey, however, located generality in the activity of productive inquiry, in operations performed with a view to determining relationships, that is, in *ways* (including the expression of habits and the use of instruments) of undertaking particular inquiries.

The position developed by Dewey was closer to the conceptualist than to either of the other two traditional positions, but it was a major departure even from that position. Because they were for the most part devoted Aristotelians, and therefore devoted essentialists, conceptualists thought that knowers are just given certain objects and that those objects come with "tags," as it were, essential properties that are the criteria for sorting them into their proper bins. This is why even the conceptualists were not bothered by talking of "natural kinds." For Dewey, however, there are no meaningful "tags" in any existential sense, or, perhaps more accurately put, there are so many tags that purely existential circumstances provide no satisfactory way of sorting them.

It was Dewey's radical proposal that generality has to do with productive activities undertaken in inference, not with things or events in terms of their status prior to inquiry and as existential. Sorting is done on the basis of need to draw certain inferences, to solve certain problems, to construct or produce certain instruments that will be effective in the resolution of experienced difficulties. Inference has to do with modes of active response. It is the source of generality, since it has to do with dispositions to act in certain ways, or what we call habits.

One of the most famous accounts of generality in the history of philosophy was provided by David Hume. Hume concluded that one particular type of generality, what is normally taken to be causal necessity, is nothing other than associations made habitually. Dewey thought that Hume was on the right track, but that he was misled by his tendency toward psychological atomism—that is, his tendency to take sense impressions as primitive data rather than the result of logical analysis. In Hume's account, once these impressions are associated they become ideas and, what is more important, ideas of objects, insofar as it makes sense to speak of objects. The idea of cause and effect, causal necessity, was then analyzed in terms of the contiguity, succession, and constant conjunction of such ideas. For Hume, the idea of causality was thus based upon habitual association. Humean association was, however, something passive. It was something that happens to human knowers, not something that they actively produce or construct.

Dewey thought this view unduly skeptical, and he thought that he had located Hume's difficulty. First, Hume had not correctly analyzed the notion of "habit." Instead of seeing it as a uniform manner of operational behavior, a recurring readiness to act in certain ways in order to achieve certain ends, he described it as just primitive and mysterious, as just "one of the principles of nature."[19] Second, Hume failed to note that once we formulate an expectation in a proposition, it can be tested against empirical data that serve either to support it or to undermine it. In Dewey's view a proposition is a proposal: as such, it can be tested. Rather than there being something done to us, there is something that we must do. Third, and most important, Hume failed to see that formulating propositions in this way "transfers expectation from the field of existential causation to the logical realm. A generality is involved in every expectation as a case of a habit that institutes readiness to act (operate) in a specified way. This involvement yields . . . potential *logical* generality" (LW12:250;LTI:251).

In other words, the generality on which science is built is neither in the data themselves, since they are particular, nor in associations of qualities given to us as a "principle of nature," since associations are produced in and for inquiry, not read out of nature. What we start with, the material for inquiry, is only a welter of detail, haphazardly arranged from the standpoint of our inquirential needs. Generality resides instead in modes of operation constructed for the purpose of a particular inquiry or brought to one inquirential situation from another, a previous one (even though that previous one may have been undertaken by someone else). As Dewey puts it, " 'common' designates, not qualities, but modes of operation" (LW12:251;LTI:253).

Qualities, as taken from a busy experienced situation, become traits characteristic of a kind when they are "the consequences of operations which are modes or *ways* of changing and acting. This fact indicates that the operations are themselves general, although in another sense from the generality attached to sets of conjoined traits. It indicates, indeed, that the type of generality which constitutes the logical form of the latter is derivative, depending upon the generality of the operations executed or possible" (LW12:252–53;LTI:254).

The importance of this position for Dewey's philosophy of technology can hardly be overestimated. Quotidian life (in which Hume took refuge after his skeptical inquiries), art, science, logic, and metaphysics are for Dewey possible only insofar as instruments (including habitual responses) with which to undertake the inquiry proper to each discipline are constructed. Further, there is only one kind of inquiry, even though its instruments and its materials differ from field to field. Each of these fields requires the successful production of instruments, including general ways of acting under certain circumstances.

X

These considerations form a bridge from the account of particular and singular propositions already given to an account of the two types of general propositions. Dewey calls "generic" those propositions that involve kinds and that are "based upon a set of related traits or characteristics that are the necessary and sufficient conditions of describing a specified kind" (LW12:267;LTI:268). "Universal" propositions are quite different from generic ones: they are "formulations of possible ways or modes of acting or operating" (LW12:263;LTI:264).

Qualities, which are the objects of particular selective discriminations from a total sensory field, as is "sweet" in the proposition "This is sweet," are grouped in various ways. So much was said by Aristotle. Aristotle, however, thought that the criteria for grouping these qualities were themselves found in nature; he thought that they were intrinsic to the qualities themselves and that some groups could be called "natural kinds."

Dewey thought otherwise. Apart from a specific inquirential situation, he argued, there are *no criteria for grouping qualities*. There are no natural kinds. Because kinds are functions of inquiry, and constructed by it and in it, they are artificial. But this does not mean that qualities are grouped arbitrarily. When qualities enter into inquiry, when they enable reasonably safe inference to be made regarding other qualities under certain conditions, they are said to be "characteristic traits." As characteristic *of* something, they allow something to be *done*. The "something" to be done is a proposal, a proposition. They become characteristic traits when they enter into a proposition.

Dewey asks why we do not take as being a kind the conjunction of certain qualities, such as being cross-eyed, being bald, and being a shoemaker. His answer is that when they are taken together as traits, as enabling reasonably safe inference, this grouping is practically worthless (LW12:267;LTI:268). Taken together, what they allow us to do is not something that we would wish to do. The construction of this conjunction of qualities is like the construction of a piece of hardware that is never used because it does not fit any task. If it is designated a "tool," that designation is by courtesy only.

The conjunction of the qualities of being cross-eyed, being bald, and being a shoemaker might function in *some* form of life as a tool for inference, but it is difficult to imagine what that form of life would be. It could be taken as an example of a conjunction of traits, just as the irrelevant and unusable piece of hardware just mentioned could be taken as an example of a tool. But in neither case is there any application to work to be done. Both instances are simply gratuitous; that is, neither is a true instrument.[20]

Conjunctions of traits may, on the other hand, be "selected and ordered with reference to their *function* in promoting and controlling extensive inference" (LW12:269;LTI:270;emphasis in original). Dewey characterizes such traits as qualities that are used as evidential signs or diagnostic marks. A high-pitched whine is in itself just an experienced quality, a change in a perceptual field, nothing more. But a high-pitched whine selected from the various sounds made by an automobile, and utilized as an evidential sign or diagnostic mark, *functions* so as to promote and control inference involved in assessing the condition of the automobile and the steps required to effect its repair, in case any are required.

Generic propositions tie selected and ordered conjunctions of traits together so that a lesser kind is included in a more extensive kind. The relation is that of species to genus, such as "Athenians are Greeks" or "All high-pitched whines in the front of an automobile are those made by belts." The relationship expressed by generic propositions, inclusion of one kind in another, is essential for scientific discourse: it "not only extends enormously the number of characteristics that are inferable, but, what is even more important, it orders observed and inferred traits in a system" (LW12:293;LTI:294). If I know that Greece has a temperate climate, for example, it takes no further existential observation to draw from "Athenians are Greeks" the inference that any person who is an Athenian was born in a temperate climate. And if I know that improperly adjusted belts are the unique source of high-pitched whines under the hood of my automobile, it takes no new observation to draw from "all high-pitched whines under the hood of my automobile are those made by belts" the inference that "any high-pitched whine under the hood of my automobile is a matter of improper tension between rubber and metal." I can make this warranted inference even before getting out of my car to see *which* of the belts needs to be adjusted, lubricated, or replaced.

Finally, there are universal propositions. As has been noted, Dewey characterizes universal propositions as those "whose subject-matter is provided by the operation by means of which a set of traits is determined to describe a kind" (LW12:253;LTI:255). Whereas generic propositions are said to have to do with "kinds," universal propositions are said to have to do with "categories." Departing from the Frege-Russell tradition, Dewey stipulates that he will use of the term "class" as a synonym of "kind."

Universal propositions may be expressed in "if-then" form. "If the sum of the three interior angles of a plane figure is equal to two right angles, the plane figure is a triangle." The two clauses of the universal proposition, however, are not such that one *follows* from the other, but such that they "represent the analysis of a single conception into its complete and exclusive interrelated logical constituents" (LW12:270;LTI:272).

There is another way of stating universal propositions, however, such that they share the linguistic form of generic propositions. "All X is Y" may represent either the generic proposition "All men are mortal," the inclusion of a kind in a more extensive kind; or it may represent "all plane figures, the sum of whose interior angles is equal to two right angles, are triangles," a statement about a mode of being a plane figure. Universal propositions function as definitions; generic propositions relate different kinds.

The point about universal propositions, concerning which Dewey is most emphatic, is that they are not about existence but, rather, prescribe possible operations that, if they were carried out, might solve a particular inquirential difficulty. Generic propositions have existential import; that is, they express concrete relations between existents. Universal propositions do not have existential import; they express relations between meanings. Universal propositions may be valid even in cases where nothing exists to fulfill the conditions laid out by them. That is why we can speak of the relation of Pegasus to the class of mythical horses.

It is important to note Dewey's assertion that grammatical form is ambiguous with respect to logical structure. As Ernest Nagel paraphrases Dewey, "The statement 'All men are mortal' is generic, if it means that all men have died or will die; it is universal, if it means that there is a necessary connection between the characters *being human* and *being mortal*."[21] Put another way, "All men are mortal" is universal just in case it expresses a relationship between the two meanings, being human and being mortal.

Universal propositions are further divisible into two significantly different types. The first type comprises what are normally called the "laws" of science. The law of gravitation, for example, is a "formulation of the interrelation of the abstract characters mass, distance and 'attraction.' But while the contents of the proposition are abstractions, nevertheless, since the proposition is framed with reference to the possibility of ultimate existential application, the contents are affected by that intent" (LW12:394–95;LTI:398).

This type of law, normally called a "physical" law, does not exhaust the possibilities and so may be abandoned for some other law, in case another can be formulated that is more adequate to the area of scientific inquiry at hand. Dewey illustrates this by means of the shift from the Newtonian law of gravitation to the Einsteinian formulation.

The second type of universal proposition comprises mathematical propositions. The proposition "2 + 2 = 4" is irrelevant to any material considerations whatsoever. Propositions of this type cannot be supplanted, according to Dewey, because they have already exhausted all the possibilities. "The final applicability of a physical law, even when stated as a universal hypothesis, demands that some preferred and therefore some limiting interpretation be placed upon the terms or contents that are related. The contents of a mathematical proposition are freed from the necessity of any privileged interpretation" (LW12:395;LTI:398). Mathematical laws have meaning only in terms of requirements of transformability within the system of maximum substitutability in which they exist.

In addition to these two senses of "law," corresponding to two types of universal proposition, there is a third sense of the term that is associated with general propositions and, thus, existential in its import. When some specified conjunction of traits has been observed to occur without exception, it is possible to speak of a "general fact" that is existential in character. "Tin melts at the temperature of 232 degrees centigrade" is an example of such a "general fact." Dewey has no objection to calling this expression of a general fact a law, but he warns that it should not be confused with laws that are nonexistential, such as those expressed by universal propositions (LW12:352;LTI:354–55).

But even Newton's law of gravitation is ambiguous; its meaning is dependent upon whether it is expressed by a universal proposition or one that is generic. In its universal sense the law is a "formulation of the interrelation of the abstract characters mass, distance and 'attraction.' " (LW12:394–95;LTI:398). In its generic sense it is a generalization concerning certain events, a "general fact."

XI

A full and detailed treatment of the logic of scientific technology would require an extensive analysis of Dewey's 1938 *Logic*, a task that is well beyond the scope of this introductory work. Nevertheless, I shall attempt to bring this chapter to a satisfactory close by means of a brief overview of what I take to be Dewey's account of how scientific inquiry functions as an *excursus* from concrete problematic situations to the realm of the type of practice he calls theory, and a *recursus* back to the data of concrete situations in order to check the warrantability of results obtained by acts of production that are abstract; that is, that involve the nonexistential manipulation of meanings.

Gail Kennedy, in what remains the best short essay on the 1938 *Logic*, has suggested that Dewey's account of the way in which inference works in the context of theory and practice may be illuminated by attending to an illustration of the difference between guided and unguided inference provided by William James in his *Principles of Psychology*:

> I am sitting in a railroad-car, waiting for the train to start. It is winter, and the stove fills the car with pungent smoke. The brakeman enters, and my neighbor asks him to "stop that stove smoking." He replies that it will stop entirely as soon as the car begins to move. "Why so?" asks the passenger. "It *always* does," replies the brakeman. It is evident from this "always" that the connection between car moving and smoke stopping was a purely empirical one in the brakeman's mind, bred of habit. But, if the passenger had been an acute reasoner, he, with no experience of what that stove always did, might have anticipated the brakeman's reply, and spared his own question. Had he singled out of all the numerous points involved in a stove's not smoking the one special point of smoke pouring freely out of the stove-pipe's mouth, he would, probably, owing to the few associations of that idea, have been immediately reminded of the law that a fluid passes more rapidly out of a pipe's mouth if another fluid be at the same time streaming over that mouth; and then the rapid draught of air over the stove-pipe's mouth, which is one of the points involved in the car's motion, would immediately have occurred to him.[22]

James says of this example that though it may seem trivial, it contains "the essence of the most refined and transcendental theorizing. The reason why physics grows more deductive the more the fundamental properties it assumes are of a mathematical sort, such as molecular mass or wave-length, is that the immediate consequences of these notions are so few that we can survey them all at once, and promptly pick out those which concern us."[23]

Dewey took over James's outline of the operation of inference in practice and theory, and developed it in terms of his classification of types of propositions as well as in terms of the relations that they exhibit. In the first instance, there is involvement of the stove *in* billowing smoke into the railway car and *with* perceived discomfort. The stove, the smoke, and the discomfort are all parts of a situation that is existentially problematic, not just logically so, and the relation among these elements, which Dewey calls "involvement" (see LW12:276–77;LTI:278–79), is an existential one, not a logical one. It is "ultimately a matter of the brute structure of things" (LW12:277;LTI:278).

Next, there is the relation between a sign and what it signifies, or what Dewey calls "inference." The smoke in the railway car, as a physical existent having certain qualities, is a natural sign of fire.

Because of its spatiotemporal qualities, however, its representative capacity is limited; it is a sign only when and where it exists. The advantage of artificial signs over natural ones is that they do not suffer from this type of restriction. The meaning of the artificial sign "smoke" is, Dewey says, "*liberated* with respect to its representative function" (LW12:58;LTI:52). It allows us to go beyond observation of what is present to inference of what is not.

It should be recalled that inference is for Dewey a mode of production. It is a tool for the construction of enduring objects as well as of kinds that are useful in inquiry. Both enduring objects and kinds "are products of the continuity of experiential inquiry. Both involve mediating comparisons yielding exclusions and agreements and neither is a truth or datum given antecedent to inquiry" (LW12:248;LTI:249). Applying this to the case of the smoke in the railway car, one could say that two different types of inference have taken place, one on the part of the passenger and one on the part of the brakeman. The passenger has inferred that the smoke is an enduring entity that can in *some* way be manipulated; it is on this basis that he asks the brakeman to do something. Or it may be said that the passenger has inferred that the smoke is one of a kind—that is, of a kind that is normally manipulated by the brakeman—and that it is, therefore, reasonable to ask him to do something about it. The inference of the passenger thus involves a singular proposition, "This is one of a kind, *viz.* smoke," as well as a generic proposition, a proposition tying a lesser kind, instances of smoke in railway cars, with a more extensive kind, the kind of things able to be controlled by brakemen.

The brakeman has also utilized inference to produce certain determinations. Trivially, there has been a singular proposition: "This is one of a kind, *viz.* smoke." But there has also been a generic proposition: "All occurrences of billowing smoke cease when the car is in motion." In terms of generality, the inference of the brakeman has proceeded further than that of the passenger.

The point of James's illustration, however, turns on a third relation, one that Dewey calls "implication" or "the relation of meanings that constitutes propositions . . . in discourse" (LW12:60;LTI:54). Dewey thought that the confusion of inference with implication was one of the great fallacies in the history of logic, but he meant this in a sense different from the usual admonitions in introductory logic texts not to confuse the two on formal grounds. When inference and implication are confused, he argued, it is but a short step to the doctrine that logic is a purely formal undertaking, cut off in terms of both origin and result from existential matters. In other words, inference, since it has to do with the relation of sign to thing signified in singular and generic propositions, is an existential relation. But implication, since it is a relation of meanings that do not have, except indirectly, to do with existential matters, and since it is therefore more open to manipulation, is often taken for the whole of logic. Put in terms of Dewey's account of signs, the relation between sign and signified is an existential relation; the relation between symbol and meaning is a logical one.

The theory to which the passenger in James's example could have appealed, and thereby spared his question, describes what we call the "venturi effect." This effect is constituted by the relationship between the meaning of a fluid passing out of an orifice and the meaning of a second fluid passing over the surface of the orifice. It is of sufficient generality to be applicable to many existential situations, but it is not simply a generalization *from* such situations. It is, rather, a theory that has been produced, albeit one that has extensively applied to concrete situations. Its generality is not in nature, but in what we are prepared to do once we hold it as a theory.

Instead of describing only this or that existential situation, it is capable of application to many situations. Its formulation is in terms of the relation of abstract characters. It does not describe existential matters, but rather defines certain possibilities. Further, it is instrumental. As a universal proposition, it is one of a class of propositions that "are operatively applied, in the first place, in deciding the special sort of data to be observationally procured—the particular occurrences that are to be discriminated out of the total welter of events actually occurring; and, in the second place, in interpretation of what the recorded events *signify*. Neither of these applications could be made on the basis simply of the data of a particular day's observation" (LW12:468;LTI:473).

One further type of relation needs to be mentioned. Besides involvement, inference, and implication, which deal with existential things, sign and signified, and symbol and meaning, respectively, there is "reference," a term that Dewey uses to designate "the kind of relation [symbol-meanings] sustain to existence" (LW12:61;LTI:55). Involvement, inference, and implication constitute the technological *excursus* by which new tools are produced with which to control problematic situations. Reference constitutes the *recursus* by means of which they are tested against existential situations.

In what was surely an overconfident assessment of his own ability to articulate this difficult material in a clear fashion, or perhaps because he thought the material less difficult than it in fact is, Dewey suggested that these "differences, when once pointed out, should be so obvious as hardly to require illustration" (LW12:61;LTI:55). He nevertheless supplied as an example the *recursus* of propositions of mathematical physics:

> (1) As propositions they form a system of *related* symbol-meanings that may be considered and developed as such. (2) But as propositions of *physics*, not of mere mathematics, they have *reference* to existence; a reference which is realized in operations of *application*. (3) The final test of

valid reference or applicability resides in the *connections* that exist among things. Existential involvement of things with one another alone warrants inference so as to enable further connections among things themselves to be discovered. (LW12:61;LTI:55)

The *excursus* and the *recursus* constitute productive activity that moves to and fro: from involvement through inference to implication, and then back to involvement through reference. The beginning and the ending of each cycle is the involvement of the concrete situation. The *terminus a quo* is unsettled and problematic; the *terminus ad quem* is ordered in a way so as to be satisfactory. Dewey suggests that the continuity of inquiry makes it difficult to establish priority with respect to inference or implication, that is, with respect to meanings or significances.

The question may be raised whether meaning-relations in discourse arise before or after significance-connections in existence. Did we first infer and then use the results to engage in discourse? Or did relations of meanings, instituted in discourse, enable us to detect the connections in things in virtue of which some things are evidential of other things? The question is rhetorical in that the question of historical priority cannot be settled. The question is asked, however, in order to indicate that in any case ability to treat things as signs would not go far did not symbols enable us to mark and retain just the qualities of things which are the ground of inference. Without, for example, words or symbols that discriminate and hold on to the experienced qualities of sight and smell that constitute a thing "smoke," thereby enabling it to serve as a sign of fire, we might react to the qualities in question in an animal-like fashion and perform activities appropriate to them. But no inference could be made that was not blind and blundering. Moreover, since *what* is inferred, namely fire, is not present in observation, any anticipation that could be formed of it would be vague and indefinite, even supposing an anticipation could occur at all. (LW12:61–62;LTI:55–56)

Dewey further suggests that the extent to which we can call a culture "civilized" depends directly on the extent to which it has been able to control its problematic situations by means of the development of symbol meanings in discourse. "If we compare and contrast the range and the depth of the signifying capacity of existential objects and events in a savage and a civilized group and the corresponding power of inference, we find a close correlation between it and the scope and the intimacy of the relations that obtain between symbol-meanings in discourse" (LW12:62;LTI:56).

The *excursus* and *recursus* become successful only when the grounds of the *excursus*, the empirical needs that generated the inquiry, are also the termination of the *recursus*. Dewey utilizes the vocabulary of business to stress his point. The refined products of the *excursus* return to their grounds "to receive their check" (LW1:37;EN:37). While this is a "check against," it is, in an even more important sense, a "check for," in the sense of a transfer of funds. Dewey indicates that it is there that refined products "inherit their full content of meaning"— that is, only in the context of the original situation that gave rise to their production.

Chapter Six: Instruments, History, and Human Freedom

> The Marxian conception of the part played in the past
> by forces of production in determining property
> relations and of the role of class struggles in social
> life has itself, through the activities it set up,
> accelerated the power of forces of production to
> determine future social relations, and has increased
> the significance of class struggles. The fact that
> history as inquiry which issues in reconstruction of
> the past, is itself a part of what happens historically,
> is an important factor in giving "*history*" a double
> meaning. (LW12:236;LTI:237)

> The fact is that it is foolish to try to draw up a debit
> and credit account for science. To do so is to
> mythologize; it is to personify science and impute to it
> a will and an energy on its own account. In truth
> science is strictly impersonal; a method and a body of
> knowledge. It owes its operation and its
> consequences to the human beings who use it. It
> adapts itself passively to the purposes and desires
> which animate those human beings . . . . It elevates
> some through opening new horizons; it depresses
> others by making them slaves of machines operated
> for the pecuniary gain of owners. (LW6:54;P:319)

I

There is probably no issue that has exercised serious critics of
technology more relentlessly than the claim advanced by some of them
that the development of technology is determined by certain necessary
laws or, put another way, that its development is "autonomous" and
thus outside human control. This claim and various objections advanced
against it are part of a larger dispute that is both ancient and profound.
Since the time of the Pre-Socratic Greeks, philosophers and theologians
have contended with one another regarding whether the universe is
"finished," in the sense of being closed to further possibilities, or
whether it is a place in which human choice is capable of modifying
consequences. Broadly speaking, determinism is the view that any

particular object or event has a cause that uniquely determines it. Looked at from another direction, it is the view that specific sets of causal antecedents are individually necessary and jointly sufficient for the occurrence of a particular consequent object or event.

Beyond this gross characterization, however, finer distinctions must be drawn if matters are to be rendered manageable. In his essay "The Dilemma of Determinism," William James distinguished between two types of determinism. "Hard" determinism, he suggested, holds that the world that now exists is the only world that could have existed. In other words, taking all events as uniquely determined, nothing that is now the case could have been otherwise than it in fact is. "It professes that those parts of the universe already laid down absolutely appoint and decree what the other parts shall be. The future has no ambiguous possibilities hidden in its womb: the part we call the present is compatible with only one totality."[1]

James may have had in mind Laplace's view that if enough information could be gathered about the initial conditions of the universe (which he took to be a mechanical system), its future states could be deduced with mathematical precision. He may also have had in mind the fatalism of Herbert Spencer, whose influence was at its zenith in 1884, when James wrote his essay. Spencer held that human progress was inevitable,[2] and his disciple John D. Rockefeller declared that its manifestation as the growth of large business is the " 'working-out' of a law of nature and a law of God."[3] James called the world of Laplace, Spencer, and Rockefeller a "block" universe.

The view that James called "soft" determinism, on the other hand, accepts all the tenets of the "hard" variety save one. Human beings are free either to accept or reject their fate; freedom is "only necessity understood, and bondage to the highest is identical with true freedom."[4]

James opposed both types of determinism with another view, which he called "indeterminism." This is the view that "the parts have a certain amount of loose play on one another, so that the laying down of one of them does not necessarily determine what the others shall be. It admits that possibilities may be in excess of actualities, and that things not yet revealed to our knowledge may really in themselves be ambiguous."[5]

The problem of "technological" determinism is thus part of this broader topic: to what extent do technological objects, events, methods, organizations, systems, and laws determine human actions, including their modes of relating to one another? If choice is possible, is it inhibited or enhanced by complex technologies? Are there inexorable technological "forces" or "laws"?

There are a number of interesting ways of approaching these questions. It is possible to begin at the top, so to speak, by means of panoramic displays of technological cultures. The units of discourse of this approach are abstractions such as historical stages, economic orders, and sociologically defined groups. This was the method chosen by Marx, and it has also been the method of Jacques Ellul, whose views, I shall argue, are more Marxist than they are usually taken to be.

Alternatively, it is possible to begin at the level of concrete individuals doing and suffering, encountering facilities and resistances with respect to their wants, wishes, hopes, and desires. The unit of discourse in this approach is the specific problematic situation that must be resolved. This was the method employed by William James and by John Dewey.

Whether inquiry into technological determinism begins abstractly or concretely, however, each approach must be ready to give an account of itself to the other. It is reasonable, for example, that a reader of *Capital* should wonder about the implications for his or her personal future of the "iron necessity" that Marx attributed to the historical laws he described in that work. It is also reasonable that the reader of Dewey's 1938 *Logic* should ask whether there are historical or cultural forces that define the boundaries of possible inquiry. It is for this reason that claims and counterclaims about technological determinism must be addressed in terms of their role in inquiry and their consequences for it, for inquiry is one unit of discourse that these very different approaches have in common.

This chapter will constitute a departure from the format of the others. Before examining Dewey's view, I shall begin with an extended treatment of the central features of four important contributions to this debate: the early "critical" Marx, the later "scientific" Marx, Jacques Ellul, and Langdon Winner. I shall then turn to Dewey's contribution to the topic, recurring to his reconstruction of the terms "necessity" and "cause and effect," which were treated in chapter 5, and adding an analysis of his reconstruction of the term "freedom." Finally, I shall return to the views of the two Marxisms, Ellul, and Winner with suggestions regarding ways in which Dewey's critique of technological determinism is relevant to them.

II

In a famous passage in *The Poverty of Philosophy*,[6] first published in 1847, the young Marx wrote: "The handmill gives you society with the feudal lord; the steam-mill, society with the industrial capitalist."[7] On its face, this comment seems to commit Marx to a rigid form of technological determinism *with respect to a given stage or type of technology*. It seems to claim that a given form of technology in a particular historical period is linked inevitably to specific forms of life during that period. Put another way, this remark seems to assert that the dominant technological instruments of a particular period—what Marx calls its forces of production—are the jointly sufficient conditions of the patterns of social organization exhibited by that period.

It is a significant feature of this claim that it is oriented toward the past. It is an attempt to characterize as "necessary" the pairing of certain forms of technology with certain forms of social relation up to and including the present. Does Marx also claim that the inertia of technohistorical pairings impel them into the future so that warranted predictions can be made?

It would seem so. In the preface to the first edition of *Capital*, published in 1867, the mature Marx compared his own work to that of the physicist who observes natural processes and designs his experiments in ways so that those processes will yield warranted predictions, and at the same time avoid artificial disturbance of the data. In other places Marx compares his work to that of biologists and chemists who struggle to formulate scientific laws applicable in all situations, including those yet to come.

So far, however, we have only a moderately strong form of technological determinism. Marx's "scientific" laws of technological development would allow prediction in new situations just in case all relevant contributory factors were the same as in previous ones. If a chemist combines two substances under specified conditions, he or she can be sure that a particular reaction will occur, whether it be next year or fifty years hence. If some culture that currently utilizes handmills introduces the steam-mill, it can be said with confidence that industrial capitalism will follow, next year or fifty years hence.

This is one way of reading Marx's warning that if the German shrugs his shoulders when he reads the account of English industrial society contained in *Capital*, he misses the point: the future of Germany is contained in the present of England. The laboratory procedure is about to be repeated.

"Intrinsically," writes Marx, "it is not a question of the higher or lower degree of development of the social antagonisms that spring from the natural laws of capitalist production. It is a question of these laws themselves, of these tendencies winning their way through and working themselves out with *iron necessity*. The country that is more developed industrially only shows, to the less developed, the image of its own future."[8] In this passage Marx contends that necessary connections between events could not only be read out of the past, but also into the future, *so long as relevant conditions are the same in each case*. I shall call this view "limited technological-stage determinism." It says that if form of technology X, which already exists in society S, is introduced into society T, social form Y will follow in T just as it did in S. This view does not hold that it is inevitable that society T will adopt form of technology X, but just in case it does, for whatever reason, social form Y will inevitably follow. There are iron laws, but they operate only insofar as a particular society chooses a specific form of technology. Further, such laws are based upon observations of technosocial configurations already in existence.

But there is another way of reading this text, one that finds in it a much stronger claim. To the previous claim, "If form of technology X is introduced, social form Y will follow," it adds: "It is inevitable that at some time in the future form of technology X will be introduced." I shall call this "unlimited technological-stage determinism." It says that society T will inevitably pass through a given technological stage.

Both limited and unlimited technological-stage determinisms look backward from the present to the past. Each view attempts to read laws of technological development out of the history of the most advanced technological society, but the predictions of each are limited to those societies that may or will follow the patterns already established in the most technologically advanced society. The future of society T is predictable only insofar as our predictions are based on generalizations about what has already been the case.

But there is an even stronger form of determinism present in the writings of Marx, one that looks to the future from the vantage point of the present. This is the view, expressed in *The Communist Manifesto*, that it is possible to read the properties of a type of technological stage that has not yet been instantiated out of the properties of a type that is now in existence. In this view, an analysis of the properties of technologically advanced capitalism would allow prediction of the properties of a consequent technological order, one that does not now exist, for that society. Such predictions would be a matter of calculation on the basis of what might be called "laws of technological development." I shall call this view "future technological-stage determinism."

But the situation is still more complex. In the same short section of *The Poverty of Philosophy* that I just quoted, Marx claims that it is human beings who produce social relations, just as it is they who produce the forces and relations of production. Cloth, linen, and silk are products, to be sure. But *forces of production*, which include tools and machines, are also products of human activity.

The same may be said of the *relations of production*, which include interactions between instruments, between human beings and instruments, and between human beings insofar as they are involved in production. Also among the products of human effort are *social relations* in the wider sense, which include those relations between human beings that have no direct connection to forces or relations of production. Marx's view in this passage seems to be that human beings freely choose their productive forces: in doing so, in changing their way of making their living, they change their social relations.[9] Forms of technology are still paired with specific social forms, but there is a good deal of play in the extent to which the variables may be manipulated. This view, which I shall call "technological-stage indeterminism," holds that within a given stage of technology there are many choices to be made, even though choices of forms of technology have definite effects within the social sphere. This view differs from limited technological-stage determinism in that it allows for more choice within a particular technological stage.

The term "product" in this material is used to refer not only to the forces and relations of production and to social relations, but also to principles, ideas, and categories. In other words, in this passage Marx seems to reject a Platonistic account of ideas, choosing instead one that is constructivist and in some respects like the one that Dewey would later advance. "Thus these ideas, these categories, are as little eternal as the relations they express. They are *historical and transitory products*. There is a continual movement of growth in productive forces, of destruction in social relations, of formation in ideas; the only immutable thing is the abstraction of movement—*mors immortalis*."[10] Marx here seems to describe these historical and transitory products as having the loose connections that James thought characteristic of an indeterminate universe.

In his letter to P. V. Annenkov, dated 28 December 1846, Marx further explicated this indeterminist view. Continuing his criticism of Proudhon, who was his target in *The Poverty of Philosophy*, Marx claimed that social relations, the way that people live together, "must necessarily change with the change and growth of the productive forces."[11] But he claims that Proudhon had fallen into the trap of the classical economists, such as Adam Smith, who saw real relations as embodiments of certain preexisting abstractions. He thus accuses Smith of Platonism. These abstractions themselves, he continues, are taken by the classical economists as "formulas which have been slumbering in the heart of God the Father since the beginning of the world."[12]

Marx's objection to the views of the classical economists in this material is *not* that they think there are laws that govern the relations between production and social relations; he, too, thinks that there are such laws. It is, rather, that they think of the laws that they have formulated as pre-existing and immutable. His criticism of Smith is the same as his criticism of Proudhon: both view the laws of production before the age of capitalism as faulty and transitional, as imperfectly reflecting the immutable laws of capitalism that they have discovered. Marx's description of the "trap" of classical liberalism is in certain respects similar to Dewey's criticism of that position in his 1938 *Logic* (LW12:498ff;LTI:504ff) and in *Liberalism and Social Action* (LW11:1–65;LSA). This is a matter to which I shall shortly return.

Examples of these two kinds of texts—those that indicate that Marx held one or another variety of technological determinism and those that indicate that he was an indeterminist—could be piled up indefinitely. In the well-known "Eleventh Thesis on Feuerbach" Marx asserts: "The philosophers have only *interpreted* the world, in various ways; the point, however, is to *change* it."[13] If the laws of technological and economic development are inevitable and rule with iron necessity, what purpose could such a call to action serve? On an indeterminist reading, effort would lead to true innovation of something not now predictable. On a "soft determinist" reading, effort would be expended in order to align oneself with the inevitable, perhaps to hasten it.

On the other hand, in his "Postface to the Second Edition" of *Capital*, published in 1873, Marx quotes with approval the remarks of a reviewer who characterizes Marx's arguments in these terms: "It is a matter of indifference whether men believe or do not believe it, whether they are conscious of it or not. Marx treats the social movement as a process of natural history, governed by laws not only independent of human will, consciousness and intelligence, but rather, on the contrary, determining that will, consciousness and intelligence."[14]

What the reviewer meant by "social movement" is not specified. One reasonable interpretation of his remarks is that the forces and relations of production—including tools, implements, methods, and whole industries—operate autonomously; that is, outside human control or will to change them. They seem to be governed by the same type of immutable, natural laws that Marx rejected in his criticism of Adam Smith. If this "hard" deterministic view of technology and history is correct, change cannot even be accelerated, since what will be the case is already fated and choice is an illusion.

III

The tone of many recent discussions of technological determinism has been set by two books by Jacques Ellul: *The Technological Society*,[15] published in French in 1954 and in English translation in 1964; and *The Technological System*,[16] published in 1977 and 1980, respectively. For reasons that will become clear, I shall term Ellul's position "technological gridlock."

Ellul's works have been characterized by some as maddeningly frustrating and obscure.[17] Nevertheless, he is clear on several points. First, he gives a precise definition of his term "technique." Borrowing his formulation from Harold Lasswell, he defines technique as "the *totality of methods rationally arrived at and having absolute efficiency* (for a given stage of development) in *every* field of human activity."[18] Little imagination is required to see the connections between this characterization of the relation between technological method and all human activity (during a particular historical stage) and the claim of the scientific Marxists that the technological infrastructure determines the political and ideological superstructure (during a particular historical stage).

Second, Ellul distinguishes "technique" from "technology." Here, with his translator's notation in parentheses, is his articulation of this distinction.

> We absolutely have to establish the difference between the concept of
> *technique* and the concept of *technology*. It is a grave error, often made by
> French intellectuals imitating Anglo-American usage, to speak of *technology*
> when they really mean *technique*. The former is a discourse on *technique*, a
> science of *technique*. First of all, it is a discourse on different *techniques*
> (English, technologies); then an attempt at discursing on *technique* (English,
> technology) in general, i.e., actually on the concept itself. This, however, is
> not intended as a study of the procedures of some—say, industrial—
> operation (That would be the subject of technical courses!); the goal here is
> a philosophical reflection.[19]

In short, technique is the ensemble of methods used in contemporary
industrial societies. Technology is the study of such methods: either one
or several at a time, or taken more generally. Thus, "technique" is for
Ellul a term of very broad application, and it corresponds closely to what
Marx called the forces and relations of production, including ideas,
categories, and methods. Technology, on the other hand, is the study or
critique of such modes of production.

Third, and perhaps most important, Ellul argues that technique (the
ensemble of methods) is no longer the subject of human control.
Technical growth is irreversible and progresses geometrically. Traditional
values evaporate before its automatic and self-augmenting growth. New
ideas must be judged in terms of its specifications. Even scientists,
technocrats, and politicians, to say nothing of philosophers and
theologians, are subject to its constraints. Individual human beings fare
even worse. "The human being," Ellul charges, "is delivered helpless, in
respect to life's most important and trivial affairs, to a power which is in
no sense under his control."[20]

In this regard Ellul appears to be in the same corner with the
"scientific" or determinist Marxists, but to lack their faith in the future.
Some scientific Marxists at least argue that the iron laws of capitalism,
its internal contradictions, will inevitably lead to its breakdown and
replacement by a form of social organization that is conducive to
improved relations between and among individuals. Ellul's view is much
more grim. In his foreword to the revised American edition of *The
Technological Society*, Ellul sketches the following "disturbances" that
might change the course of history. First, a general war might break out.
In this event, destruction would be so extensive that technological
society as we know it would be at an end. Second, an increasing
number of people might become convinced that technology poses a
threat to human "spiritual" life and might decide to alter matters in a
decisive way. Third, "if God decides to intervene, man's freedom may
be saved by a change in the direction of history or in the nature of
man."[21]

Although there is a glimmer of hope in Ellul's second scenario, its
suggestion is no less cataclysmic than the other two. What Ellul in effect

contrasts are (1) the orderly evolution of the present self-augmenting and geometrically progressing technological regime, and (2) several radical cultural discontinuities, radical revolutions that will upset its course. There is more than a hint of Luddism in these alternatives.

With the exception of his third scenario, then, which is un-Marxist on its face, Ellul writes very much like a scientific Marxist gone grim. Like Marx himself, however, he is a writer of many moods and views, some of them patently incompatible with others. In an interview with David C. Menninger, Ellul reveals yet another scenario, in addition to the three forms of radical discontinuity and one form of continuing evolution we have just seen. Drawing on Marx's description of the conditions of the proletariat during his own time, he suggests that the very appearance of hopeless deadlock could be just the needed stimulus for change. "If man does decide to act, he doesn't have many possibilities for intervention, but some do continue to exist. And he can change the course of social evolution."[22] Despite its lack of concrete proposals, this call for revolution would be quite acceptable to many "critical" or indeterminist Marxists.

Fourth, technique is for Ellul not neutral. It obeys its own agenda, which is ever-greater self-augmentation and "rationalization" of whatever is left of hitherto resistant pockets of competing methods. His view thus exhibits a marked contrast to at least one moment within Marx's complex view, the position Marx expressed in his letter to Annenkov: "The application of machinery in the present day is one of the relations of our present economic system, but the way in which machinery is utilized is totally distinct from the machinery itself. Powder remains the same whether it is used to wound a man or to dress his wounds."[23]

IV

In his 1977 book *Autonomous Technology* (AT),[24] Langdon Winner sought to contrast what he called the "traditional" interpretation of the technological society with his own view, which he called "technological politics." As Winner characterizes it, the traditional interpretation holds that a given society has at its disposal a set of tools and methods that are capable of being marshaled toward the attainment of certain preselected ends. In addition, whatever tools exist for the society in question are generally responsive and adaptable to whatever ends are selected. Effective control is thus unidirectional; it has its source in the political sphere and is applied to tools in order to achieve chosen ends.

A significant component of the traditional view is what Winner calls the "straight-line" notion of tool use. This is the "straight-line" instrumentalism that Dewey's critics almost universally accused him of, but he himself criticized it as inadequate for successful inquiry. It is the view that perceived problems come more or less furnished with ready-made *desiderata* that function as inflexible ends. The resolution of the original difficulty is, then, only a matter of choosing the appropriate instruments, putting them to use, and judging the success of the entire operation in terms of the degree to which there has been a satisfactory arrival at the ends originally projected (AT:228). Implicit in this traditional view is the contention that valuation comes from outside experimental technology, that goals are formulated by nontechnological means.

Winner's model of the technological system departs substantially from this traditional view. For one thing, he thinks that contemporary large-scale systems are altogether too complex to exhibit "straight-line" instrumentalism. It is increasingly unlikely, for example, that any person or group of persons is capable of effectively controlling a complex technological process such as the delivery of a new model of automobile from inception in the design stage to the end point—in this case its use by a consumer, and its repair and maintenance by service people (or even the recycling or disposal of its parts once it becomes unserviceable).

Winner thinks that technological complexity is of two types. First, there is the *manifest* complexity of advanced technological societies that engenders extraordinary events, functions, and interconnections that are no longer comprehensible in the sense that no person is able to get an overview of the entire picture (AT:284). Winner thinks that manifest complexity makes it very difficult to approach problems scientifically, whether those problems be quotidian or specific to a particular discipline. With Mannheim, he thinks that most contemporary forms of inquiry are more religious than scientific because of their heavy dependence on faith.

Concealed complexity is in Winner's view much more dangerous. This is a kind of Kafkaesque complexity that operates within the environs of electronic interchanges utilized by bureaucratic institutions. The speed and efficiency of such complex configurations is overwhelming, but decision procedures tend to become opaque to public scrutiny (AT:285).

Another point at which Winner's view differs from traditional straight-line instrumentalism is that he views the technological system as more than simply a toolbox from which instruments may be selected; it is a real, active, objective system. Like Ellul, Winner pointedly refuses to anthropomorphize the technological system, though in both his work and Ellul's certain anthropomorphisms sometimes tend to creep in. He further denies that the technological system is in any way occult. But for Winner, as for Ellul, the system possesses inertia and goals of its own. The size, complexity, and mutual interdependence of the components of the megatechnical system create demands to which society is forced to yield. "Confronted with these imperatives—the system's need to control supply, distribution, and the full range of circumstances affecting its operations—the immediate and expressed needs of society may seem capricious" (AT:251).

Also like Ellul (in one of his moods), Winner inverts the traditionally conceived relationship between political power and technological instrumentation; political power has in both of their views become subservient to the goals of the technological system. The technological system, because of its size and complexity, and because of the interdependence of its parts, is not only unresponsive to political control, but also is able to make demands to which those in political office must yield or else face unacceptable consequences.

Winner thus rejects the view of some critics of technology, including Ellul (in another of his moods),[25] that "the movement of advanced technology is universally centralizing and that this centralizing tendency eventually culminates in control by an extremely powerful, technologically oriented state" (AT:252). Both Ellul and Mumford, for example, citing electrical generation and transmission as examples, have argued that technological societies tend to concentrate control of production and distribution in very few hands, and that these hands are ultimately those of political autocrats. It is their view that regardless of political intent in this and other cases, the very nature of large-scale technological phenomena dictates inevitable political reaction and restructuring.

Winner also rejects the mirror image of this view—that is, that "within an organized system, control originates in a central source and emanates outward through the other parts" (AT:253) and that that central source is a state driven by technocratic concerns. In Winner's view, then, control neither originates in the sector responsible for technological production and then gravitates to a public political center, nor does it originate in a political center and then become diffused throughout a private technical sector.

In Winner's view, the technological system *really has no core*, but is nonetheless a real system with real effects, even though those effects are often at cross-purposes. He thus rejects the view of those such as Galbraith, who argue that power increasingly rests in the hands of the members of a managerial elite who pass back and forth through a revolving door between public and private sectors, so that public and private sectors share the power in the new industrial state. In Galbraith's view such power sharing is, to be sure, anything but equitable. Major industrial decisions are made in the private sector, then ratified by government-agency heads who are once and future members of the directorial boards of the industries with whose regulation they are charged.

In order to understand Winner's objections to these theses, variously advanced by Ellul, Mumford, and Galbraith, it is necessary to combine the concepts of manifest and concealed complexity with two others: the "technological imperative" and "reverse adaptation." Stanley

Carpenter has summarized and characterized these concepts with great precision:

> The concept of the technological imperative goes to the heart of the matter. The kinds of decisions required by the technological order itself, rather than consciously selected ends directed either toward human purposes or special interests, turns out to dominate. Providing for basic needs, food, clothing, shelter, mobility, etc., is replaced by technologically specific objectives—more oil, increased electric power, wider roads, higher buildings, etc. Such redefinitions of original human demands in terms of large-scale, sophisticated, and intermeshed technologies result in man, the ostensible master, acquiring a pathological dependence on technology, the supposed slave. Winner pushes the analyses deeper along Marxist lines. As the technological order respecifies objectives, human expectations themselves change to match the respecification. Perceptions, judgments, feelings, desires are reshaped under the lordship of the order itself. Ways of speaking, thinking, behaving along with patterns of work the individual must tolerate are transformed. A mode of life is defined and so ultimately is human consciousness itself.[26]

According to Winner, then, "technologies are structures whose conditions of operation demand the restructuring of their environments" (AT:100). As such, technological imperatives are consummately practical. In order to have X, it is necessary to have Y. But the means to Y—call them M, N, and O—must also be put into place. One reason why this procedure amounts to an imperative is that M, N, and O are rarely "chosen" in and of themselves. In fact, if there were to be a choice, they would most likely be rejected.

The consumption of electrical power is one of many possible examples of the effects of the technological imperative. What appears to be a free choice of X, to use more electrical appliances, requires Y, the construction of more power plants. But the means to more power plants may include M, the burning of high-sulfur coal; N, the generation of nuclear waste that cannot be safely disposed of; and O, special legislative provisions for the nuclear-power industry to protect it from financial liability in the case of an accident that results from poor design, improper maintenance, or human error.

In this case it is theoretically important to have increasing access to electrical power. This is a goal that is consciously chosen. The proximate and practical means of generating more electrical power may be less desirable but are at least theoretically acceptable. At the level of actual production, however, means that are quite remote from the original goal (theory) begin to dominate patterns of life in ways that are unavoidable and, at times, unacceptable. The deforestation of large areas due to acid rain, consequence of high-sulfur-coal furnace emissions; amorphous but nagging concerns about radiation leaks; the perception that special interests are able to operate with impunity outside the structure of democratic accountability—taken together, the consequences of these remote means begin to precipitate fear, cynicism, and a crisis of confidence in the political system. Somewhat naive original expectations of cheap and plentiful electricity are changed by the technological system itself into attitudes that are debilitating and even destructive.

This is but one aspect of the technological imperative. There are many other examples, some more positive but no less exacting. Technological media may be thought of as tools that produce news and entertainment, but in Winner's analysis they alter the ways in which technological men and women perceive the content and function of news and entertainment. Human beings become molded by the electronic slave. Such are the workings of the technological imperative.

Winner is quick to point out that analysis of ways in which technological change generates imperatives is much more useful than a simpler analysis of "unintended consequences." It might be thought, for example, that the destruction of rain forests is just an unintended consequence of industrialization in Brazil or Mexico. But Winner's model is much richer. He speaks of requirements met *beforehand*. "The environment is modified to make room for the thing or things demanding that modification; in a certain sense the effects antedate the cause" (AT:104). Those responsible for technological decision-making in developing countries seek to emulate the techniques and procedures utilized in countries that are more developed. "Preconditions" are put into effect, even if it means ripping apart the cultures of the countries to be developed.

Regarding "reverse adaptation," Carpenter once again precisely distills in one paragraph what Winner has developed over many pages. He thinks that the notion helps to explain the situation faced by the supermarket shopper who must accept "tomatoes bred for picking rather than tasting or when one is willing to put out good money for armor-plated oranges that must be believed to be eaten." Carpenter clearly sees that "reverse adaptation does not suggest that technological means are totally divorced from human wants, needs, cultural standards, political decisions, but rather that ' . . . technical systems become severed from the ends originally set for them and, in effect, reprogram themselves and their environments to suit the special conditions of their own operation.' "[27]

In short, Winner sees reverse adaptation at work when "technical systems become severed from the ends originally set for them and, in effect, reprogram themselves and their environments to suit the special conditions of their own operation. The artificial slave gradually subverts the rule of its master" (AT:227).[28] This amounts to "the adjustment of human ends to match the character of the available means" (AT:229).

Beyond oranges and tomatoes, other examples of reverse adaptation lie close at hand. A person working at a job that requires high standards of exactitude may find that those standards begin to encroach on other areas of his or her life. What functions as means in one situation becomes the end of other situations. Another way of putting this is that ends become capable of articulation only in terms of available means, that the store of available means has been shrunk as a result of the pressures of high-level performance in a specific task, and consequently imagination and inventiveness suffer.

Winner offers the example of standardized college-entrance exams. What once was taken as a means to the end of ascertaining a general level of educational competence becomes a specialized end that replaces the original end. The successful taking of the test becomes the end, and education comes to be identified with the means to that end.

In this matter Winner is in general agreement with Ellul. Like Ellul, he believes that the technological system increasingly limits free choice because of its emphasis of standardized practices. Like Ellul, he believes that technique has become operative in all areas of life, and that original human goals and responses have atrophied. Decisions are made automatically and instrumentally—like clockwork. "Once such conditions take effect, only an extraordinary act of will can reopen the process of evaluation, choice, and action, for all situations in social life turn out to be those in which a known instrument is available to do the job and a corresponding instrument ready to make the right selection" (AT:235).

Carpenter has suggested that Winner's position exhibits a "love-hate relation" with that of Ellul.[29] This is, I would argue, an important insight into Winner's program. I have already suggested some of the ways in which Winner's views differ from those of Ellul, as well as from those of the two Marxisms. Winner's most important departure from Ellul's position, however, is that he has a number of concrete suggestions to make with respect to what he terms the regaining of technological control. He takes technologies as forms of life, he thinks that forms of life generate forms of political organizations, and he therefore holds that concerted efforts to introduce new forms of technology will be more productive of expanded choice than efforts to overhaul the political system directly. This view is quite similar to what was called "limited technological-stage determinism," and it places Winner's view quite close to that of some of the critical Marxists.

V

As I indicated in the previous chapter, Dewey undertook an extensive reconstruction of the notions of cause and effect and necessity. His argument, in fine, was that cause and effect and necessity are logical tools only, and are not found in existential situations. He further argued that the determinist who looks for causes, effects, and historical necessities elsewhere than among tools of inquiry commits the philosophic fallacy, taking something that has been developed as an instrument within inquiry for something that has existence in itself prior to inquiry. It was, further, his view that these tools—cause and effect, and necessity—can easily be dispensed with once inquiry has grasped the whole situation, which was formerly divided into parts for the sake of analysis.

Another way of putting this is that Dewey rejected technological determinism not simply by issuing the counterclaim, as did James, that it would be better if human beings were free and that they therefore had a right to act as if they were. Dewey undercut the ontological assumptions of determinists and indeterminists alike as a part of his critique of Aristotelianism. He thought that the error of both positions lay in their acceptance of the assumptions of Aristotelian essentialism. He argued that it is not the discovery of ontological categories that allows control of future action, including scientific control, but differentiation among modes of experience in terms of their relation to production. Categories may serve as tools for inquiry, but they should not be thought to pre-exist inquiry. They function in inquiry because they are constructed to serve a function, not because they are discovered fully formed in some reality external to human productive activity. In other words, Dewey substituted a critique of production for a cataloging of essences and accidents as instrumental to the growth of knowledge, although he acknowledged that catalogues and taxonomies often were very handy tools for doing certain jobs.

"We learn," he writes, "(but only at the end) that instead of discovering and then connecting together a number of separate realities, we have been engaged in the progressive definition of one fact" (EW4:21). The fact thus produced is neither there previous to our production of it nor invented from nothing. It is the result of technical manipulation of data in order to achieve some goal or purpose.

VI

Whereas Marx, Ellul, and to some extent Winner preferred to start with abstract institutions, Dewey's focus was on concrete situations. In his essay "Philosophies of Freedom," published in 1928, Dewey tied the development of the concept of freedom to the concept of choice: "There is an unexpugnable feeling that choice *is* freedom and that man without choice is a puppet, and that man then has no acts which he can call his very own. Without genuine choice, choice that when expressed in action makes things different from what they otherwise would be, men are but passive vehicles through which external forces operate" (LW3:92–93).

Dewey suggested that one of the reasons why this problem of human freedom is so difficult is that what he calls the "fact of choice" got mixed up early on with a number of other issues. Tendency to praise and blame became codified in terms of legal punishment. Such practice in turn sought metaphysical support from a doctrine that came to be known as "the freedom of the will." And if the will were truly free, the locus of moral and legal liability, it must be "equally free to choose one way or another unmoved by any desire or impulse, just because of a causal force residing in will itself" (LW3:93).

There is, Dewey argued, a serious fault in the traditional account of the will as exercising unmotivated choice. Human beings are concrete existential beings. They embody a complex matrix of habits, desires, and purposes. If there is an absolutely free will somehow independent of the concrete human individual who is to be held responsible, how could responsibility be legitimately placed on that concrete human individual?

Dewey's solution to this difficulty is twofold. First, he dehypostatizes the will. Augustine, Descartes, and Kant, whom Dewey seems to have in mind in these remarks, wrote of the will as a separate faculty or entity. Dewey not only rejected these and all other versions of faculty psychology, but also thought hypostatizing of this sort pure nonsense.

Second, Augustine, Descartes, and Kant analyzed human action in terms of the antecedent influences of the will upon it. For Dewey, however, the resolution of the question of liability lies not in the past, but in the future: what can be expected in terms of future behavior? It is at this point that Dewey's evolutionary naturalism and behaviorism come into play. He argues that selective behavior can be found everywhere in nature, from atoms to human beings. Atoms and molecules have a tendency to hook up in certain ways, and not in others. If this were not so, there would be no science, and it would be impossible to practice medicine. Further, these preferences express the "natures" of atoms, molecules, rocks, plants, and animals, including human beings. Dewey does not commit himself to "essentialism," however, simply because he talks of natures. His theory of inquiry makes this matter quite clear: he characterizes "natures " operationally, in terms of interactions among objects as known, not as fixed essences.

The basis for choice in human beings, then, is the same kind of preferential action that is exhibited throughout the rest of nature. But choice among human beings is more than simple preferential action, though it is at least that. This is so because human beings are more sensitive to their environments, more complex in terms of their organization, and more capable of taking into account a wider variety of experiences than are lower animals and plants. Dewey speaks of human beings as having, and as being more or less aware of, their own *life histories*.

This is just to say that whereas other natural beings are more or less "pushed into action from behind" (LW3:96), human beings are aware of a great number of factors that compete for the role of determinants. This awareness is coupled in human beings with the ability to transcend, to a certain extent, environmental pushes. This transcendence has two elements: human beings are able to project their future actions, and they are capable of complex sign behavior that serves as a tool for rising above the fray of natural exigencies. "As observation and foresight develop, there is ability to form signs and symbols that stand for the interaction and movement of things, without involving us in their actual flux" (LW3:96).

In short, human beings are capable of choice in the following sense: though they are caught in a nexus of natural behavioral preferences, such preferences function for human beings as complex, competing, flexible, and capable of being anticipated by means of symbolic behavior such as warnings, mathematical calculations, and analogical thinking.

It may be objected that to speak of animals being "pushed into action from behind" and to speak of human beings as being subject to certain natural exigencies, as Dewey does, is to sneak in through the back door the very notions of cause and effect and necessity that he has so noisily and publicly ejected through the front door. Realist and essentialist treatments of necessity, after all, describe as "necessary" the ways in which atoms of hydrogen and oxygen combine to form water, as well as certain constraints that all human beings feel (for example, the need to eat).

It is not that Dewey denies such constraints: it is simply that he thinks that until they are dealt with in inquiry, ordered in some useful way, they are no more than unformed aesthetic features of situations in which human beings find themselves. Thus the requirement felt by all human beings for food *means* different things in and for different cultures. Food, as well as the nexus of cultural practices we call eating, is constructed differently in different cultures. Choice is then a matter of appreciation, in the sense that perceived possibilities have gained interest by means of productive work undertaken.

To constitute a contribution to the problems of technological determinism, then, concrete human choice and freedom must be examined in terms that are broad and overtly public. Choice may be obstructed or facilitated not only by natural exigencies, but also by laws, economic systems, technical constraints, and other human artifacts. It is trivially true that some institutions operate so as to constrict human activities to a greater extent than do others. Some technical decisions tend to broaden avenues of choice, to produce what Dewey calls "increased significance," whereas others tend to constrict available meanings and provide only cul-de-sacs.

What is regarded as a technical success can suddenly and inexplicably turn into a situation that is deeply problematic. Unintended and deleterious consequences can, and often do, arise from matters thought satisfactorily settled. Dewey finds the source of difficulties of this type not in "technology," in the sense of the application of technical methods to unsettled situations, but in the very precariousness of existence. There is no guarantee, indeed no agency to issue such a warrant, that problems once solved will forever remain so. "Technological" problems indicate that further technical work needs to be done, not that such work needs to be abandoned in lieu of search for "spiritual" or other types of values, or, worse, that nothing at all can be done because the future is already determined.

One of the impediments to meaningful choice most often mentioned by Dewey was the dead weight exercised by methods, habits, and institutions that have ceased to be properly instrumental, that is, instrumental to the ends for which they were chosen. Perhaps the instruments have themselves become worn, or perhaps the ends that they once served are no longer desirable. The framers of eighteenth-century liberalism were well aware of this problem, but unfortunately did not see their own movement as subject to it. They argued that institutional impediments to individual choice should be reduced so far as possible. Institutions were regarded as supportive of freedom only insofar as they allowed "the unobstructed play of wants in industry and commerce and . . . the enjoyment of the fruits of labor" (LW3:97). This official doctrine was, and still is, called laissez-faire.

Dewey suggested that there was a popular psychological correlative that grew out of the liberal doctrine of political and economic laissez-faire. If wants and commerce could proceed unobstructed by institutional interference, why not instincts and impulses as well? Freedom came to be identified, in popular thinking, as self-expression: the unimpeded expression of "natural" instincts and impulses.

What the popular theory overlooked, however, was that individual human instincts and impulses are in large measure products of social environments. Dewey saw in the popular theory the remnants of one that was much older than the classical liberalism of Locke, Bentham, and Mill, one that was present in Augustine and even in Plato, that natural tendencies are the gift of God and artificial institutions are either a necessary evil or, worse, an occasion for falling away from love of God or the knowledge of the Forms.

Dewey thought that classical liberalism was immensely successful in its initial stages. It was a great good that stultifying feudal institutions were dismantled as the interests associated with new forms of manufacture and trade became more powerful. But these new institutions themselves became, in time, a burden to members of the working classes.

Among the criticisms of classical liberalism, however, has been the view that it placed too much emphasis on the individual. Dewey rejected this criticism on the grounds that it was overly timid. He suggested that "it would be equally pertinent to say that it was not 'individualistic' enough. Its philosophy was such that it assisted the emancipation of individuals having a privileged antecedent status, but promoted no general liberation of all individuals" (LW3:100).

The fallacy of classical liberalism, according to Dewey, was that it assumed that all human beings are equally capable of taking advantage of existing laws and institutions.

> Since actual, that is, effective, rights and demands are products of interactions, and are not found in the original and isolated constitution of human nature, whether moral or psychological, mere elimination of obstructions is not enough. The latter merely liberates force and ability as that happens to be distributed by past accidents of history. This "free" action operates disastrously as far as the many are concerned. The only possible conclusion, both intellectually and practically, is that the attainment of freedom conceived as power to act in accord with choice depends upon positive and constructive changes in social arrangements. (LW3:100–101)

Dewey thought the problem of human freedom could be put simply (though he by no means regarded it as a simple problem): it is "the problem of the relation of choice and unimpeded effective action to each other" (LW3:104). I have argued that Dewey's talk of "effective action" is in fact talk of pro-duction, that is, technical problem solving. His solution to this problem is thus a further expression of his instrumentalism. Successfully exercised technique, as effective control of the environment, generates increased freedom because it "enlarges the range of action, and this enlargement in turn confers upon our desires greater insight and foresight, and makes choice more intelligent" (LW3:104). An important component in intelligence is the ability to see situations that are doubtful and problematic *as* doubtful and problematic.

VII

Taken together, Dewey's reconstruction of three concepts—necessity, cause and effect, and freedom—sharply undercuts the naive realism exhibited by both Marx and Ellul. Dewey meets the question of whether choice exists with an argument that might be called "transcendental." The very fact of asking that question indicates that choice at some level has been exercised, for the term "choice"—like the terms "necessity," "causality," and "freedom"—is itself a technical artifact, the product of a procedure in which choice has been exercised in the context of inquiry.

But the larger questions put by Marx, Ellul, and Winner remain. Are there iron laws of technological development, as the scientific Marxists claim? Has contemporary technology significantly limited human freedom by its apparatus of domination, as the critical Marxists claim? Is there technological gridlock such that human choice is squeezed to a bare minimum, as Ellul claims? Has technical choice passed out of the hands of political control because of its size and complexity, as Winner claims?

It follows from Dewey's remarks on the doctrine of necessity that he rejects all claims that there are inevitable laws operative in history.

His view might be taken as a trivial expression of the obvious unless it is recalled that at least nominally, the basic body of belief held by a majority of the world's inhabitants includes some form of historical determinism. In their most common popular formulations, Christianity, Marxism, Judaism, and Islam contain some measure of commitment to the predictability of the future on grounds of fixed historical determinants, some of which are immanent and some of which are regarded as imposed by a transcendent God.

Dewey rejects the judgment that there is an overall direction to history because of external supernatural forces, whether personal or impersonal; and he rejects both the judgment that history exhibits laws that are internally "dynamic," as well as the judgment that history involves "single"- or "multiple"- factor causal accounts.

Historical judgments are for Dewey just a special type of narrative account, and narrative accounts are those into which temporal and spatial relations enter. In nature, however, there are no absolute temporal or spatial relations. The event we call "daybreak," to use one of his examples, may serve as the initiation, the termination, or an intermediate point in a particular narrative. Its place is overtly chosen and is relative "to the objective intent set to inquiry by the problematic quality of a given situation" (LW12:221;LTI:222). To refer to another of his examples, a mountain is taken in one inquiry as permanent. In another inquiry, however, the geologist takes "the same" mountain as expressive of a temporal sequence of birth, growth, maturation, decay, and death. In short, "events" exist not in nature but in judgment.

More specifically, however, historical judgments present a restricted form of a problem that is properly logical. Once it is understood that temporal continuity is produced or constructed as a part of directed inquiry, "what is the relation of propositions about an extensive past durational sequence to propositions about the present and future? Can the historical continuum involved in admittedly historical propositions of the past be located in the past or does it reach out and include the present and future?" (LW12:230;LTI:230–31).

Dewey's answer to these questions is that historical accounts involve concerns and leading principles that exist at the time historical inquiry is undertaken. What are claimed to be the "iron" laws of history are in fact judgments made about data available at a particular time, and on the basis of conceptual materials and interests that are important at that particular time and to that particular inquiry. "History cannot be written *en masse*. Strains of change have to be selected and material sequentially ordered according to the direction of change defining the strain which is selected" (LW12:234;LTI:234).

Historical judgment, like all other types of judgment, is selective. The history of the modes of production is in fact wrung from a larger set of events, one into which factors such as religious practice, military successes, and aesthetic considerations also enter in.

"History" is in Dewey's view an ambiguous term. It is both a body of judgments about what happened in the past and a purposive reconstruction of those events. The writing of history cannot escape its own eventuality as a part of history. Like other human constructions, historical judgments are tools: they are "instruments for estimating the force of present conditions as potentialities of the future. Intelligent understanding of past history is to some extent a lever for moving the present into a certain kind of future" (LW12:238;LTI:239).

The strong claims of technological determinism advanced by the scientific Marxists are from an instrumentalist perspective yet another example of the philosopher's fallacy, that is, the taking of consequents as antecedents. "Laws" of history are in fact historical judgments in the sense just described. They are instruments that arise not *by* but *from* inquiry; consequently, they are necessary only in that limited sense. Not only do they represent a partial understanding of past events and of the import that those events have for the future, but they also undergo continual revision as new interests emerge and new inquirential techniques are brought into play.

If there is any meaning to Marx's claim in *Capital* that a culture that is more technologically developed shows one that is less developed an image of its own future, it is that specific (although not necessarily well-informed) decisions are often made by politicians and planners in less technologically developed cultures on the basis of information (and misinformation) gleaned from cultures that are more technologically advanced. As so frequently happens in all forms of inquiry, the method of authority is substituted for the experimental method as a means of resolving a problematic situation.

A concrete example of this phenomenon is what has been called "the green revolution." If scientific Marxists were correct in their view that a particular means of production uniquely determines both relations of production and social relations, it would have been possible to make accurate predictions about the application of large-scale farming in Mexico and Brazil on the basis of patterns visible in the United States. Mechanized farming techniques in the United States have, in fact, so far been accompanied by large harvests, and more plentiful and cheaper food.[30] In the case of Mexico, however, productivity actually decreased after the introduction of large-scale farming. Following its "green revolution," Mexico, a country rich in cheap labor and low annual per-capita incomes, became a net importer of food for the first time in its history. As one critic suggested, farming (or large-scale, moderately efficient food production) replaced gardening (or small-scale, highly efficient food production). Displaced from their traditional occupations as gardeners of small plots, the formerly productive rural poor who were capable of feeding themselves became the urban destitutes who were dependent upon unstable and unsustainable levels of exports and trade balances for their sustenance. This pattern is now being repeated in Brazil, with consequences that are even more devastating.

This should not be taken to indicate that actions do not have consequences that can be predictable; it is evident that they do. Moreover, Dewey never tired of repeating his view that consequences are predictable and controllable just to the extent that they are the results of technical inquiry—that is, the results of the purposeful enlargement of meanings and expansion of the substitutability of variables in the context of the kind of practice he calls theory. However, technical inquiry and technical control are matters of the utilization of what Dewey called "checks and cues," not of the operation of necessary historical laws.

Dewey's differences with the scientific Marxists, then, are profound and irreconcilable. When instrumentalism is put alongside the work of the critical Marxists, however, the situation is quite different. Whereas scientific Marxists seek an absolute, decontextualized knowledge of the laws of history that utilizes the physical sciences as paradigm, critical Marxism, like instrumentalism, emphasizes the contextuality of knowledge and the importance of human choice. Critical Marxists, like instrumentalists, regard existing social institutions as historically conditioned, conditioned in the sense that they are the results of decisions made in the past by members of human societies, not in the sense that they are the products of iron laws. Social institutions are thus treated by critical Marxists and instrumentalists alike as capable of change in the present for the sake of the future, and change is regarded as the result of human activities.

Instrumentalists and critical Marxists do eventually part company, however. Although it is something of an oversimplification, it may be said that the former emphasize the activities of individuals for bringing about social change; the latter emphasize the activities of groups. The question for both schools, then, becomes not so much the proper reading of the iron laws of history as the kinds of practices that will motivate and inform intelligent social choice. It is in this spirit that Jürgen Habermas, a dominant figure within critical Marxism, has turned to the theories of communication developed by British analytic philosophy, especially in the work of J. L. Austin, and by American pragmatism, especially in the work of G. H. Mead.[31]

Habermas and Dewey are both indeterminists, although in somewhat different senses. Whereas Habermas seems to be content to work within the boundaries of the problem of determinism, as it has been defined by traditional metaphysics, Dewey seeks to undercut that tradition. It is also crucial to remember that the young Marx who is the favorite of the critical Marxists treated ideas, categories, and institutions as products. He did not, however, treat these products as instrumental in the extended sense in which Dewey would treat them.

The situation with respect to Ellul's version of "technological gridlock" is somewhat more complex because of the vagueness of his presentation. From the standpoint of instrumentalism, Ellul's work represents an egregious case of the philosopher's fallacy. The "technological system," an abstraction, is claimed to be causally operative, according to internal laws that it itself has generated and that are just discoverable by competent sociologists of technique.

I believe that Dewey would have been quick to argue that the "totality of methods rationally arrived at and having absolute efficiency (for a given stage of development) in every field of human activity"— Ellul's definition of the technological system, taken either as a "totality" or as a "system"—is just a tool in inquiry that has been claimed to be much more than that. It has been claimed to be an essence discovered outside and prior to inquiry.

If the situation described by Ellul is taken as the empirical generalization that technical methods have limited possibilities, his view is not a variety of technological determinism at all. From an instrumentalist standpoint, this reading of Ellul's view would constitute a claim that technical methods have not been sufficiently or adequately applied, that instruments once used and no longer appropriate have become dead weight. For the instrumentalist, the measure of technical methods is the extent to which meaning is enriched and significance broadened. Dewey thought that enriched meaning and broadened significance are the means of intelligent choice.

Ellul seems to be of two minds regarding the relationship of technique to political control. At times he argues that technical control has been concentrated in the hands of state technocrats who utilize such control to augment their own status. Dewey explicitly regarded such concentration of power as an impediment to technical control.

At other times Ellul argues that it is the technological system itself that is the locus of power, and that even elected politicians and technocrats must obey its laws. If it is meant by this that institutions tend to become ossified and recalcitrant, Dewey would have regarded such a situation as a call for further inquiry. If it is meant that there is an active impersonal force at work, we once again have the philosopher's fallacy.

There is yet another possible reading of Ellul. It might be said that certain forms of technology tend not only to limit choice, but also to anesthetize awareness that choice has been limited. But even if this description were an accurate one, it would not follow that there are historical or technological "forces" at work, just that men and women have chosen tools to do their bidding that are dangerous or even potentially disastrous. What is being pointed to is at least a fact, at most a trend (which in Dewey's vocabulary is but a larger fact) but in no sense an inevitability.

VIII

Winner's view of what he calls "autonomous technology" is far less open to the sort of criticism that Dewey's instrumentalism can bring to bear on Marx and Ellul, even though Winner finds much of value in the work of both of those thinkers. This may be so because Winner's notion of technology as a "form of life" has its roots in Wittgenstein and because, as I have already suggested, Wittgenstein's work has much in common with Dewey's.

Both Winner and Dewey consider "straight-line" instrumentalism inadequate. Both reject its view that technological control is just a matter of employing the proper political tools required to achieve preselected ends. Both argue that means and ends interpenetrate, even to the extent that what may be the *result* of a technological decision in one situation often becomes the *condition* for it in another setting. As I have indicated, Winner even has a name for this phenomenon: he calls it "reverse adaptation." Deforestation, for example, which is a result of technological decisions in country A, becomes a condition for them in country B.

But Winner seems to think that the unease felt by contemporary men and women—their perception that the manifest complexity of their situation has become too great, and that the system in which they live is incoherent and ungovernable—is a unique feature of advanced technological societies. He also takes this complexity as an indication that technology does not have a "core."

Dewey would, I think, have argued that manifest complexity is not new to technological societies, but was also a feature of political entities as small as the Greek city-states. His discussion of the social organization of the Athenian *polis* emphasizes the powerlessness that the majority of its constituents must have felt. Against Dewey, it might be replied that the difficulty for the Athenians was not so much that their situation was complex, but that political power was utilized in an unenlightened manner. But in the view of certain perceptive insiders, such as Aristophanes, complexity was precisely the Athenian Achilles heel. He depicts the Athenians as overly litigious, and as inextricably enmeshed in the web of their own economic and military imperialism. As far as Winner's claim that technology does not have a "core," I think Dewey would have suggested that the expectation that technology should have a "core" betrays a previous commission of the philosopher's fallacy.

Winner is worried about the concealed complexity exhibited by apparatus of various types. He thinks that the fact that we don't understand how our machines work is an important piece of the larger picture of diminished personal freedom within advanced technological societies. The astounding speed and power of computers, for example, render their users dependent. Internal parts are not user-friendly; certain machine-language codes are proprietary and unavailable to the public.

On this matter, at least, Dewey saw matters quite differently. He continually argued that complexity is just a functional relation between available skills and the degree to which situations are perceived as in need of attention. Insofar as I can tell, Dewey never argued against the introduction of any tool *per se*; he did, however, warn that inquiry into the possible ways in which new tools can be used is frequently terminated before they have been fully explored.

Early in Dewey's career the telephone was a novel tool. Telephones of the 1890s must have appeared quite complex to their users, as ours do to us now. Then, as now, special skills and tools were required to repair telephones. Dewey saw the telephone not as an obstacle or a danger, however, but as the bearer of great potential for increased communication.

It is also possible to question Winner's contention that the concealed complexity of the electronic culture leads to massive centralization of power in the hands of a few. Whereas it is undeniable that centralization does occur, electronic communication seems to have had the effect of decentralizing important elements of cultural and political power. Minority groups such as blacks, Hispanics, gays, and lesbians have been able to communicate with one another and to take their cases before larger publics in ways not possible before electronic communication. Even in a matter as mundane as regional accents, television seems to have removed some of the stigma from nonstandard American English. Further, there has probably never been a time in the history of the United States when there was more interest in local "support" groups oriented toward myriad interests.

If one substitutes Dewey's terms "habits" and "institutions" for what Winner calls "technique," the claim of both is that increased human freedom lies in the continuing reconstruction and reassessment of the results of previous decisions in order to maintain appropriate adjustment with respect to overlapping environmental demands. This task is rendered difficult wherever specific tools are habitually coupled with particular tasks, as they generally are in the exercise of established "cookbook" techniques, because such situations facilitate acquiescence to solutions that are not adequately adjustive. There is a tendency in such situations to muddle through with existing tools, rather than face the difficult task of developing new ones. Part of the appeal of straight-line instrumentalism is that it is simply a less-demanding method than the dynamic type of instrumentalism favored by both Dewey and Winner.

For both Dewey and Winner, then, the most persistent barrier to the exercise of technological choice is the enormous body of tools, skills, institutions, and apparatus that are utilized in habitual ways. But at the same time, both Dewey and Winner recognize that technopolitical inertia is not without certain benefits. Habits, institutions, laws, and cookbook technical recipes are not developed without effort. Dewey refers to this body of social habits as the "flywheel" and the "mainspring" of technological cultures. But both Dewey and Winner also see such social habits as contributing to the frequent failure of technological cultures to develop and utilize skills that allow problematic situations to be seen as problematic, as well as tending to entrench class and economic interests.

To an uncritical reader, Winner might appear to be arguing that technology must be returned to its former place as subservient to political will. He has written, for example, that technology must be "disciplined by the political wisdom of democracy."[32] Taken at face value, this would set him at odds with Dewey, who argued that whatever wisdom a democracy exhibits is itself a technological artifact, conditioned upon technical progress in the sphere of material life and generating ideals from intelligent technological practice.

But read closely, Winner's argument turns out to be very much like Dewey's. It is not that there are two modes of human production—technology and politics—and that technology must be subordinated to politics. It is not Winner but the straight-line instrumentalists who attempt to split technology from politics. It is not he but they who define "efficiency" narrowly and establish it as *summmum bonum*. To use one of Winner's examples, the generation of the cheapest possible electric power may in fact not be efficient in a larger sense. The social costs that are usually labeled "political" are in fact part of a larger technological situation. Like Dewey, Winner thinks that the United States now has an implicit technological constitution in addition to its explicit political one, but that its approved political doctrine, straight-line instrumentalism, has tended to obscure that fact. Also like Dewey, Winner thinks that the platforms of both classical liberalism and Marxism exhibit defective technological planks, since both regard material abundance as the sufficient condition of human freedom.

Nevertheless, Winner does think that certain technical problems are just too large to be solved, and that this is true because of the very size of the investment in the status quo. In this respect, at least, he is much more pessimistic than was Dewey. Since Winner's book appeared, however, an excellent counterexample to his thesis has developed. The governor of New York has taken steps to purchase and close the Shoreham nuclear reactor. The motivation for this action is a large technical problem, namely the inability of its builder to develop adequate evacuation procedures in the event of an accident. Even an investment of $4 billion was ultimately deemed of lesser import than the safety of the residents of Long Island. Some might suggest that this is a case of the technological being brought under the control of the political. But Dewey would have argued that political inquiry, like other forms of inquiry, is technological. In the next chapter, I shall indicate some of the ways in which he thought this to be so.

Chapter Seven: Publics as Products

> Only geographically did Columbus discover a new world. The actual new world has been generated in the last hundred years. Steam and electricity have done more to alter the conditions under which men associate together than all the agencies which affected human relationships before our time. There are those who lay the blame for all the evils of our lives on steam, electricity and machinery. It is always convenient to have a devil as well as a savior to bear the responsibilities of humanity. In reality, the trouble springs rather from the ideas and absence of ideas in connection with which technological factors operate. (LW2:323;PP:141)

> Roughly speaking, tools and implements determine occupations, and occupations determine the consequences of associated activity. In determining consequences, they institute publics with different interests, which exact different types of political behavior to care for them. (LW2:263;PP:44–45)

> Democracy is belief in the ability of human experience to generate the aims and methods by which further experience will grow in ordered richness. (LW14:229)

I

It is an incontrovertible fact of contemporary life that the problems we term public, in societies that are democratic as well as those that are authoritarian, have come to be associated in one way or another with the growth, the implementation, and the prospects of technology. This attitude is a common feature of societies that are otherwise quite diverse. East and west, among Marxists as well as laissez-faire capitalists, and north and south, among nations that are developed as well as those that are developing, public problems are now almost universally viewed as having technological origins as well as technological solutions.

Dewey's concern with the technological dimensions of public problems was coterminous with his long career, and his publications on that subject were voluminous. His major works in this area, which include *The Public and Its Problems* (1927), *Individualism Old and New* (1930), *Liberalism and Social Action* (1935), and *Freedom and Culture* (1939) were written between the two world wars. But his active involvement with social issues antedates these works by decades.[1] The title of Dewey's lecture to the Philosophical Union of the University of Michigan in 1888 was "The Ethics of Democracy," and he was an active participant during the 1890s in the intellectual movement that led to the Progressive era of the first two decades of this century.

Dewey's work this in area was influenced by hands-on experience. During Dewey's decade at the University of Chicago, from 1894 to 1904, that city was regarded as "the center of radical thought in the United States."[2] This was also the time of Dewey's involvement with Jane Addams's Hull House, among whose other associates were Florence Kelley, a translator of Engels, and Henry Demarest Lloyd, a muckraker whose targets included Standard Oil. By 1916, Dewey had published *Democracy and Education*, which contains the substance of what he continued to refine as his public philosophy.

Dewey's aim in this sphere, as in the others to which he turned his attention, was demystification. Here, as elsewhere, he constructed an alternative to the extreme positions widely regarded by his peers not just as incommensurable and irreconcilable, but as requiring a commitment to one side or the other. Unlike many of his contemporaries, who felt it necessary to choose either communism or laissez-faire capitalism as their working political and economic ideology, Dewey rejected both.[3]

In this domain, as elsewhere, his method was widely misunderstood. For example, he was accused by C. Wright Mills, one of his many critics on the left, of not having a coherent political position, of being a "mugwump,"[4] and of failing to come to terms with the "kinds of action occurring within and between struggling, organized political parties."[5] Mills thought Dewey's suggestion that intelligence could operate at the level of complex political organizations dangerously naive: taking his cues from Marx and Weber, he regarded political parties as organizations for social fighting. "Their 'theory,' e.g., platform, has to be dogmatized, not only to insure, in a time of quick mass communication, uniformity among party workers, but because they are organizations. Some party workers become functionaries, hence it is not permitted that they think through independently problems in a 'free' and 'intelligent' manner."[6] This criticism, similar to one advanced by Reinhold Niebuhr, is one that many of Dewey's readers have taken as vitiating his political theory. I shall return to the attacks launched by Mills and Niebuhr against Dewey.

II

What are the themes within Dewey's social and political philosophy that play a role within his critique of technology? And what guidance does his critique of technology provide us for action in social and political matters?

First, Dewey rejected the social-contract theory in all its numerous manifestations. It was his view that social-contract theories neither provide what they have historically claimed to, that is, causal explanations, nor do they do any useful work when regarded, as they now most often are, as a hypothetical "limit." Observation led him to conclude that the search for "state-forming forces" uniformly leads to myths that are at best unhelpful and at worst misleading. Inquiry into social and political activity, like inquiry of other sorts, must begin where human beings find themselves—*in medias res*. Regardless of how it came to be the case, the unavoidable fact is that the activities of human beings, both singly and in groups, tend to produce consequences for themselves and for others.

Wherever this is recognized to be the case, means are sought to control consequences: to ensure that some outcomes are secured and that others are avoided. It is to this end that artifacts, including instruments of all sorts, are developed and used, and it is within this context that human social and political life is technological—pro-ductive and con-structive—where and everywhere it is encountered.

Just as Dewey's critique of traditional forms of epistemology sought to avoid the extremes of realism and idealism, his critique of traditional social and political theories sought to avoid the absolutism present in many versions of Marxism, as well as the atomism that characterizes most political theories in the West. One need only examine the most influential works in social and political philosophy in the past two decades to appreciate the fact that Dewey's program has still not been widely accepted as a critique of either his predecessors or his (or our) contemporaries.

The highly abstract reconstruction of the social-contract theory advanced by John Rawls, for example, reveals the same fault lines that Dewey thought weakened the social-contract theories of Locke and Rousseau.[7] And Robert Nozick's reworking of theories of absolute natural rights,[8] to mention another influential example, can best be described as "mythical" in the sense intended by Dewey in the passage quoted at the beginning of this chapter. Both Rawls and Nozick treat human individuals as logically, ontologically, and perhaps historically prior to and independent of human societies. This is a position against which Dewey argued forcefully more than half a century earlier by identifying it as an example of the unacceptably naive realism consequent upon the commission of the philosophic fallacy. It is quite remarkable that neither of these major works of political philosophy—

works that most impartial observers would place among the most influential of the 1970s and 1980s within the classical liberal tradition— takes into account the actual historical and cultural context of live, decision-making human beings. Both proceed as if the ends of political inquiry could be fixed once and for all, as if it were simply a matter of finding the proper means to reach those ends. In other words, both exhibit what Langdon Winner has called "straight-line instrumentalism." Put another way, it is remarkable that neither Rawls or Nozick seems to take into account the technological factors of group life.

The situation is somewhat more complex with respect to Marxist thought. The past few years have witnessed a gradual eclipse of "scientific" Marxism at the same time that "critical" Marxism has been ascendent. Not only Marxist theorists, such as Jürgen Habermas, but also those Marxists such as Mikhail Gorbachev, who wield real political power on a daily basis, have moved increasingly toward a stance that has been popularly termed "pragmatic." By this it is usually meant that rigid ideologies have begun to yield to the more resilient politics of communicative interaction, centralized control has begun to give way to new forms of cultural pluralism, and personality cults have begun to be supplanted by experimentalism.

Because he was more interested in what could and ought to be done in the sphere of the social and the political than he was in attempts to undertake ontological analyses of such material, Dewey argued that the time-honored *structural* distinction between "individual" and "society," upon which rests the work of the members of the Frankfurt School no less than that of Rawls and Nozick, is of less import than the *functional* distinction between what is private and what is public. Dewey thought the concept of individuality advanced by the empiricists, by those of the "classic" school no less than those who are our contemporaries, an empty abstraction. He argued that individuals are identifiable as such only after being abstracted from historical and cultural contexts. They are neither found, nor could they find themselves, in a state of nature prior to associations with other human individuals. Nor are they the bearers of absolute natural rights apart from and independent of any human society. The reason for this is a technological one. There are no individuals before there is communication, for communication is a technological artifact that is a necessary condition of awareness of oneself as an individual.

Dewey's reconstruction of the traditional problems of "individual versus society" is reminiscent of his critiques of mind-body dualism and of cause and effect. There is a problem of reconciling the extremes only if one has made the mistake of separating them in the first place. Groups may be opposed to each other, and individuals may also be opposed to each other. An individual may be divided within him- or herself in terms of conflicting memberships, roles, and obligations. But to take these facts as grounds for hypostatizing "the individual" and

"the social" as fundamentally opposed entities is to create what Dewey
calls an "unreal" problem. "Because *an* individual can be dissociated
from this, that and the other grouping . . . there grows up in the mind an
image of a residual individual who is not a member of any association at
all. From this premise, and from this only, there develops the unreal
question of how individuals come to be united in societies and groups:
the individual and *the* social are now opposed to each other, and there
is the problem of 'reconciling' them. Meanwhile, the genuine problem is
that of adjusting groups and individuals to one another"
(LW2:355;PP:191).

Dewey thought it empirically obvious that individuals discover
themselves, and in fact are capable of such discovery, only within social
matrices whose connections are technological; that is, that consist of
artifacts constructed for use and enjoyment. It is only by means of
technological artifacts that human beings are able to *mean* their worlds;
only by means of them are community, and individuality, possible. The
concepts "individual" and "society" are thus abstractions from rich
contexts of linguistic and other technological meanings. Neither
concept—the individual or the social—is primitive: not historically, not
ontologically, not logically. Dewey went so far as to call "the problem of
the relation of individuals to associations—sometimes posed as the
relation of *the* individual to society," a meaningless one
(LW2:278;PP:69).

Dewey argued that the term "society" has no univocal reference. In
a remark that bears a striking likeness to what would later be termed
Wittgenstein's "family-resemblance" theory of universals, Dewey argued
that "since there is no one *thing* which may be called society, except
[an] indefinite overlapping, there is no unqualified eulogistic connotation
adhering to the term 'society' " (LW2:279;PP:70).

When Dewey abandoned the *structural* concept pair individual/
society, an instrument that commonly serves Marxist as well as classical
liberal laissez-faire social theories, he chose as an alternative the
functional concept pair private/public. As functional concepts, what is
private and what is public are treated by Dewey as tools that may be
brought to bear on problematic situations in ways that "individual" and
"society," because of the ontological baggage they carry, cannot.
Dewey's delineation of the public and the private is in terms of control:
"private" people are those who are deprived of public position, and a
public consists "of all those who are affected by the indirect
consequences of transactions to such an extent that it is deemed
necessary to have those consequences systematically cared for"
(LW2:245–46;PP:15–16).

Each human being is associated with other human beings in the *de
facto* sense that his or her very coming to existence and childhood
survival are dependent upon previously functioning human associations.
But human beings are also associated with one another in the *de jure*

sense that what they desire, hope for, and value—and thus what they are able to become—is bound by material conditions that include membership and participation within matrices of human technological achievement: human groups.⁹ Conversely, novel action undertaken by any group, any *new* idea, is always the action of this or that concrete individual. "Every *new* idea, every conception of things differing from that authorized by current belief, must have its origin in an individual" (MW9:305;DE:296). For Dewey the significant contrast is not between individual and group, since there are no individuals (in the full sense of that term) who are not associated with other individuals, but between individuals who are productive and creative, and therefore able to contribute to group life, and individuals who are caught up in what is unproductive and unimaginative, and therefore not capable of doing so. Thus, the "actual alternative to deliberate acts of individuals is not action by the public; it is routine, impulsive and other unreflected acts also performed by individuals" (LW2:247;PP:18).

Unlike Nozick and Rawls, who see the primary struggle as that between individuals and other individuals, or between individuals and social groups, Dewey argued that "men were not actually engaged in the absurdity of striving to be free from connection with nature and one another. They were striving for greater freedom *in* nature and society. They wanted greater power to initiate changes in the world of things and fellow beings; greater scope of movement and consequently greater freedom in observations and ideas implied in movement. They wanted not isolation from the world, but a more intimate connection with it" (MW9:302–3;DE:294).

Dewey's removal of the primary tension within social and political theory from its customary place, between the individual and the group, and his relocation of it to the qualitatively different space between the private and the public is thus expressed in terms of consequences of actions undertaken. Friendships, religious associations, and professional organizations are examples of groups that are *prima facie* "merely" social, that is, in a nonpolitical sense. The most basic activities of such groups tend to turn inward, to have effects that do not extend beyond their own boundaries. But such private groups may also undertake activities whose consequences continue well beyond the confines of their immediate membership and interests. When this occurs, various publics are brought into existence.¹⁰ "The characteristic of the public as a state springs from the fact that all modes of associated behavior may have extensive and enduring consequences which involve others beyond those directly engaged in them" (LW2:252;PP:27).

Publics, in order to be effective, require officials and agencies. When officers and agencies of various publics, including those we call "states," function *for* their respective publics, they constitute governments that are effective and responsible. The source of most of the problems usually called "political" or "public" arise when officers and agencies that are nominally public operate either covertly or overtly for ends that are private.

It follows from this analysis that many forms of political organization may function so as to exercise effective control of the problematic situations that call various publics—and the larger public called the state—into existence. Dewey thus seeks to avoid what he sees as a rigidity characteristic of most standard political theories. "The only statement which can be made is a purely formal one: the state is the organization of the public effected through officials for the protection of the interests shared by its members. But what the public may be, what the officials are, how adequately they perform their function, are things we have to go to history to discover . . . there is no *a priori* rule which can be laid down and by which when it is followed a good state will be brought into existence" (LW2:256;PP:33).

Dewey's analysis of the state is thus quite unlike that of Aristotle, for example, since it seeks to determine what any particular state can become, rather than seeking to determine what it is and therefore in which category it should be placed. But if Dewey has no ontology of the state, he has a clear methodology, a clear "criterion for determining how good a particular state is" (LW2:256;PP:256). A state is to be measured in terms of the extent to which a public is organized so as to solve certain difficulties, and in terms of the extent to which public officials are capable of and do in fact exercise effective control of public interests.

States that perform this function well are said to be "representative" in the sense of "democratic." They are formed when a public "adopts special measures to see to it that the conflict [between public and private interests] is minimized and that the representative function overrides the private one" (LW2:283;PP:66–67). Not every society is a state, let alone a democracy. Indeed, the state is in Dewey's view a relatively recent development. States are formed when a public becomes sufficiently aware of itself that it can construct and maintain regulative functions through its officers.

There is in Dewey's account no room for divine purpose in the formation of and maintenance of the state, no room for blind obeisance to the "original intent" of its founders, no room for mythical causal forces such as social contracts, and no room for the state-supplanting mystical forces that have been systematically hypostatized and termed "technological" by theorists such as Jacques Ellul.

Each of these approaches to social and political matters was regarded by Dewey as backward-looking and desiccated: none of them was capable of providing meaningful, testable, self-correcting plans for future action. His view was that the public called the state is what that particular public under the leadership of its officers *does* in order to secure more effective control of problematic situations. The state is a means of social inquiry by and for its constituents. It is a constructed artifact like other tools and utensils. Its nature is its function, and its function may not only be different for societies having different cultural histories, but also may change for any given society according to changing conditions.

Among these altered and altering conditions are changes with respect to material culture. If the larger public called the state is a consequence of the formation of smaller publics, each of those publics is in turn a consequence of the occupations of its constituents. And occupations are tied up with forms of culture, which is to say varieties of tool use (LW2:263;PP:44).

Dewey's view of the state thus stands in stark contrast to those that are essentialist; that is, to those that regard the state as having an archetypical essence or as growing organically. Dewey is unequivocal in his view that the state is a technological artifact; it is neither found nor discovered as something existing prior to its construction, nor is it invented in the sense of being arbitrarily conventional.[11] Not only is the state constructed, in the rich sense in which Dewey uses that term, but it is also in need of continual reconstruction, in the equally fecund sense in which Dewey also uses *that* term.

III

Dewey argued that the theory advanced by laissez-faire liberal thinkers since Locke (and as I have suggested, we can now add both Rawls and Nozick to that list) largely ignored the history of technological facilities and constraints upon the generation and operation of various publics. The original idea of the classical liberals was a good one. Existing institutions, ecclesiastical as well as political, had become an impediment to the exercise of intelligent choice and effective action. But the revolt against established authority was couched in terms of what was said to be another authority, at once more primitive, sacred, and inalienable: the fundamental rights and powers of protesting individuals. "Thus 'individualism' was born, a theory which endowed singular persons in isolation from any associations, except those which they deliberately formed for their own ends, with native or natural rights. The revolt against old and limiting associations was converted, intellectually, into the doctrine of independence of any and all associations" (LW2:289;PP:86–87). In the work of Locke, the sole end of government became the protection of individual natural rights.

This political doctrine was by no means isolated from its broader cultural context. It was accompanied by the epistemology and psychology of the era from which it arose. Seventeenth-century rationalism and empiricism, the schools of Descartes and Locke, were in agreement on at least one central point: the search for foundations ends with an ego, an independent mind, a private self.

Dewey argued that there was an important consequence of their position that these thinkers had failed to recognize, a consequence that has still not been fully grasped by those who continue to practice political philosophy in their manner. That point is that laissez-faire liberal political thought was conditioned by technological considerations. Mechanical appliances, including the lens and pendulum, had come to be utilized in organized ways. The organization of simple tools led to the production of machinery; and machinery, to the construction of new forms of commerce.

Dewey especially condemned his contemporaries who were members of this laissez-faire school, which he labeled "the older humanism" in his *Democracy and Education*. He charged them with having "omitted economic and industrial conditions from [their] purview" (MW9:298;DE:289). He thought it ironic that even though many of their number were unashamed apologists for big business, they failed to examine the influence of changes wrought in the history of business and industry upon the history of their own ideas. It was not theories of social contracts and political atomism that gave rise to new sciences and new forms of individualism: these things came in the wake of "the rise of free cities, the development of travel, exploration, and commerce, the evolution of new methods of producing commodities and doing business" (MW9:303;DE:294). Dewey even thought that the methods of Galileo, Descartes, and their successors were *analogues* to the methods that had already begun to be tested in a literal marketplace by experimental means.

Dewey found yet another deep irony in the doctrines of the laissez-faire liberals. Although their efforts were attempts to limit the operations of existing institutions because those institutions were judged guilty of impeding new forms of production and distribution, the language used to justify these efforts was the language of "nature," taken over from an older metaphysics. "Natural" laws, laws of the creation of wealth, laws of supply and demand, and laws of the rights of the individual naked of all associations were set over the "artifice" of political laws and institutions.

Dewey thought that there was an obvious correlation between the circumstances that surrounded the rise of laissez-faire liberalism and those that attended the rise of seventeenth-century science (a matter that I discussed at length in chapter 4). In both cases there was a kind of practical resolution of perceived difficulties. But at the same time there was in both cases an attempt to justify actual, successful, productive outcomes by means of theories that made irrelevant appeals to outworn and counterproductive metaphysical doctrines. In other words, there was within both groups, among the liberals as well as the physical scientists, a disparity between what was being *produced* and what was being provided as a theoretical description and justification of what was being produced.

In the case of the physical scientists, the productive use of tools and implements to solve perceived difficulties, to enlarge the domain of problems to be solved, and to render scientific concepts more instrumental was accompanied by an anti-instrumentalist metaphysics of fixed and finished essences. In the case of the liberals, concrete action taken to stem the influence of antique and dysfunctional restrictions upon technological production and commerce—activities that are artifactual and instrumental by definition—was accompanied by appeals to a fixed and finished nature that had endowed all individuals with certain equally fixed rights and powers.

The view of these matters advanced by Dewey is unequivocally technological in its import. The rise of modern forms of democratic government has had less to do with the theories of Locke and the utilitarians than with the development and widespread use of technological artifacts: "What has happened sprang from no theory but was inherent in what was going on not only without respect to theories but without regard to politics: because, generally speaking, of the use of steam applied to mechanical inventions" (LW2:294;PP:95).

Nation-states arose not out of sophisticated and well-honed political theories, but out of the need to control and regulate the new forms of technological production. "The transition from family and dynastic government supported by the loyalties of tradition to popular government was the outcome primarily of technological discoveries and inventions working a change in the customs by which men had been bound together. It was not due to the doctrines of doctrinaires" (LW2:326;PP:144).

Such control has not, however, always been such as to liberate further technological advances. Old forms of economic and political control, inherited from feudal and semifeudal periods of human history, have tended to hamstring the working out of technological solutions to emerging problems. "The same forces which have brought about the forms of democratic government, general suffrage, executives and legislators chosen by majority vote, have also brought about conditions which halt the social and humane ideals that demand the utilization of government as the genuine instrumentality of an inclusive and fraternally associated public. 'The new age of human relationships' has no political agencies worthy of it. The democratic public is still largely inchoate and unorganized" (LW2:303;PP:109).

IV

C. Wright Mills argued that Dewey's social and political philosophy was based upon models that were agricultural and rural, and thus not appropriate to the problems of national corporations and political institutions, to say nothing of transnational corporations and global political alliances.[12] But although it is true that Dewey did take primary face-to-face relationships as a starting point for his theory of communication and therefore of communities, there is also in his work a profound understanding of the ways in which new technologies have created new kinds of communities whose gigantism is entirely dependent upon them. "Our modern state-unity," he wrote in 1927, "is due to the consequences of technology employed so as to facilitate the rapid and easy circulation of opinions and information, and so as to generate constant and intricate interaction far beyond the limits of face-to-face communities" (LW2:306–7;PP:114). Thus, in the 1920s Dewey was already advancing a position that Marshall McLuhan would popularize in the 1960s: global communication creates global communities—in McLuhan's words, a "global village"—and forms of political life are, in relation to any given state of communication technology, always in arrears.

In Dewey's boyhood home of Burlington, Vermont, there were by 1870 nearly as many foreign-born residents as there were native Americans.[13] His ten years in Chicago (1894–1904) and his nearly half-century in New York (1904–1952) included periods of enormous immigration. He thought it quite marvelous that so many millions of people could have been absorbed into the political life of the United States without the major upheavals that had characterized lesser migrations in Europe. He attributed this fact in large part to advancing communications technologies. But he was also aware that "mass production is not confined to the factory" (LW2:307;PP:116), that rich and varied forms of life have been crushed and obliterated by the great American culture machine. As the members of the Frankfurt School were later to do, Dewey warned of the dangers of technologically induced uniformity, mediocrity, and domination.

There were during Dewey's time those who prophesied that the waves of Irish, Poles, Italians, and Jews that hit the American shores would introduce great pockets of alien and undigested cultures into the midst of their new land. There are those now who issue the same dark warnings with respect to more recent arrivals: Cubans, Mexicans, Salvadoreans, Vietnamese, and Cambodians. Dewey, who was by no means a distant observer of such matters, thought that such pessimists failed to take into account an essential ingredient of the situation: "They ignored the technological forces making for consolidation" (LW2:308;PP:116).

As McLuhan would be some forty years later, Dewey was well aware during the 1920s that enhanced communicative interaction does not mean the absence of conflict. If technological innovations provide means of consolidation in one area, they can occasion disintegration and fragmentation in another. What might otherwise constitute a public is often made mobile and scattered as a consequence of technological factors. Communities whose cohesion is based on long traditions may be rent asunder by a highway, a bridge, telephones, television sets, or (in the case of the Native Americans of Alaska) snowmobiles. Sports, popular entertainment, and even the purely aesthetic dimensions of technological artifacts such as automobiles may function as distractions from communication with respect to matters requiring conjoint action— the communication that is essential to the formation of enlightened publics.

For Dewey, community is ultimately a matter of "face-to-face intercourse" (LW2:367;PP:211). He thought the family and the neighborhood the most basic instrumentalities of debate, education, and interaction. The larger technologically based community might enrich local ones and help order their relations, but he thought that it could never embody the qualities that render them uniquely important. As had Emerson, Dewey thought that we lie "in the lap of an immense intelligence. But that intelligence is dormant and its communications are broken, inarticulate and faint until it possesses the local community as its medium" (LW2:372;PP:219).

Dewey was aware that in drawing attention to the technologically necessary conditions for various forms of social organizations, he might be read as a determinist. It was for this reason that he repeatedly emphasized his view that "what actually happens in consequence of industrial forces is dependent upon the presence or absence of perception and communication of consequences, upon foresight and its effect upon desire and endeavor" (LW2:333;PP:156). Unlike the determinists, Dewey's concern was not with *sufficient* conditions, but with *necessary* ones. "The object of the analysis will be to show that *unless* ascertained specifications are realized, the Community cannot be organized as a democratically effective Public. It is not claimed that the conditions which will be noted will suffice, but only that at least they are indispensable" (LW2:333;PP:157). Dewey thought the machine age a necessary (but not sufficient) condition for "what is needful as the precondition of a free, flexible and many-colored life" (LW2:370–1;PP:217).

For all his talk of the technological bases for public life, Dewey refused to take the turn later urged by Jacques Ellul. He never reified technology, and it never became for him a justification for any ideology—either utopian or dystopian. He regarded technology as neither the means of *deus ex machina* salvation nor the source of ultimate doom. "It is," he wrote, "always convenient to have a devil as well as a savior to bear the responsibilities of humanity. In reality, the trouble springs rather from the ideas and absence of ideas in connection with which technological factors operate" (LW2:323;PP:141).

V

In the preceding chapter I discussed at length Dewey's views regarding evolution and progress with respect to the claims of his critics that he held some variety of technological determinism. It is now time to review his notion of progress as it touches on his wider account of the public and its problems.

Dewey's contributions to *A Cyclopedia of Education*, published in 1912 and 1913, include an article entitled "Progress." Like its near synonyms "development," "evolution," and "growth," the term "progress" indicates cumulative change in which continuity is present. But devastating viruses as well as healthy young children are capable of development, evolution, and growth. What differentiates progress from its near cognates is that unlike them, it also indicates amelioration, or change toward a more desirable state of affairs.

Dewey traces the notion of progress to Francis Bacon. Whereas even the Greeks had the notion of evolution, the idea of progress was foreign to them. They took wants and needs to be imperfections, not, as did Bacon, as motivations for improvement. Bacon regarded technology as both offspring and source of ideas of progress. The rise of modern technology in the seventeenth century provided realistic grounds for expecting that improvements would continue. It offered the prospect of relief from sickness, poverty, and despotism. But it also spawned unrealistic utopian dreams and millennial schemes.

Dewey explicitly rejected the notion of progress as "natural" or "automatic." He argued that it requires "trained intelligence and forceful character," and that "progressive societies depend for their very existence upon educational resources" (MW7: 333). Progress is brought about by release of the strictures of outworn and irrelevant customs, conventions, and habits. But without education, the loosing of such bonds tends toward destructive and uncontrolled results.

Dewey expanded on these remarks in a longer article with the same title, published in the *International Journal of Ethics* in 1916. The events of that year might have offered Dewey reasons to question the very notion of progress: it was a year that saw the first zeppelin raid on Paris, gas masks and steel helmets first used by the German army, and troops of the United States in both Mexico and the Dominican Republic. But the very conditions that many writers saw as occasions for pessimism and discouragement were seized by Dewey as an opportunity for renewed emphasis upon the necessity for the unrelenting application of intelligence in order to secure continued progress.

Rapidity of change, he argued, cannot be identified with progress, nor can simple gains in comfort and ease be taken as a sign of cosmic well-being. Rapid change may afford the *opportunity* for progress, but is not itself progress. He raised a question that indicates his awareness that the mechanized war then being fought in Europe was of a different and more terrible kind than had theretofore been known. His question is even more appropriate to our own milieu of research into space-based nuclear weapons than it was to his of tanks and machine guns, and it is as fresh as Jeremy Rifkin's latest assault upon research with recombinant DNA: "Has man subjugated physical nature only to release forces beyond his control?" (MW10:236).

Far from yielding to Luddism, however, as Rifkin sometimes does, Dewey was convinced that the events of 1916 called for more work, more planning, more responsibility—in short, more technology, in the reconstructed sense in which he used the term. The future of progress would be secure only when and as long as men and women worked to make it so. The history and present of technology could furnish both sound methods and unlimited examples of progress: the telephone, irrigation, and the self-binding reaper provide concrete instances of progress, and the methods by which they were developed are well known. Why not, then, apply the methods of technology to the problems of public life we call social and political? Why not address the problems of hunger and malnutrition, unemployment, homelessness, and social security for the elderly and the ill with the same methods and with the same care and energy that have achieved palpable results in science and industry?

Here, as elsewhere, Dewey's position is rendered much clearer when one understands the extremes between which his position was hewn. On this matter there were in fact two pairs of extremes against which Dewey argued.

The first pair involved on one of its sides the Spencerian evolutionists, whose root metaphors were passive adjustment to fixed natural laws and gradual organic growth. On its other side were those who claimed to be members of the same school, but whose root metaphors were the very different ones of active red-in-tooth-and-claw struggle and the inevitable march of evolutionary progress.[14]

The branch of Spencerian evolutionary theory that Dewey identified as espousing "something ended and admitting of no change" (LW4:195;QC:244) was represented best by Spencer himself. Spencer wrote in 1864 in his *Social Statics* as if the future were already an accomplished fact. "The ultimate development of the ideal man is logically certain—as certain as any conclusion in which we place the most implicit faith; for instance that all men will die . . . . Progress, therefore, is not an accident, but a necessity. Instead of civilization being artificial, it is a part of nature; all of a piece with the development of the embryo or the unfolding of a flower."[15] Spencer's influence in the United States was at its peak about the time that he made his triumphant visit to New York City in 1882, the year that Dewey was beginning his graduate studies at Johns Hopkins.

It is not surprising that Spencer's thought should have been the subject of considerable revision by his followers in America. The growing, impatient, brawling culture on this side of the Atlantic provided a somewhat different environment than the more stable and subtle English one from which Spencerianism had sprung. Here his views became the doctrine of the survival of the strongest individual in the

boom-and-bust world of business and industry. Spencerians of this
stripe included William Graham Sumner, professor of political and social
science at Yale, and Andrew Carnegie, the industrialist. Sumner argued
that millionaires are the product of natural selection, that laws and rights
are relative to particular cultures, and that democracy was but a passing
phenomenon.[16] Carnegie wrote of the human "march to perfection."[17]

Richard Hofstadter has argued, in *Social Darwinism in American
Thought*, that one of the reasons why pragmatism became the dominant
American philosophy in the first two decades of this century—the
Progressive era—was its rejection of the conservative Spencerian
evolutionary philosophy.[18]

> Spencer had apotheosized evolution as an impersonal process, the
> omnipotence of circumstances and the environment, the helplessness of
> man to hasten or deflect the course of events, the predetermined
> development of society in accordance with a cosmic process toward a
> remote but comfortable Elysium. By defining life and mind as the
> correspondence of inner to outer relations, he had portrayed them as
> essentially passive agencies. The social counterpart of this approach was
> his gradualistic fatalism. The pragmatists, beginning without any special
> interest in ulterior social consequences, at first approached the uses of
> ideas in an individualistic vein, but in time drifted toward a socialized
> philosophical theory in the form of Dewey's instrumentalism . . . . The
> pragmatists' most vital contribution to the general background of social
> thought was to encourage a belief in the effectiveness of ideas and the
> possibility of novelties—a position necessary to any philosophically
> consistent theory of social reform. As Spencer had stood for determinism
> and the control of man by the environment, the pragmatists stood for
> freedom and control of the environment by man.[19]

Although Dewey's attacks on Spencer and his heterodox American
disciples date from his earliest works, it was in 1929, in *The Quest for
Certainty*, that one finds his clearest characterization of the two
Spencerian positions as extremes and his alternative to them. His
suggestion was that nature is neither fixed and static, nor does it involve
any inevitable march. It is precarious in a way that can be made stable
only by direct human intervention.

> The conditions and processes of nature generate uncertainty and its risks
> as truly as nature affords security and means of insurance against perils.
> Nature is characterized by a constant mixture of the precarious and the
> stable. This mixture gives poignancy to existence. If existence were either
> completely necessary or completely contingent, there would be neither
> comedy nor tragedy in life, nor need of the will to live. The significance of
> morals and politics, of the arts both technical and fine, of religion and of
> science itself as inquiry and discovery, all have their source and meaning in
> the union in Nature of the settled and the unsettled, the stable and the
> hazardous. Apart from this union, there are no such things as "ends,"

either as consummations or as those ends-in-view we call purposes. There is only a block universe, either something ended and admitting of no change, or else a predestined march of events. There is no such thing as fulfillment where there is no risk of failure, and no defeat where there is no promise of possible achievement. (LW4:194–95;QC:243–44)

The second pair of extremes was set out by Thomas Huxley in his influential Romanes Lectures on "Evolution and Ethics" in 1893. Huxley accepted an Hobbesian interpretation of evolutionary theory, to which he gave the term "cosmic process," although he could as well have used the term "natural law." To this he opposed what he called "the ethical process," the artificial correctives that human beings bring to the cosmic process but that lie outside that grand scheme. Dewey had no more patience with this second set of extremes than he had with the first, and in fact accused Huxley of defaulting to Spencer's "insipid millennium" (EW5:47).

Huxley used an analogy of a garden in trying to shore up his dualism. The plants in possession of a plot of ground in its natural state thrive there because they are adapted to their particular environment. But when the plot is turned into a garden, those plants are uprooted and the environment modified. The soil is changed by fertilization, a portion of the garden may be shaded by a wall, and the plot is watered at regular intervals. The garden is, in Huxley's analogy, outside and opposed to nature in the same way that the ethical process is outside and opposed to the cosmic process. Artifice requires continual attention and is a hedge against the forces of nature.[20]

Dewey's essay "Evolution and Ethics," published in the *Monist* on the eve of the Progressive era in 1898 (EW5:34–53), was one salvo of a broad counterattack mounted by Progressives against reactionary Spencerians, an assault that consisted in the appropriation of the metaphors of evolution by the Progressives for their own social agenda. In this essay Dewey reconstructs the terms "fit," "struggle for existence," and "natural selection."

Dewey professed shock at the dualism that Huxley set up with his garden analogy, and he reworked the analogy to turn it against him. He had no quarrel with Huxley's conclusion that the ethical process, like the activities undertaken by the gardener, involves constant attention and effort. In Dewey's progressive vocabulary, lack of struggle is synonymous with retrogression.

What Dewey objected to was Huxley's conclusion that the ethical process was outside the natural process. Utilizing the very metaphor that Huxley had found so attractive, he argued that technology is not over nature, but instead a part of the natural processes by which human beings, who are after all within and part of nature, alter their environment to make it serve their interests more adequately. Technology is the use of one part of the environment to alter another part of it. "The plants which the gardener introduces, the vegetables and fruits he wishes to cultivate, may indeed be foreign to this particular environment; but they are not alien to man's environment as a whole. He introduces and maintains by art conditions of sunlight and moisture to which this particular plot of ground is unaccustomed; but these conditions fall within the wont and use of nature as a whole" (EW5:37–38).

Though Dewey did not accuse Huxley of succumbing to the vulgar version of evolutionary theory advanced by Carnegie and Rockefeller, as well as by the thousands of business boosters throughout the country, he nevertheless thought that Huxley's dualism gave comfort to that cult of rugged individualism. Dewey argued that if evolution is to be taken seriously, the "laws" of evolution must themselves evolve.

Huxley's dualism led him to use the term "fit" in two senses, corresponding to fitness for the natural process and fitness for the ethical process. Since Dewey does not allow Huxley the initial dualism, he sees no reason to allow him the two senses of "fit." To use the term "fit" as it might have been applicable to some period prior to the advent of mankind is therefore little more than self-serving nonsense. "The conditions with respect to which the term 'fit' must *now* be used include the existing social structure with all the habits, demands, and ideals which are found in it. If so, we have reason to conclude that the 'fittest with respect to the whole of the conditions' is the best . . . . The unfit is practically the anti-social" (EW5:39).

"Fitness" is itself doubly instrumental. As a concept, it has been developed as part of the broader theory of evolution, itself an instrument, to do certain kinds of work associated with particular ends-in-view. Moreover, the fitness of any individual human being is a matter of his or her skill in adjusting to changed and changing conditions. And among the conditions in which human societies now function is the requirement of group loyalty and solidarity.

Huxley also argued for two senses of "struggle" corresponding to his two processes. The struggle for existence takes place in the cosmic process, and the struggle for happiness occurs within the ethical process. Dewey argued that Huxley's distinction breaks down not only in human life, but also in the life of lower animals. The wolf that preys on the sheep does not struggle for existence, but to exist *as a wolf*. Dewey hypothesizes that if existence were all the wolf was after, the sheep might have compromised with it, "including even an occasional bowl of mutton broth" (EW5:45). It does not take much imagination to see in Dewey's remarks about wolves and sheep, made against the backdrop of a growing national sentiment for reform of antitrust laws, a veiled reference to then-current American business practices.

There is indeed a difference between the struggle within the human world and that within the world of the lower animals, Dewey suggests, but it is not the one that Huxley describes. The difference is that animals operate largely by chance, and human beings have technological skills at their disposal. Intelligence and controlled foresight, the ability to reconstruct habits and institutions while they are still in use, and the use of artifacts such as novel ideas to operate upon and improve other artifacts, such as habits and ideals—these constitute struggle in human terms.

Finally, Dewey turns his attention to "natural selection." Though he thought Huxley's position on this matter somewhat unclear, he does not hesitate to provide his own reconstruction of the term. To identify natural selection, as did some of the vulgar Spencerians and perhaps Huxley himself, as a kind of ordeal by death in which the strong inherit the earth seemed to Dewey overly gross. Dewey suggests that the idea of Malthus—that nature spreads a feast that is not quite large enough for all the invited guests—might account for the extinction of certain species, but it could not be responsible for the rise of any new ones. "The selection which marks progress is that of a variation which *creates* a new food supply or amplifies an old one. The advantage which the variation gives, if it tends towards a new species, is an organ which opens up a wider food environment, detects new supplies within the old, or which makes it possible to utilize as food something hitherto indifferent or alien . . . . *The new species means a new environment to which it adjusts itself without interfering with others* . . . . The unwritten chapter in natural selection is that of the evolution of environments" (EW5:51–52;emphasis in original).

Dewey was thus in 1898 already arguing for two theses that are the subject of extensive debate almost a century later, in acclaimed works of social theory such as Robert Bellah's *Habits of the Heart*[21] and Robert Reich's *Tales of A New America*.[22] The first is the abandonment of the Malthusian model of the zero-sum society. The second is the notion that the future of the present is quite different from the future of the past; that is, that intervention into existing circumstances changes the conditions under which new predictions and adjustments must be made. But if these theses prove to be useful ones, it should not thereby be inferred that human society is no longer subject to "selection." Quite the contrary is true. Modern forms of industry, communication, and transportation allow for rapid change and adaptation, as well as for increased "flexibility of function, the enlargement of the range of uses to which one and the same organ, grossly considered, may be put." Selection has not ceased but has become technologically driven, with all that means for increased possibilities of progress.

In short, Dewey's rejection of Huxley's view is his rejection of the dualism between the natural and the human or, put another way, the cosmic and the ethical. Technology is no new force outside of nature, but the cutting edge of nature in its social dimension.

Though no one who took the trouble to read carefully this call for responsible social experimentation could have mistaken Dewey's view for any variety of fatalism, he was aware that there were those who insisted upon reading pragmatism as an apologetic for the form of social Darwinism embraced by American laissez-faire business boosterism. Lest he be misunderstood, Dewey repeatedly sought to distance himself from the American Spencerians who argued that evolution was both wholesale and inevitable; that both business and nature are red in tooth and claw; and that the inevitable triumph of the strongest individual is, by definition, progress. Eighteen years after his essay on Huxley, in his 1916 essay on "Progress" in the *International Journal of Ethics*, Dewey was still attempting to inform his critics.

There is a touch of conscious irony in Dewey's use of the vocabulary of the salesman to make the central point of this essay. "Progress is not automatic; it depends upon human intent and aim and upon acceptance of responsibility for its production. It is not a wholesale matter, but a retail job, to be contracted for and executed in sections" (MW10:238). In short, Dewey sees "progress as a responsibility and not as an endowment" (MW10:238).

As he would do later in his 1922 *Human Nature and Conduct*, Dewey argued that the failure of progress, when it occurs, is not the result of technology so much as it is the result of lazy reliance on unreconstructed impulses, sentiments, and emotions. The impulses of progressed man are undoubtedly the same as those of his less-progressed forebear; the difference is the tools that have been developed to refine and control those impulses, including not only institutions but also those tools more commonly identified as technological.

What are the enemies of progress? Dewey mentions unreconstructed instincts or impulses, and especially the laissez-faire philosophy that entrusts "the direction of human affairs to nature, or Providence, or evolution, or manifest destiny—that is to say, to accident—rather than to a contriving and constructive intelligence" (MW10:240). Another enemy of progress is the conservative attitude that accepts existing conditions not as starting points for improvement, but as results of what has already transpired.

Dewey developed this theme still further in his postwar book *Reconstruction in Philosophy* (1920). "These four facts," he wrote, "natural science, experimentation, control and progress have been inextricably bound up together" (MW12:103;RP:42). Two years later, in *Human Nature and Conduct*, he would argue that "all conduct is *interaction* between elements of human nature and the environment, natural and social. Then we shall see that progress proceeds in two ways, and that freedom is found in that kind of interaction which maintains an environment in which human desire and choice count for something" (MW14:9;HNC:10).

Real progress is for Dewey always both orderly and reformative (MW14:67;HNC:93). Some of what has been termed progress has been precipitated by chance events breaking down old habits and the consequent necessity of reconstructing them, whether or not we wish to do so. Progress is also linked with the fact that men and women have so many conflicting instincts that they cut across one another in ways that are both confusing and ultimately debilitating, unless some way of directing that busy traffic is learned. What separates human beings from the lower animals, Dewey suggested, is that "in learning habits it is possible for man to learn the habit of learning. Then betterment becomes a conscious principle of life" (MW14:75n;HNC:105:n).

VI

Dewey's critics have been, and continue to be, numerous. One of his most vocal opponents on the left was Reinhold Niebuhr, who targeted Dewey in his 1932 book *Moral Man and Immoral Society*.[23] Niebuhr lays bare the lines of his polemic at the outset of that work. He takes on those "moralists" and "modern educators" who believe that egoism can be held in check by the development of rationality, which if sufficiently continued will be sufficient to establish cooperation between human societies and races. What they fail to recognize, he says, is that collective power "can never be dislodged unless power is raised against it."[24] Conscience and reason can modify, but not abolish, such struggles.

Niebuhr already has Dewey in his crosshairs three pages into his introduction. More than half a page is devoted to a long quotation from *Philosophy and Civilization*, which Dewey published the previous year. Dewey wrote of building up the social sciences just as the physical sciences had been built up, by the active use of "techniques of tools and numbers in physical experimentation" (LW6:62;PC:329). Niebuhr thought it "the most persistent error of modern educators"[25] (by which he clearly meant Dewey and his disciples) that they have operated on the assumption that social difficulties arise from the failure of social sciences and values to keep pace with the rapid progress of technological innovation.

Niebuhr charges Dewey with a broad range of errors. He accuses him of lack of clarity, of failure to understand the profundity of the predatory self-interest of the owning classes, of mislocation of the grounds of social conservatism at the door of ignorance, and of being excessively preoccupied with education as a means to social planning. He further argues that Dewey failed to exhibit a program for overcoming social inertia, that he confused the methods of the social sciences with those of the physical sciences, and that he failed to see that social situations are by their very nature not fully rationally objective. Niebuhr viewed Dewey's work as betraying a middle-class prejudice that treats the poor as ignorant and slothful.

For Niebuhr, social injustice "cannot be resolved by moral and rational suasion alone . . . . Conflict is inevitable, and in this conflict power must be challenged by power."[26] The problem in forming power groups is to create cohesion, and such cohesion—or "morale," as Niebuhr calls it—is the result of "the right dogmas, symbols and emotionally potent oversimplifications."[27] It is not that Niebuhr rejects the methods of science as the means for projecting social goals and as the means for choosing the proper instruments for attaining them. It is just that a more powerful motive force than rational experimentation must be present and operative if they are to succeed. In short, social ills will yield to reason only if reason uses tools that are not themselves rational.[28]

According to Niebuhr, liberals, especially liberal Christians, usually fail to see the difference between "the problem of charity within the limits of an accepted social system and the problem of justice between economic groups."[29] "Social intelligence" (one of Dewey's key phrases) may, in Niebuhr's view, serve to "mitigate the brutalities of social conflict, but [it] cannot abolish the conflict itself."[30] Niebuhr regards Dewey as a "typical and convenient example" of the social philosophers who regard the function of reason as the cutting of channels for the stream of life. Absent this, they suggest, life is guided by ungoverned impulse and habit, and fails to reach solutions to its problems. Niebuhr thinks this view both naive and unresponsive to the complexities of human behavior, as well as to the inevitable conflicts between the objectives determined by reason and those of the total body of impulse.[31]

Niebuhr's prescription for situations in which intelligence fails is what he calls a "religious ethic":

> A rational ethic aims at justice, and a religious ethic makes love the ideal. A rational ethic seeks to bring the needs of others into equal consideration with those of the self. The religious ethic, (the Christian ethic more particularly, though not solely) insists that the needs of the neighbor shall be met, without a careful computation of relative needs. This emphasis upon love is another fruit of the religious sense of the absolute. On the one hand religion absolutises the sentiment of benevolence and makes it the norm and ideal of the moral life. On the other hand it gives transcendent and absolute worth to the life of the neighbor and thus encourages sympathy toward him. Love meets the needs of the neighbor, without carefully weighing and comparing his needs with those of the self. It is therefore ethically purer than the justice which is prompted by reason.[32]

The application of the religious ethic can, however, justify the use of violence. Niebuhr thinks that

> if a season of violence can establish a just social system and can create the possibilities of its preservation, there is no purely ethical ground upon which violence and revolution can be ruled out . . . . Once we have made the

> fateful concession of ethics to politics, and accepted coercion as a
> necessary instrument of social cohesion, we can make no absolute
> distinctions between non-violent and violent types of coercion or between
> coercion used by governments and that which is used by revolutionaries. If
> such distinctions are made they must be justified in terms of the
> consequences in which they result. The real question is: what are the
> political possibilities of establishing justice through violence?[33]

Niebuhr is particularly hard on the educational program advanced by
Dewey and his disciples. "The very terms in which they state the
political problem proves that they are themselves bound by middle-class
perspectives, which will naturally increase in force and narrowness in
proportion to the distance from the ideal of the educator."[34] He argued
that Dewey's program was bound to fail, not, as some of Dewey's
critics had claimed, because the intelligence of the general community
could never be raised to the heights thought possible by Dewey, but
rather because there *is* no such general community.[35]

VII

To what extent can we now determine—more than a half-century after
the publication of *Moral Man and Immoral Society*—whether Niebuhr's
attacks on Dewey found their mark? One way of answering this
question is to examine Dewey's views on the use of violence. A second
is to examine his treatment of religion and symbol manipulation. A third
is to see whether Niebuhr's criticisms of his educational program are
valid. Dewey's treatments of these matters lead to the very heart of his
critique of technology, for they are couched in the language of
production, construction, and control.

In 1916 Dewey published an article called "Force and Coercion"
(MW10:244–51), which was reprinted in *Characters and Events*[36] two
years before the appearance of Niebuhr's book. Writing in terms that
could have been a paraphrase of Niebuhr's introduction, Dewey termed
it a "hard fact" that social difficulties usually concern the application of
force of some sort, and he objected to the "idealistic" talk current in
1916 about a "moral and common will" (MW10:245). Nevertheless,
unlike Niebuhr, he rejected the use of violence and did so on grounds
that were ultimately technological: his argument, in fine, is that violence
is inefficient.

Dewey sets up his argument by distinguishing among three
concepts: power or energy, coercive force, and violence. It is significant
that his remarks apply equally to the production of what are commonly
called technological artifacts and to the production of political and social
artifacts. Another way of putting this is that Dewey uses models and
metaphors from technological production in order to develop and
explicate his social philosophy.

Power, in Dewey's vocabulary, means just an "effective means of operation; ability or capacity to execute, to realize ends" (MW10:246). Power, as such, is neutral: it may be directed toward ends (by which he means ends-in-view) that are worthwhile, or it may be allowed to work in an unregulated way and consequently to frustrate purpose. He thinks that political and social theories that refuse to take power seriously are little more than exercises in sentimentality, just as (other) technological projects that abjure the use of energy do not deserve the name "technological." Dewey's constant emphasis on the fact that human beings confront a world of constraints and opportunities, of pushes and pulls, is just another form of this view that power is a datum that may be either cultivated and productive or uncultivated, and potentially dangerous and destructive.

Dewey's engineering metaphors become even more dominant when he comes to describe the relation of power to its relatives, coercive force and violence. Coercive force is used when a vehicle is turned to the right in traffic in an orderly fashion. Violence ensues when a driver fails to use the proper force to constrain the energy of the vehicle and to direct it in a direction that is desirable. This is, of course, a description of a relation between a human being and a machine, but the same is true with respect to the relation between public officials or public laws and individual activities.

Energy brought to bear to enforce traffic regulations is an example of coercive force. If used directly, it may be an instance of violence. But used indirectly, to secure the end of orderly traffic flow, it is constructive. "Constraint or coercion, in other words, is an incident of a situation under certain conditions—namely, where the means for the realization of an end are not naturally at hand, so that energy has to be spent in order to make some power into a means for the end in hand" (MW10:246).

Dewey thought that what are called the laws of science share important traits with what are called the laws of human society. This is a view that was, and remains, controversial. Scientific laws, like rules of the road or other social laws, are statements "of the conditions of the organization of energies which, when unorganized, conflict and result in violence—that is, destruction or waste" (MW10:246). Dewey is here very close to a theme that dominated his early and middle work, and that continued in his later work as a leading idea. Moral action does not need to be justified by a transcendent ground of values; neither is it unjustifiable. Moral action is, quite simply put, what is most efficient and appropriate to the resolution of a given problematic situation.

Likewise, scientific laws are for Dewey not justified by appeals to a Laplacian block universe; neither are they just arbitrarily conventional. They are grounded in the needs of individuals and communities to change some situation—to produce or construct something not previously available. Perhaps the most demanding of possible counterexamples to Dewey's notion of law are the laws of astronomy. These are laws in which "control," in the sense in which straight-line instrumentalism uses the term, is not possible. But Dewey substituted a dynamic sense of the term "control" for the static one of the straight-line instrumentalists. Control means more than simply alteration of stars, planets, or nebula, and it certainly means more than simple accommodation to their influences. In Dewey's reconstruction of the term, control means adjustment with respect to a total situation; something not present is sought. Such control—in the sense of adjustment—is effected by means of instruments such as spectrometers and radio telescopes, as well as by means of the instruments we call models, hypotheses, and scientific laws.

The situation is not different in the domain of social interaction; that is, in the realm in which the effects of actions undertaken by various publics are felt by constituents of publics different from themselves. The energy expended by various publics is palpable and, for Dewey, a datum. The question is what is to be done with it. Left just as a raw material, it can become destructive, just as an undammed, unchannelled river may be destructive. Some type of coercive force must be brought to bear on situations in which great energy is present if that energy is to be controlled. Such organization of force Dewey simply terms "efficiency" (MW10:247).

Is the use of force ever justified, as, for example, in the case of industrial struggles? Dewey's answer is quite different from Niebuhr's. Niebuhr attempted to bifurcate the moral and the political, a realm of ethics from a realm of force opposing force. Dewey rejects this split, arguing that what is moral on a small scale is acceptable or justifiable for precisely the same reasons why certain activities of the state and of other publics are acceptable on a larger one. For Dewey, to be moral is to exercise efficient intelligence. On small scales and large, force is justified only insofar as it serves the purposes of economy and efficiency; and it should be remembered that the law, which Dewey calls "legal machinery," has been set up as an "energy saver."

Though it may in some ways be defective, legal machinery has been set up at great cost; if it is ignored or abrogated to solve some local problem, it should be remembered that its available energy for the solution of wider problems may be dissipated or jeopardized. Finally, except in unusual circumstances, legal institutions are more finely tuned than is overt force, and their procedures should be exhausted before extraordinary force is used. "The fine mechanism which runs a watch is more efficient than the grosser one which heaves a brick" (MW10:247). Violence is usually unethical because it is wasteful.

The solution offered by Dewey to the problem of the use of force is thus neither conservative nor radical; it is situational and expressed in terms of the deeply technological metaphor of efficiency. Dewey had been developing that metaphor at least since his 1891 essay "Moral

Theory and Practice," in which he treated ethics as a species of engineering problem. But his is not the efficiency of the straight-line act or rule utilitarian, since it is his view that ends are not fixed but flexible and under constant revision. They are ends-in-view.

Dewey was also aware of the claim made by some that, as Tolstoy put it, "the State is the arch-criminal" because of its use of wholesale force. But Dewey does not call upon the state to renounce force: indeed, he thinks that the regulation necessary for orderly progress is possible only as force is applied to situations that would otherwise be haphazard and chaotic. The point is simply that the state must develop techniques of force that are intelligent, which is to say appropriate and effective. "An immoral use of force is a stupid use" (MW10:249).

One of Dewey's examples of the inefficient (thus, immoral) use of force was then-current labor practices. Since they were coercive, they failed to "enlist greater individual interest and attention, greater emotional and intellectual liberty" (MW10:251). One could say the same of the shameful problems of hunger and homelessness in the United States during the 1980s. Malnourished children and adults have handicaps that prevent the fullest development of their potentials. The difficulty with arguing that the hungry should be fed because of the prescriptions of one or another of the religious communities within the United States is that religious values differ widely. Further, arguments that the hungry should be fed on altruistic grounds, or even on grounds of fairness, notoriously fail to elicit the support of those who are financially comfortable.

Dewey's suggestion is unambiguous. The problem of hunger will be solved once American citizens have been educated to the fact that hunger is more than just a disgrace or a shame: it is inefficient and a major debilitating force within any society in which it is allowed to occur. His answer is a technological answer: people who are malnourished cannot be constructive and productive. Their ability to exercise intelligence is diminished. Their condition is therefore a ticking time bomb in any society in which it is allowed to exist.

Passive resistance was counted by Dewey as being among possible efficient (moral) uses of force: "Given certain conditions, passive resistance is a more *effective* means of resistance than overt resistance would be. Sarcasm may be more effective than a blow in subduing an adversary; a look more effective than sarcasm" (MW10:249–50).[37] The key word here, however, is "possible." Characteristically, Dewey did not recommend passive resistance where and everywhere there was a political problem to be solved. Different problematic situations call for different solutions. Passive resistance was for Dewey a tool, not a panacea or a rigid ideology. It was simply one more instrument at the disposal of those who would engage in thoroughgoing technological inquiry.

VIII

Niebuhr also charged Dewey with failure to understand that social change takes place by means of the formation of power groups, that "dogmas, symbols and emotionally potent oversimplifications" are the adhesive that binds such groups, and that the most effective of such dogmas was Christian love, the "transcendent and absolute worth" attributed to the life and well-being of one's neighbor. In short, Niebuhr argued that the mass of human beings are deeply irrational; in order to be effective, rational activity must utilize the irrational.

There is much in this statement with which Dewey agreed. But he did not think so much in terms of the "rational" and the "irrational" as in terms of impulsions (a tendency of the whole organism); impulses (more focused tendencies to act in certain ways); habits (ways of behaving that have worked in the past); and intelligent, adjustive behavior (the refined product of these raw materials). Impulsions, impulses, and habits are not as productive as adjustive behavior because they are not properly focused. They are not the result of experimentation and, hence, not as well adapted to the specifics of a problematic situation.

Must, as Niebuhr suggested, a religious ethic intervene in situations in which intelligence fails? Is it necessary to turn to the transcendent and absolute as the grounds for justice and sympathy?

Dewey did not, as some who have taken offense at his part in the formulation of "Humanist Manifesto"[38] have suggested, argue that religious experience was fraudulent or self-deceptive. What he argued in *A Common Faith*, published a year after that manifesto and two years after Niebuhr's book, was that "elements and outlooks that may be called religious" (LW9:8;CF:8) should be emancipated from particular doctrines, ideologies, and institutions. It is in this regard that he proposed to write of "religious" as adjectival in place of the substantive "religion." "Religious" was a character of experience, not an experience in itself.

Dewey was in fact amplifying in 1934 a position he had already taken in his 1891 "Moral Theory and Practice." Theories and ideals are things to be done. Divorced from any particular theological or ideological stance, faith is a "conviction that some end should be supreme over conduct" (LW9:15;CF:20). Further, "conviction in the moral sense signifies being conquered, vanquished, in our active nature by an ideal end; it signifies acknowledgment of its rightful claim over our desires and purposes. Such acknowledgment is practical, not primarily intellectual. It goes beyond evidence that can be presented to *any* possible observer" (LW9:15;CF:20–21).

However, the difficulty with most religions, including the Christian religion as it is usually practiced, is that faith is taken as a substitute for knowledge; its object is taken as an intellectual object already existing, not as something desirable and to be worked for. The difficulty with most religions is that "faith that something should be in existence as far as lies in our power is changed into the intellectual belief that it is already there in existence. When physical existence does not bear out the assertion, the physical is subtly changed into the metaphysical. In this way, moral faith has been inextricably tied up with intellectual beliefs about the supernatural" (LW9:16;CF:21–22).

But not all moral faith is religious faith. Dewey characterizes the religious as "morality touched by emotion." In complex situations in which ideals give rise to emotions that are integrative, they touch the whole person: this is where the religious quality of certain experiences occurs. Thus defined, the religious character of certain experiences has been and can be a source of motive and binding force with respect to social groups. In Dewey's remarks on religious experience, as elsewhere in his work, one finds both a warning against default to the status quo and to the unorganized forces of nature, and a call to take intelligent, instrumental, technological control of problematic situations.

Even during those periods of the past that we regard as the most religious, Dewey suggested, it was not religious doctrine *per se* that united men and women in common undertakings; such doctrines were merely a symbol of "conditions and forces that gave unity and a centre to men's views of life" (LW5:71;ION:62). The implication is that Niebuhr's "Christian love" does not function in the foundational way he holds for it; it functions, rather, as one expression among many, itself a symbol of more general ideals of "loyalty, of solidarity, and common devotion to a common cause" (LW5:71;ION:61).

Dewey thought that this view—that only through religious myths, advertising icons, and other types of symbol-manipulation could common goals could be advanced and common action undertaken—put the cart before the horse. "Religion," he suggested, "is not so much a root of unity as it is its flower or fruit. The very attempt to secure integration for the individual, and through him for society, by means of a deliberate and conscious cultivation of religion, is itself proof of how far the individual has become lost through detachment from acknowledged social values. It is no wonder that when the appeal does not take the form of dogmatic fundamentalism, it tends to terminate in either some form of esoteric occultism or private estheticism" (LW5:72;ION:64).

If I read him correctly, an essential component of Niebuhr's critique of Dewey turns on his assertion that some social situations are so problematic that intelligent action cannot be exercised. Dewey's counterargument is, first, that we cannot know in advance which situations are impervious to intelligent action, and second, that situations change, undergoing alteration and maturation over time. A situation that seems insoluble at one moment may in the next display clear avenues of resolution. There were once those who thought that French, Germans, and British would never be capable of living in peace with one another, to say nothing of engaging in economic cooperation. And during the early portion of Dewey's career, there were those who argued that young women were incapable of adapting to the rigors of college life and that co-education would lead to the destruction of higher education. But economic cooperation and co-education were held as ideals to be worked for, and the means of bringing those ideals into existence were produced.

One of the primary candidates advanced by Dewey as an instrument for weaning the members of the public, young and old alike, away from metaphysical absolutes, whether associated with backward-looking ideologies or forward-looking utopias, was progressive education. Whereas Niebuhr had called for "dogmas, symbols and emotionally potent oversimplifications" as tools to bind and motivate the uneducated, Dewey thought that education could improve the quality of ideals to the extent that they would no longer need to be dogmatic or oversimplified. For Dewey, education is the opening of dogmas to the work of intelligence and the development of what is simple, to see whether it can work in a complex environment.

Although Dewey's educational program is far too rich to treat adequately here, it should nevertheless be noted that it is his recommended method for refining public tastes. Karl Mannheim saw this clearly, and extended an enormous tribute to Dewey in his *Freedom, Power, and Democratic Planning*, published posthumously in 1950.[39] In the context of a discussion of the enormous power of what the Freudians called "cathexis," the investment of emotional energy in certain objects of one's life world, Mannheim suggested that when these bonds are loosened because of war, economic depression, or any sudden shock, the unattached energy is like electric power. If guided into the proper channels, it can be a source of great creativity. If unmanaged, it becomes destructive. Grasping a point that Niebuhr missed, Mannheim saw that Dewey rightly understood that it is not rationality that is the proper instrument of such rechannelling, but "refined passions."

By the end of his career, after experiencing the trauma of European Fascism, Mannheim had become convinced that art and religion must once again become a "significant part of the fabric of human life."[40] He thought that the latent irrationalism that lies beneath the surface of even the most civilized modern human beings can be counterbalanced only by "refinement of passion at all levels of human action and co-operation."[41] Dewey of course differed with Mannheim regarding the necessity or desirability of institutionalized religion as a means to human solidarity, suggesting that it had far more often been a divisive force. Nevertheless, he would certainly have agreed with Mannheim's general prescription, that the best antidote to the barbaric appeal of the Fascists was the cultivation of refined passions: he had

spent the major portion of his life articulating the educational methods
by which this could be undertaken.

IX

I believe that Dewey's treatment of this material—his analyses of force,
religion, and education—not only lays bare the extent to which Niebuhr
misunderstood him, but also tends to blunt the criticism of C. Wright
Mills, who attacked Dewey using arguments obtained from Max Weber
and Karl Mannheim. Mills accused Dewey of "technologizing" and
"biologizing" inquiry, of treating all inquiry as if it were a species of
laboratory or experimental science undertaken for the purposes of
adaptation.[42] And so Dewey did—at least, all inquiry that can be termed
successful. But in Mills's account, this becomes a sticking point. He
charged Dewey's concept of action with lacking a political dimension.
"Reality to him [Dewey] is seen *technologically* or *socially*, in his
peculiar, complex and freighted meaning of social, which is not peculiar
and complex when viewed against a small town of artisans or a farming
community. His concept of action is *of an individual*. It is not the action
of a petty official nor of an administrator who is acting within 'routine
affairs of state.' It is the conduct of an individual in non-rationalized
spheres or types of society. It is conduct that makes decisions about
situations that have not been regulated."[43]

What Mills thought wrongheaded—or at least old-fashioned—about
Dewey's analysis of social inquiry was also Niebuhr's complaint: Dewey
failed to take into account the fact that power groups, such as economic
classes, often run head-to-head in ways that are not open to intelligent
resolution. Mills's example is Dewey's treatment of the waves of
immigrants that hit the cities of the United States in the last decades of
the nineteenth century and the first decades of the twentieth. He faults
Dewey for his inability to see the problem as a class problem,
suggesting that he had viewed it instead through technological and
biological spectacles: he thought that the solution lay in assimilation and
adaptation, rather than in direct confrontation. Dewey was, Mills
asserted, guilty of "the assumption that no 'problems' will arise that will
be so deep that a third idea-plan would not unite in some way the two
conflicting plans."[44] But how can such a model work in a context in
which two social interests are locked in a "death clutch"? "Whenever
opposing groups are confronting one another and can not be 'adapted'
to one another because of the structural antagonisms of society, the
'answer' we get from Dewey is not a choice supporting one or the
other. More than likely there is the plea that when social science
develops like physical science, we can solve or obviate such problems,
or define them so as to permit their solution."[45]

For Mills, the "entire issue" came down to what he regarded as
Dewey's failure to understand the excellence and exigencies of the

method of straight-line instrumentalism as a method of achieving ideological goals.[46] He thought that Dewey's view that "instruments imply the ends to which they are put" was the sheerest nonsense. "There is," Mills argued, "no value trademark placed upon airplanes or even upon educational procedures. By their character, physical instruments set limits to their use, but obviously the limits are very wide indeed. The professionalizing or methodizing of value and of value questions already assumes for its happy operation a kind of community that nowhere exists."[47]

But in picking the example of immigrants, Mills compromised his own case. In terms of size and complexity, there has probably never been a greater social experiment than the acceptance and absorption of the world's people by the United States. The experiment has certainly not been without difficulties and local failures, and it is by no means finished. But overall, the fact that Mills's class struggles have not materialized even during the worst of times and the fact that publics have been created across lines of ethnic and social-class membership in order to solve perceived problems, both militate against Mills's thesis.

Like Niebuhr, Mills made the mistake of reading Dewey as a failed straight-line instrumentalist. Neither Niebuhr nor Mills was able to see what John J. McDermott thought central in Dewey's work: instruments were for him not good, bad, or neutral. They are all of those things. They teem with values. They present matrices of facilities and constraints with which we have the opportunity to come to terms. Far from there being "no value trademark" placed on automobiles or telephones or airplanes, there are many such trademarks. Whereas Mills focuses on the limits to the uses of instruments, Dewey is concerned with their possibilities.

It would be a mistake, however, to think that Dewey regarded every public problem as soluble. Some problematic situations have been so complicated, pushed to the brink of chaos by the failure of involved individuals and groups to apply intelligence, that there is little hope for satisfactory solution in the short term. But one thing is sure: apart from blind luck, there is no better method of solving perceived problems than the experimental method that Dewey terms "instrumentalism."

Epilogue: Responsible Technology

What empirical method exacts of philosophy is two
things: First, that refined methods and products be
traced back to their origin in primary experience, in all
its heterogeneity and fullness; so that the needs and
problems out of which they arise and which they
have to satisfy be acknowledged. Secondly, that the
secondary methods and conclusions be brought back
to the things of ordinary experience, in all their
coarseness and crudity, for verification. In this way,
the methods of analytic reflection yield material which
form the ingredients of a method of designation,
denotation, in philosophy. (LW1:39;EN:33)

Just as there is no ontological dualism within the self,
classically known as body and soul, so too there is
no ontological dualism between the self and the
world. Now the startling consequence of this view
. . . is that if man and the world are made of the
same reality and only function differently, then the
things of reality as made by man are ontologically
similar. Artifacts, then, are human versions of the
world acting as transactional mediations, representing
human endeavor in relational accordance with the
resistance and possibility endemic to both nature and
culture.—John J. McDermott[1]

I

In a paper presented in 1959, at a celebration of the hundredth
anniversary of Dewey's birth, Edwin A. Burtt suggested that if he had to
pick a single word to typify Dewey's philosophical work, it would be
"responsibility." Burtt was quick to point out that he did not intend the
term in the limited sense that it has had in law, or even in the sense that
it has usually had in ethics, but "in the meaning it might convey when
applied by a reflective moralist to all philosophical issues."[2] Burtt
suggested that sometime around 1890 the idea must have occurred to
Dewey that "*all human action, including thinking as an important part of
action, has consequences; and that the vital difference which men in*

general and philosophers especially are concerned about is whether
responsibility for those consequences is accepted or not.''[3]

I have pointed out that Dewey was the only major figure of the
classic period of American philosophy who took it as *his* responsibility to
enter into the rough-and-tumble of public affairs. I have also indicated
some of the ways in which his work was influenced by the concrete
social difficulties that he experienced firsthand. In the 1890s he was
already constructing an account of personal responsibility that reflected
his sensitivities to the problems of labor practices, immigration, and
education, to name just a few. "Responsibility," he wrote in *The Study*
of Ethics, "is a name for the fact that we are, and are something definite
and concrete—specific individuals. I am myself, I am conscious of
myself in my deeds (self-conscious), I am responsible, name not three
facts, but one fact" (EW4:342). And further, "Every bad man is (in the
substantial sense) irresponsible; he cannot be counted upon in action,
he is not certain, reliable, trustworthy. He does not respond to his
duties, to his functions. His impulses and habits are not co-ordinated,
and hence do not answer properly to the stimuli, to the demands made.
The vicious man is not socially responsible" (EW4:343).

But even those who might have been expected to be among
Dewey's natural allies have not always understood his position with
respect to these matters. It must have been a matter of considerable
disappointment to Dewey, for example, that the response of C. S.
Peirce to his 1903 *Studies in Logical Theory* was to chastise him for
being irresponsible, for engaging in a "debauch of loose reasoning,"[4]
and to suggest that Dewey's life in Chicago—a city that, as Peirce put
it, "hasn't the reputation of being a moral place"—had apparently
weakened his sense of dyads such as right and wrong, true and false.[5]

Dewey has fared little better among some of our contemporaries
who claim to be sympathetic to his views. Richard Rorty, for example,
misreads pragmatism as viewing "science as one genre of literature—
or, put the other way around, literature and the arts as inquiries, on the
same footing as scientific inquiries. Thus [pragmatism] sees ethics as
neither more 'relative' or 'subjective' than scientific theory, nor as
needing to be made 'scientific.' "[6]

If I have made my case in chapters 3 and 5, it should be clear not
only that Dewey held no such view, but also that he argued quite
strenuously that while science and literature utilize the same general
method of inquiry (a method that is briefly reiterated in the epigraphs to
this chapter), their respective tools, their respective ends-in-view, and
their respective materials are quite different. I must confess that I cannot
understand how it is possible to read Dewey, as Rorty has apparently
done, as saying that the advances made by the scientific-technological
revolution—advances based upon its novel utilization of instruments,
among which was its new conception of maximum substitutability of
variables—could have been made equally well with the tools and

materials of literature. If this view of Rorty's is deconstructivist, it is clear that Dewey's work is not in the family tree of that school of thought: Rorty's view of this matter has little resemblance to the positions Dewey clearly and consistently held for more than sixty years. More specifically, Dewey spent hundreds of pages in his 1938 *Logic* arguing against just this kind of position.

The responsibility that Dewey held to be a characteristic trait of good men and women has a correlate in inquiry: inquiry is good if it is *reliable*. Inquiry that leads to the warrantable assertions that are its reliable products is inquiry that is successful, in the sense that it produces testable results. Rorty seems to have missed the central point of Dewey's account of inquiry as technological: inquiry issues products that are testable, and our concrete experience either "buys" those products by issuing checks for them, or it returns them as bad merchandise.

There is indeed a sense in which inquiry is as Rorty characterizes it: an ongoing conversation. But it is a distinguishing mark of Dewey's instrumentalism that conversations are themselves tools that enable practiced interlocutors to distinguish men and women who are responsible from those who are not, as well as to distinguish assertions that are better and more reliable from those that are less so. Far from being a "vocabulary . . . for unjustifiable hope,"[7] as Rorty has described it, Dewey's technological method is in fact a blueprint for the production of reliable consequences by responsible men and women.

Ralph Sleeper has, I think, correctly seen the central problem in Rorty's well-known version of Dewey's work. He thinks that the difficulty with Rorty's position lies not in his recognition and appropriation of Dewey's antifoundationalism, but rather in what he takes to be the consequences of that position. Rorty's Dewey leaves us with "ungrounded social hope," and this is a far cry, if Sleeper and I are correct, from what Dewey actually said. What offends Sleeper most of all is what he calls "Rorty's insouciant reductionism." Dewey's version of pragmatism, in Sleeper's view, "had seemed to offer us more than that. It had seemed to be teaching us how to transform the culture that is decaying around us, rather than just how to 'cope' with its collapse."[8]

II

It is a widely accepted view among professional philosophers that the most innovative and influential philosophers of the twentieth century are Wittgenstein, Heidegger, and Dewey. Of those three, only Dewey wrote extensively about public philosophy; only Dewey advanced a philosophy of education; and only Dewey had a coherent program to produce practical social amelioration.

In their very different ways, the responses of Wittgenstein and Heidegger to the communities in which they lived were somewhat mystical. Despite his early training as an engineer, Wittgenstein seems to have had a profoundly private agenda that necessitated his withdrawal from public life for extended periods—to teach elementary school, to tend a garden, and even while occupying a place within an academic community to lead a life that was ascetic and to a great extent reclusive. Nevertheless, he served in the First World War as a volunteer on the side of Austria, and during the Second World War as an orderly in a hospital in England. When he came to reassess the position he had taken in the *Tractatus*, in which he began to treat language as instrumental, it was almost as if language became for him a tool that reflected his own introspective project; it became for him a tool whose principal use was the examination of language itself.

Heidegger, too, seemed unwilling to use, or incapable of using, language as a tool for producing extralinguistic products. His self-described peers are not engineers and social reformers, but poets: the German Romantic poets were the only ones beside himself, as Rorty has insightfully suggested, who seemed to Heidegger to inhabit the mountain peaks of European culture.

The case of Heidegger is more tragic even than that of the tormented Wittgenstein. Wittgenstein's mysticism was that of the sensitive thinker seeking to overcome what at times must have appeared to him to be insurmountable personal difficulties. Heidegger's mysticism, however, especially that of his mature work, was rooted in arrogant appropriation of the irrational blood and soil myths of a highly romanticized German-Greek cultural axis, and in the deeply destructive eschatalogical myths that have influenced European culture at least since the time of Augustine.

The more we learn of Heidegger's brief political career as *Führer-rector* of Freiburg University,[9] the more deplorable and even despicable seem his limited attempts at public praxis. No more than six months after Hitler suspended civil liberties, arrested eighty-one legally elected deputies to the *Reichstag*, began a systematic program of burning books and banning their authors, and announced the opening of the concentration camps (one of which was close by Heidegger's hometown, Messkirch), Heidegger "publicly sent Hitler a telegram stating his willingness to cooperate in the 'alignment' (*Gleichschaltung*) of the universities with the NSDAP's programs."[10]

Heidegger, like many other Germans of his generation, later claimed to have known nothing of the treatment of Jews at the hands of his fellow Nazi Party members. But the Jewish population of Baden, where he lived, "dropped dramatically from 20,600 in 1933 to 6400 in 1940, and . . . virtually all of the 6400 who remained were deported to France on October 22, 1940, and thence to Izbica, the death camp near Lublin. As Heidegger was lecturing on Nietzsche in the Forties, there were only 820 Jews left in all of Baden."[11]

What would have been John Dewey's response to the forcible

removal and detention of thousands of his neighbors, to the suspension of civil liberties, and to the burning of books? It is possible to read the answer to these questions from the pages of his productive political life. Dewey loudly and consistently sided with those who he thought were the objects of unjust treatment. He was a founding member of the National Association for the Advancement of Colored People (NAACP) and a member of the Men's League for Women's Suffrage.[12] He was a leading member of the American Civil Liberties Union. He defended Bertrand Russell (who had for decades been one of his harsher critics) in 1940, when Russell was dismissed from the City College of New York on grounds of "atheism" and "hedonism." He was the chair of the Trotsky inquiry in Mexico City. It was Dewey's view that responsible men and women work to take control of barren and problematic situations in ways that attempt to ameliorate them and render them productive, and he worked to prove himself responsible.

Seen from this perspective, the criticism advanced during the height of World War II by Max Horkheimer—that the pragmatists were incapable of caring about "murders perpetrated behind closed frontiers"—seems particularly inappropriate. In *The Eclipse of Reason*, based on lectures he delivered in 1944 at Dewey's own Columbia University, Horkheimer was particularly critical of Dewey (whom he misread as an idealist in the same camp with F. H. Bradley), for abandoning the idea of "objective truth."[13] "According to pragmatism," he wrote, "truth is to be desired not for its own sake but in so far as it works best, as it leads us to something that is alien or at least different from truth itself."[14]

What this meant for Horkheimer was that by undercutting the objectivity of "God, cause, number, substance [and] . . . soul,"[15] pragmatism (whose "most radical and consistent form" he regarded as Dewey's) was reduced to the claim that "knowing is literally something which we do."[16] What had been regarded by Dewey as one of the great insights of the pragmatists thus became for Horkheimer, steeped in the static and contemplative metaphysics of the European tradition, an occasion for offense.

> If the world should reach a point at which it ceases to care not only about such metaphysical entities but also about murders perpetrated behind closed frontiers or simply in the dark, one would have to conclude that the concepts of such murders have no meaning, that they represent no "distinct ideas" or truths, since they do not make any "sensible difference to anybody." How should anyone react sensibly to such concepts if he takes it for granted that his reaction is their only meaning?[17]

But when Horkheimer advanced this criticism, he was not just exhibiting a failure to understand the written texts of Dewey's instrumentalism as well as a lack of knowledge of Dewey's actual political career; he was also begging his own question. He set up examples that were patently incapable of being known—they were behind closed frontiers and in the dark—and then he berated Dewey and the other pragmatists for their contention that it is impossible to take action with respect to matters about which there is no information. If such murders were perpetrated behind truly closed borders, that is, if he did not know about them, then Horkheimer, too, would be unable to care about them. And if the borders were not completely closed, if some evidence were to leak out, a "sensible difference," to use the pragmatist phrase he mocks, would have been made in whoever had access to that evidence.

Horkheimer also misread Dewey's view of the nature of scientific change. From Dewey's point of view, he made a mistake that typifies the very straight-line instrumentalism that he and the other members of the Frankfurt School professed to despise when he wrote that "if Dewey means to say that scientific changes usually cause changes in the direction of a better social order, he misinterprets the interaction of economic, technical, political and ideological forces. The death factories in Europe cast as much significant light on the relations between science and cultural progress as does the manufacture of stockings out of air."[18]

Dewey's reply would, I think, have been that the European death factories were anything but scientific or technological. Their fixed agenda utilized technical means (in the sense of the straight-line instrumentalists) to further programs based, for example, on faulty eugenic studies. But the death camps were not for Dewey an example of technology in his reconstructed sense. They were instead the worst example of the straight-line instrumentalists's adherence to fixed ends, a program that was in that particular case rendered even more disastrous because intransigent ends were coupled with reliance on slovenly technical means, and therefore neither goals nor means had been checked.

Dewey's disciple C. E. Ayres, writing in 1943, shortly before the world came to know the enormity of what the Nazis had done, put this matter better than Dewey ever did. Though he writes of "nightmares" and "engines of destruction" in another sense, his remarks are equally applicable to the death factories.

> The truth is, of course, that the prophets of scientific doom are invoking not science but metaphysics; and they are doing so not altogether because they feel the weight of the dead hand of immemorial tradition, but in part from sheer ignorance. We are only just now beginning to realize that science and technology, the fine and the mechanical arts, contain within themselves the criterion of value by which they must be judged. Technological progress is not "meaningless apart from ends"; on the contrary it is the locus of meaning. What is wrong with the nightmares is that they are contrary to the actualities of science and technology, and what is wrong with the use of scientific tools as "engines of destruction" in war is not that war is an "unworthy end" but that it is a calamitous interruption of the activities by which alone civilization has made progress.[19]

III

What, in Dewey's view, constitutes responsible technology? This book is an attempt to suggest some answers to that question. By way of review and conclusion, it may be said that Dewey rejected what I have called "straight-line instrumentalism," or the view that neutral tools are brought to bear on ends that are valued for reasons external to the situations within which those tools have been developed. Drawing on the metaphors that accompanied Darwinian evolutionary theory, Dewey argued that human beings are organisms within nature and that their tool use is one of the developmental edges of natural activity. Tools and artifacts are no more neutral than are plants, nonhuman animals, or human beings themselves: they are interactive within situations that teem with values.

Responsible technology involves for Dewey the choice, the implementation, and the testing of goals that arise from those situations. There is no need for divine intervention to point the way, and the quest for absolute truth constitutes an impediment. Values arise out of inquiry, and once they are refined by inquiry they are brought back to the situations from which they originated in order to ascertain whether they are appropriate. Tools that are utilized in choosing, implementing, and testing enter into the articulation of ends, or things to be done, modifying those ends as the need arises. Evolving ends demand the modification of existing tools. Responsible technology thus remains flexible because it must accommodate changing situations. In addition to being resilient, responsible technology is redundant: it does not allow undue risks, and it backs itself up, both in terms of parallel development and in terms of the establishment of plateaus as possible fallback positions. Responsible technology is not so much radical as regenerative.

Responsible technology is not a thing, as Jacques Ellul and others have suggested. Nor should it be surprising that technology has no "core," since experience itself, of which technological activities and products are parts, is accessible only by shifts of interest and focus. Technology is instead the sum of concrete activities and products of men and women who engage in inquiry in its manifold forms: in the sciences, in the fine and useful arts, in business, in engineering, and in the arts we call political.

Where technology fails to be responsible, it is not because technology as method has failed, but because inquiry and testing have been misdirected, subsumed to nontechnological ends, or aborted. Ends have been dissociated from means. Fixed religious or political ideologies have taken the place of legitimate, testable inquiry. Economic and class interests have intervened where experimentation would have been appropriate.

I have suggested that Dewey would probably have been delighted at what appears to be a possible outcome of the long struggle concerning the Shoreham nuclear reactor, for that outcome indicates that it is now at least thinkable that even the largest industrial projects can be altered or canceled in response to the growth of new knowledge.

To those such as Hans Jonas, who have argued that responsibility to future generations must be based upon some metaphysical principle, such as an ontological responsibility to the "idea of Man,"[20] I think that Dewey would have argued that if we act responsibly, if we insist upon reliable forms of technology, the future will be as successful as it is possible for it to be. Dewey consistently argued that appeals to abstract metaphysical principles may serve as goals and patterns that can be taken back to the details of concrete situations, but if they are treated as immutable starting points they only tend to confuse otherwise productive debates.

Dewey also argued that we have no guarantee of success. Natural events could terminate human life, and human greed, laziness, or error could have the same result. The special place of human beings on earth lies in their development and use of intelligence: if intelligence fails or is thwarted, human beings will have lost their ecological niche. There is no god to save us.

Dewey was confident that the social problems of his time, which were not so different from our own, were tractable. Given the resources of material production, there is no reason why all the people of the world cannot have adequate food, shelter, and clothing. There is no reason why they cannot be weaned away from anachronistic and counterproductive outlooks and educated in the self-corrective methods of experimental science. Where the material commodities necessary to human development are lacking, it is not a failure of technology but a failure of imagination, a failure of diligence, or a failure of nerve.

But there was also a sense of urgency in Dewey's critique of technology. Failure to be responsible sets in motion trends and events that are increasingly difficult to divert or overcome. I think that Dewey would have argued that the destruction of the tropical rain forests, the desertification of vast areas of Africa, and the destruction of the environment due to acid rain and other industrial pollutants are not technological failures in the sense commonly intended by that term: they are instead problems that are consequent upon the failure to sharpen and use the technological tools required for intelligent social planning. And if intelligence is not exercised now, it may be increasingly difficult to do so. The opportunity may even be lost entirely.

For Dewey, technology was clearly identified as the tools and methods of productive inquiry, the tools and methods that are applicable even to those problems commonly described as the most intractable. Technology has worked well in the domain of natural sciences, but it is a method that men and women seem unwilling to apply beyond that sphere.

Appendix: Pagination Key to Works Cited

CRITICAL EDITION TO PRECRITICAL EDITIONS

THE EARLY WORKS

EW3:93–109 "Moral Theory and Practice," *International Journal of Ethics* I (January 1891), 186–203.

EW3:125–41 "The Present Position of Logical Theory," *Monist* II (October 1891), 1–17.

EW3:211–35 "Introduction to Philosophy: Syllabus of Course 5, Philosophical Department, University of Michigan, February, 1892." Preserved in the University of Michigan Historical Collections.

EW4:19–36 "The Superstition of Necessity," *Monist* III (April 1893), 362–79.

EW4:219–362 *The Study of Ethics* (Ann Arbor: The Inland Press, 1894).

EW5:3–24 *The Significance of the Problem of Knowledge* (Chicago: The University of Chicago Press, 1897). Reprinted "with slight change" in *The Influence of Darwin on Philosophy* (New York: Henry Holt and Co., 1910), 271–304.

EW5:34–53 "Evolution and Ethics," *Monist* VIII (April 1898), 321–41.

EW5:96–109 "The Reflex Arc Concept in Psychology," *Psychological Review* III (July 1896), 357–70.

THE MIDDLE WORKS

MW1:151–74 "Some Stages of Logical Thought," *Philosophical Review* 9 (1900), 465–89. Revised and reprinted in *Essays in Experimental Logic* (Chicago: The University of Chicago Press, 1916), 183–219. Page references are to the Dover reprint (New York: Dover Publications, Inc., n.d.).

MW2:39–52 "Interpretation of Savage Mind," *Psychological Review* 9 (1902), 217–30. Reprinted in *Philosophy and Civilization* (New York: Minton, Balch and Co., 1931), 173–87.

MW2:293–375 *Studies in Logical Theory* (Chicago: The University of Chicago Press, 1903). The first four essays in this book were revised and reprinted in *Essays in Experimental Logic* (Chicago: The University of Chicago Press, 1916), 75–156. Page references are to the Dover reprint (New York: Dover Publications, Inc., n.d.).

MW4:78–90 "The Control of Ideas by Facts," *Journal of Philosophy, Psychology and Scientific Methods* 4 (1907), 197–203, 253–59, 309–19.

Revised and reprinted in *Essays in Experimental Logic* (Chicago: The University of Chicago Press, 1916), 230–49. Page references are to the Dover reprint (New York: Dover Publications, Inc., n.d.).

MW4:91–97 "The Logical Character of Ideas," *Journal of Philosophy, Psychology and Scientific Methods* 5 (1908), 375–81. Revised and reprinted in *Essays in Experimental Logic* (Chicago: The University of Chicago Press, 1916), 220–29. Page references are to the Dover reprint (New York: Dover Publications, Inc., n.d.).

MW4:98–115 "What Pragmatism Means by Practical." Originally published as "What Does Pragmatism Mean by Practical?", *Journal of Philosophy, Psychology and Scientific Methods* 5 (1908), 85–89. Revised and reprinted in *Essays in Experimental Logic* (Chicago: The University of Chicago Press, 1916), 303–29. Page references are to the Dover reprint (New York: Dover Publications, Inc., n.d.).

MW5:1–540 *Ethics* by John Dewey and James Hayden Tufts (New York: Henry Holt and Co., 1908). Page references are to the 1913 Holt reprint. In 1932 Dewey and Tufts published a substantially revised edition (New York: Henry Holt and Co., 1932).

MW6:103–22 "Brief Studies in Realism," *Journal of Philosophy, Psychology and Scientific Methods* 8 (1911), 393–400, 546–54. Revised and reprinted as "Naive Realism vs. Presentative Realism" and "Epistemological Realism: The Alleged Ubiquity of the Knowledge Relation" in *Essays in Experimental Logic* (Chicago: The University of Chicago Press, 1916), 250–80. Page references are to the Dover reprint (New York: Dover Publications, Inc., n.d.).

MW7:331–33 "Progress," *A Cyclopedia of Education*, ed. Paul Monroe (New York: The Macmillan Co., 1912–1913).

MW8:14–82 "The Logic of Judgments of Practice," *Journal of Philosophy, Psychology and Scientific Methods* 12 (1915), 505–23, 533–43. Revised and reprinted in *Essays in Experimental Logic* (Chicago: The University of Chicago Press, 1916), 335–442. Page references are to the Dover reprint (New York: Dover Publications, Inc., n.d.).

MW8:83–97 "The Existence of the World as a Logical Problem." Originally published as "The Existence of the World as a Problem," *Philosophical Review* 24 (1915), 357–70. Revised and reprinted in *Essays in Experimental Logic* (Chicago: The University of Chicago Press, 1916), 281–302. Page references are to the Dover reprint (New York: Dover Publications, Inc., n.d.).

MW9:1–370 *Democracy and Education* (New York: The Macmillan Co., 1916). Page references are to the 1961 reprint (New York: The Macmillan Co., 1961).

MW10:3–48 "The Need for a Recovery of Philosophy," *Creative Intelligence: Essays in the Pragmatic Attitude* (New York: Henry Holt and Co., 1917), 3–69. This is a volume of essays by various authors.

MW10:89–97 "Logical Objects." Address to the Philosophical Club, 9 March 1916. From unpublished typescript, Papers of the Philosophical Club, Columbia University Special Collections.

MW10:234–43 "Progress," *International Journal of Ethics* 26 (1916), 311–22. Reprinted in *Characters and Events*, ed. Joseph Ratner (New York: Henry Holt and Co., 1929), vol. 2, 820–30.

MW10:244–51 "Force and Coercion," *International Journal of Ethics* 26 (1916), 359–67. Reprinted in *Characters and Events* , ed. Joseph Ratner (New York: Henry Holt and Co., 1929), vol. 2, 782–89.

MW10:320–65 "Introduction," *Essays in Experimental Logic* (Chicago: The University of Chicago Press, 1916), 1–74. Page references are to the Dover reprint (New York: Dover Publications, Inc., n.d.).

MW10:366–69 "An Added Note as to the 'Practical,' " *Essays in Experimental Logic* (Chicago: The University of Chicago Press, 1916), 330–34. Page references are to the Dover reprint (New York: Dover Publications, Inc., n.d.).

MW12:77–201 *Reconstruction in Philosophy* (New York: Henry Holt and Co., 1920). Page references are to the enlarged edition (Boston: Beacon Press, 1957).

MW14:1–230 *Human Nature and Conduct* (New York: Henry Holt and Co., 1922). Page references are to the revised edition (New York: The Modern Library, 1957).

THE LATER WORKS

LW1:1–326 *Experience and Nature* (Chicago and London: Open Court Publishing Co., 1925). Page references are to the second edition (La Salle, Ill.: Open Court Publishing Co., 1965).

LW1:329–64 "The Unfinished Introduction" (to a reissue of *Experience and Nature*). Appendix 1 to LW1 of the critical edition.

LW1:365–92 "Experience and Philosophic Method." Appendix 2 to LW1 of the critical edition.

LW2:235–372 *The Public and Its Problems* (New York: Henry Holt and Co., 1927). Page references are to the enlarged edition (Athens, Ohio: Swallow Press Books, 1954).

LW3:3–10 "Philosophy and Civilization." From an address to the Sixth International Congress of Philosophy, Harvard University, 15 September 1926. First published in *Philosophical Review* 36 (1927), 1–9. Reprinted in *Philosophy and Civilization* (New York: Minton Balch & Co., 1931), 3–12.

LW3:92–114 "Philosophies of Freedom," *Freedom in the Modern World*, ed. Horace M. Kallen (New York: Coward-McCann, 1928), 236–71.

LW4:1–250 *The Quest for Certainty* (New York: Minton, Balch and Co., 1929). Page references are to the 1960 reprint (New York: Capricorn Books, 1960).

LW5:41–123 *Individualism Old and New* (New York: Minton, Balch and Co., 1930). Page references are to the 1962 reprint (New York: Capricorn Books, 1962).

LW6:53–63 "Science and Society," *Philosophy and Civilization* (New York: Minton, Balch and Co., 1931), 318–30.

LW8:105–352 *How We Think: A Restatement of the Relation of Reflective Thinking to the Educative Process* (Boston: D. C. Heath and Co., 1933). This is a major revision of *How We Think* (Boston: D. C. Heath and Co., 1910).

LW9:1–58 *A Common Faith* (New Haven: Yale University Press, 1934). Page references are to the 1962 Yale reprint.

LW9:91–95 "Why I Am Not a Communist," *Modern Monthly* 8 (April 1934), 135–37.

LW10:1–352 *Art as Experience* (New York: Minton, Balch and Co., 1934). Page references are to the 1958 reprint (New York: Capricorn Books, 1958).

LW11:1–65 *Liberalism and Social Action* (New York: G. P. Putnam's Sons, 1935). Page references are to the 1980 reprint (New York: Perigee Books, 1980).

LW12:1–527 *Logic: The Theory of Inquiry* (New York: Henry Holt and Co., 1938).

LW13:1–62 *Experience and Education* (New York: The Macmillan Co., 1938).

LW14:224–30 "Creative Democracy—The Task Before Us," *John Dewey and the Promise of America*, Progressive Education Booklet No. 14 (Columbus, Ohio: American Education Press, 1939), 12–17.

PRECRITICAL EDITIONS TO CRITICAL EDITION

	"An Added Note as to the 'Practical,' " *Essays in Experimental Logic* (Chicago: The University of Chicago Press, 1916), 330–34. Page references are to the Dover reprint (New York: Dover Publications, Inc., n.d.).	MW10:366–69
AE	*Art as Experience* (New York: Minton, Balch and Co., 1934). Page references are to the 1958 reprint (New York: Capricorn Books, 1958).	LW10:1–352
	"Brief Studies in Realism," *Journal of Philosophy, Psychology and Scientific Methods* 8 (1911), 393–400, 546–54. Revised and reprinted as "Naive Realism vs. Presentative Realism" and "Epistemological Realism: The Alleged Ubiquity of the Knowledge Relation" in *Essays in Experimental Logic* (Chicago: The University of Chicago Press, 1916), 250–80. Page references are to the Dover reprint (New York: Dover Publications, Inc., n.d.).	MW6:103–22
	"A Comment on the Foregoing Criticisms," *The Journal of Aesthetics and Art Criticism* 6 (1948), 207–9.	Not yet reprinted in the critical edition
CF	*A Common Faith* (New Haven: Yale University Press, 1934). Page references are to the 1962 Yale reprint.	LW9:1–58
	"The Control of Ideas by Facts," *Journal of Philosophy, Psychology and Scientific Methods* 4 (1907), 197–203, 253–59, 309–19. Revised and reprinted in *Essays in Experimental Logic* (Chicago: The University of Chicago Press, 1916), 230–49. Page references are to the Dover reprint (New York: Dover Publications, Inc., n.d.).	MW4:78–90
	"Creative Democracy—The Task Before Us," *John Dewey and the Promise of America*, Progressive Education Booklet No. 14 (Columbus, Ohio: American Education Press, 1939), 12–17.	LW14:224–30
DE	*Democracy and Education* (New York: The Macmillan	MW9:1–370

Co., 1916). Page references are to the 1961 Macmillan reprint.

EEL *Essays in Experimental Logic* (Chicago: The University of Chicago Press, 1916), 1–74. Page references are to the Dover reprint (New York: Dover Publications, Inc., n.d.).

E *Ethics* by John Dewey and James Hayden Tufts. (New York: Henry Holt and Co., 1908). Page references are to the 1913 Holt reprint. In 1932 Dewey and Tufts published a substantially revised edition (New York: Henry Holt and Co., 1932).   MW5:1–540

"Evolution and Ethics," *Monist* VIII (April 1898), 321–41.   EW5:34–53

"The Existence of the World as a Logical Problem." Originally published as "The Existence of the World as a Problem," *Philosophical Review* 24 (1915), 357–70. Revised and reprinted in *Essays in Experimental Logic* (Chicago: The University of Chicago Press, 1916), 281–302. Page references are to the Dover reprint (New York: Dover Publications, Inc., n.d.).   MW8:83–97

EE *Experience and Education* (New York: The Macmillan Co., 1938).   LW13:1–62

EN *Experience and Nature* (Chicago and London: Open Court Publishing Co., 1925). Page references are to the second edition (La Salle, Ill.: Open Court Publishing Co., 1965).   LW1:1–326

"Experience and Philosophic Method." Appendix 2 to LW1 of the critical edition.   LW1:365–92

"Force and Coercion," *International Journal of Ethics* 26 (1916), 359–67. Reprinted in *Characters and Events*, ed. Joseph Ratner (New York: Henry Holt and Co., 1929), vol. 2, 782–89.   MW10:244–51

HWT *How We Think: A Restatement of the Relation of Reflective Thinking to the Educative Process* (Boston: D. C. Heath and Co., 1933). This is a major revision of *How We Think* (Boston: D. C. Heath and Co., 1910).   LW8:105–352

HNC *Human Nature and Conduct* (New York: Henry Holt and Co., 1922). Page references are to the revised edition (New York: The Modern Library, 1957).   MW14:1–230

ION *Individualism Old and New* (New York: Minton, Balch and Co., 1930). Page references are to the 1962 reprint (New York: Capricorn Books, 1962).   LW5:41–123

"Interpretation of Savage Mind," *Psychological Review* 9 (1902), 217–30. Reprinted in *Philosophy and Civilization* (New York: Minton, Balch and Co., 1931), 173–87.   MW2:39–52

EEL "Introduction," *Essays in Experimental Logic* (Chicago: The University of Chicago Press, 1916), 1–74. Page   MW10:320–65 references are to the Dover reprint (New York: Dover Publications, Inc., n.d.).

"Introduction to Philosophy: Syllabus of Course 5, Philosophical Department, University of Michigan, February, 1892." Preserved in the University of Michigan Historical Collections.   EW3:211–35

LSA *Liberalism and Social Action* (New York: G. P. Putnam's Sons, 1935). Page references are to the 1980 reprint (New York: Perigee Books, 1980).   LW11:1–65

"The Logic of Judgments of Practice," *Journal of Philosophy, Psychology and Scientific Methods* 12 (1915), 505–23, 533–43. Revised and reprinted in *Essays in Experimental Logic* (Chicago: The University of Chicago Press, 1916), 335–42. Page references are to the Dover reprint (New York: Dover Publications, Inc., n.d.).   MW8:14–82

LTI *Logic: The Theory of Inquiry* (New York: Henry Holt and Co., 1938).   LW12:1–527

"The Logical Character of Ideas," *Journal of Philosophy, Psychology and Scientific Methods* 5 (1908), 375–81. Revised and reprinted in *Essays in Experimental Logic* (Chicago: The University of Chicago Press, 1916), 220–29. Page references are to the Dover reprint (New York: Dover Publications, Inc., n.d.).   MW4:91–97

"Logical Objects." Address to the Philosophical Club, 9 March 1916. From unpublished typescript, Papers of the Philosophical Club, Columbia University Special Collections.   MW10:89–97

"The Need for a Recovery of Philosophy," *Creative Intelligence: Essays in the Pragmatic Attitude* (New York: Henry Holt and Co., 1917), 3–69. This is a volume of essays by various authors.   MW10:3–48

"Moral Theory and Practice," *International Journal of Ethics* I (January 1891), 186–203.   EW3:93–109

"Philosophies of Freedom," *Freedom in the Modern World*, ed. Horace M. Kallen (New York: Coward-McCann, 1928), 236–71.   LW3:92–114

PC *Philosophy and Civilization* (New York: Minton Balch & Co., 1931).

"Philosophy and Civilization," from an address to the Sixth International Congress of Philosophy, Harvard University, 15 September 1926. First published in *Philosophical Review* 36 (1927), 1–9. Reprinted in *Philosophy and Civilization* (New York: Minton Balch & Co., 1931), 3–12.   LW3:3–10

"The Present Position of Logical Theory," *Monist* II (October 1891), 1–17.   EW3:125–41

PM   *Problems of Men* (New York: Philosophical Library, 1946).

"Progress," A *Cyclopedia of Education*, ed. Paul   MW7:331–33
Monroe (New York: The Macmillan Co., 1912–1913).

"Progress," *International Journal of Ethics* 26 (1916),   MW10:234–43
311–22. Reprinted in *Characters and Events*, ed.
Joseph Ratner (New York: Henry Holt and Co., 1929),
vol. 2, 820–30.

PP   *The Public and Its Problems* (New York: Henry Holt and   LW2:235–372
Co., 1927). Page references are to the enlarged edition
(Athens, Ohio: Swallow Press Books, 1954).

QC   *The Quest for Certainty* (New York: Minton, Balch and   LW4:1–250
Co., 1929). Page references are to the 1960 reprint
(New York: Capricorn Books, 1960).

RP   *Reconstruction in Philosophy* (New York: Henry Holt   MW12:77–201
and Co., 1920). Page references are to the enlarged
edition (Boston: Beacon Press, 1957).

"The Reflex Arc Concept in Psychology," *Psychological*   EW5:96–109
Review III (July 1896), 357–70.

"Science and Society," *Philosophy and Civilization*   LW6:53–63
(New York: Minton, Balch and Co., 1931), 318–30.

The Significance of the Problem of Knowledge (Chicago: EW5:3–24
The University of Chicago Press, 1897). Reprinted "with
slight change" in *The Influence of Darwin on Philosophy*
(New York: Henry Holt and Co., 1910), 271–304.

"Some Stages of Logical Thought," *Philosophical*   MW1:151–74
Review 9 (1900), 465–89. Revised and reprinted in
Essays in Experimental Logic (Chicago: The University
of Chicago Press, 1916), 183–219. Page references are
to the Dover reprint (New York: Dover Publications, Inc.,
n.d.).

SLT   *Studies in Logical Theory* (Chicago: The University of   MW2:293–375
Chicago Press, 1903). The first four essays in this book
are reprinted in *Essays in Experimental Logic* (Chicago:
The University of Chicago Press, 1916), 75–156. Page
references are to the Dover reprint (New York: Dover
Publications, Inc., n.d.).

The Study of Ethics (Ann Arbor: The Inland Press,   EW4:219–362
1894).

"The Superstition of Necessity," *Monist* III (April 1893),   EW4:19–36
362–79.

"The Unfinished Introduction" (to a reissue of   LW1:329–64
Experience and Nature). Appendix 1 to LW1 of the
critical edition.

"What Pragmatism Means by Practical." Originally   MW4:98–115
published as "What Does Pragmatism Mean by
Practical?", *Journal of Philosophy, Psychology and
Scientific Methods* 5 (1908), 85–89. Reprinted in *Essays*

in Experimental Logic (Chicago: The University of Chicago Press, 1916), 303–29. Page references are to the Dover reprint (New York: Dover Publications, Inc., n.d.).

"Why I Am Not a Communist," *Modern Monthly* 8 (April 1934), 135–37.　　LW9:91–95

Notes

1. LOCATING DEWEY'S CRITIQUE OF TECHNOLOGY

1. Webster Hood was correct in his assertion that Dewey had an "abiding interest" in technology and that he was probably the first contemporary philosopher to make technology a central concern and "to see it as posing genuine philosophic problems." See Webster F. Hood, "Dewey and Technology: A Phenomenological Approach," *Research in Philosophy and Technology* V (1982), 190.

2. General anthologies in this field include: Carl Mitcham and Robert Mackey, eds., *Philosophy and Technology: Readings in the Philosophical Problems of Technology* (New York: The Free Press, 1972); Albert H. Teich, ed., *Technology and the Future*, 4th ed. (New York: St. Martin's, 1986); Alex C. Michalos, ed., *Philosophical Problems of Science and Technology* (Boston: Allyn & Bacon, 1974); George Bugliarello and Dean B. Doner, eds., *The History and Philosophy of Technology* (Urbana, Ill.: University of Illinois Press, 1979); Larry Hickman and Azizah al-Hibri, eds., *Technology and Human Affairs* (St. Louis: C. V. Mosby, 1981); and Larry Hickman, ed., *Philosophy, Technology and Human Affairs* (College Station, Texas: Ibis Press, 1985). Only the last two collections include selections from Dewey's work.

3. These rare essays include: Webster F. Hood, "Dewey and Technology: A Phenomenological Approach," *Research in Philosophy and Technology* V (1982), 189–207; and Edith Wyschogrod, "The Logic of Artifactual Existents: John Dewey and Claude Lévi-Strauss," *Man and World* XIV (1982), 235–50.

4. A notable exception to this pattern are the works of John J. McDermott. See especially *The Culture of Experience* (New York: New York University Press, 1976), and *Streams of Experience* (Amherst, Mass.: The University of Massachusetts Press, 1986).

5. See Richard Rorty's essay "Dewey's Metaphysics," in his book *The Consequences of Pragmatism* (Minneapolis: The University of Minnesota Press, 1982).

6. Dewey exhibited a curious lack of interest in keeping his works in print. Systematic research into his work was extremely difficult prior to the availability of the critical edition of his work, undertaken by Jo Ann Boydston and her staff at the Center for Dewey Studies at Southern Illinois University.

7. This is Max Eastman's designation. See Eastman's article "America's Philosopher," *Saturday Review of Literature*, 17 January 1953, 23–24, 38.
8. Charles A. Beard and Mary R. Beard, *The Rise of American Civilization*, rev. ed. 1934, reprinted 1946 (New York: The Macmillan Company, 1946), 789.
9. Robert H. Walker, *Life in the Age of Enterprise* (New York: Capricorn Books, 1971), 44–45.
10. In his introduction to *Essays in Religion and Morality*, the ninth title and the eleventh volume of *The Works of William James* (Cambridge: Harvard University Press, 1982), John J. McDermott gives the following assessment of that occasion:

> The occasion of James' oration was the unveiling of a monument to Robert Gould Shaw, the commander of the Fifty-Fourth Regiment of Massachusetts Volunteers, the first regiment of black soldiers to fight for the Union Army. James was both a likely and an unlikely candidate for the honor of giving this address. It was fitting for James to speak, for his younger brother Garth Wilkinson James had been an adjutant in the Fifty-Fourth Regiment and had been wounded in the assault on Fort Wagner. Yet William James, though of age and surrounded by peers who enlisted, chose not to serve in the Civil War and offered no excuses or explanations (xx).

McDermott characterizes James's stance on the events symbolized by that occasion:

> Missing . . . is any sense of the enormous importance of the abolition movement and of the end of slavery in the United States. Not having participated in that movement in either a military or a political manner, he seems to view the Civil War at too great a distance, a distance that no doubt contributed to his estrangement from his two military brothers (xxi).

11. See Siegfried Giedion, *Mechanization Takes Command* (1948; reprint, New York: W. W. Norton, 1969), 83.
12. A fascinating analysis of Dewey's audiences has been done by C. Wright Mills in his *Sociology and Pragmatism*, Irving Louis Horowitz, ed. (New York: Oxford University Press, 1966).
13. Sidney Ratner *et al.*, eds., *John Dewey and Arthur F. Bentley: A Philosophical Correspondence, 1932–1951* (New Brunswick, NJ: Rutgers University Press, 1964), 646.
14. Irwin Edman, *John Dewey: His Contribution to the American Tradition* (Indianapolis: Bobbs-Merrill, 1955), 11.
15. Lewis Mumford, *The Golden Day* (New York: Dover Publications, 1968), 130.
16. FBI New York File No. 100-25838, New York, New York, 29 April 1943, p. 2. Copy at Center for John Dewey Studies, Carbondale, Ill.
17. H. L. Mencken, *Letters of H. L. Mencken*, Guy J. Forque, ed. (New York: Alfred A. Knopf, 1961), 316. Quoted in Earl James Weaver, "John Dewey: A Spokesman for Progressive Liberalism." Ph.D. diss., Brown University, 1963, 288n.
18. Stephen Toulmin, introduction to vol. 4 of *The Later Works* (LW1:xi).
19. John J. McDermott, *The Philosophy of John Dewey*, vol. I (New York: G.P. Putnam's Sons, 1973), xxviii.
20. Toulmin, introduction to vol. 4 of *The Later Works* (LW4:xi).
21. Carl Mitcham and Robert Mackey, eds., *Philosophy and Technology* (New York: The Free Press, 1972), 1. See also Carl Mitcham. "Types of Technology," in *Research in Philosophy and Technology*, vol. I, Paul Durbin, ed. (Greenwich, Conn.: JAI Press, 1978), 229–94.

22. Mitcham (1978), 230–31.
23. Ibid.
24. Ibid., 232.
25. Mitcham is one of only a handful of philosophers who hold this view. Others include I. C. Jarvie and Emmanuel G. Mesthene. See I. C. Jarvie, "The Social Character of Technological Problems: Comments on Skolimowski's Paper," in Mitcham and Mackey (1972), 50–61. "Technology for me, then, is coterminous with our attempts to come to terms with our world; that is, our culture and our society; and, as such, it contains within it both pure tools and all knowledge" (p. 61).

    See also Emmanuel G. Mesthene, *Technological Change* (New York: New American Library, 1970). For Mesthene, who received three academic degrees from Columbia University, technology is "tools in a general sense, including machines, but also including such intellectual tools as computer languages and contemporary analytic and mathematical techniques. That is, we define technology as the organization of knowledge for the achievement of practical purposes" (p. 25).
26. Mitcham and Mackey (1972), 2.
27. See R. W. Sleeper, *The Necessity of Pragmatism* (New Haven: Yale University Press, 1986).
28. Beard and Beard (1946), 789.
29. A very good example of the extent to which pragmatism has influenced sociologists to consider the meanings of quotidian objects is Mihaly Csikszentmihalyi and Eugene Rochberg-Halton, *The Meaning of Things: Domestic Symbols and the Self* (Cambridge: Cambridge University Press, 1981).
30. Albert Borgmann, *Technology and the Character of Contemporary Life* (Chicago: The University of Chicago Press, 1984). Borgmann writes of his categories: "These summaries distinguish a multitude of approaches, but all distinctions fit well one of three essential types: the substantive, the instrumentalist, and the pluralist views of technology" (p. 9).
31. See Jacques Ellul, *The Technological Society*, John Wilkinson, trans. (New York: Random House, 1964). See also Jacques Ellul. *The Technological System*, tr. Joachim Neugroschel, trans. (New York: Continuum, 1980).
32. Borgmann (1984), 9.
33. Ibid., 10.
34. Ibid.
35. Ibid.
36. Victor Ferkiss, *Technological Man: The Myth and the Reality* (New York: New American Library, 1969).
37. See Allan Bloom, *The Closing of the American Mind* (New York: Simon and Schuster, 1987). See also an excellent review of Bloom's book by Martha Nussbaum, "Undemocratic Vistas," *The New York Review of Books*, 5 November 1987, 20–26.
38. Borgmann (1984), 10.
39. Ibid., 11.
40. Ibid., 10.
41. William Barrett, *The Illusion of Technique* (Garden City, NY: Anchor Press/Doubleday, 1978), 18–19.
42. Ibid., 19.
43. Mitcham (1978), 233.
44. Ibid.
45. Mitcham (1978), 243.
46. Ibid., 242–57.
47. All references to Aristotle will be by means of Bekker's standard 1831 edition of the Greek text of Aristotle. Notation consists of a page number, a

column letter, and a line number. The translation I have used throughout this book is that collected by Jonathan Barnes in his edition of *The Complete Works of Aristotle* (Princeton: Princeton University Press, 1984), 2 volumes, Bollingen Series LXXI 2.
48. See Abraham Edel, *Aristotle and His Philosophy* (Chapel Hill: University of North Carolina Press, 1982). "We make things in order to use them in living. But contemplation is in his view the highest end" (p. 388).
49. Mitcham (1978), 258.
50. Francis Bacon, *The Works of Francis Bacon*, vol. IV, J. Spedding et al. eds. (1857–1874; reprint, New York: Garrett Press, 1968), 405.

2. KNOWING AS A TECHNOLOGICAL ARTIFACT

1. F. E. Peters, *Greek Philosophical Terms* (New York: New York University Press, 1967), 190.
2. Wolfgang Schadewaldt, "The Concepts of Nature and Technique According to the Greeks," in *Research in Philosophy and Technology*, vol. 2, Paul T. Durbin, ed. (Greenwich, Conn.: JAI Press, 1979), 166.
3. Ibid. (This is a paraphrase of Aristotle's *Nichomachean Ethics* VI 4, 1040a, 10 ff).
4. See *Nichomachean Ethics,* 1139b18, ff. "of things capable of being otherwise we do not know, the object of knowledge is of necessity. Therefore the object of knowledge is of necessity. Therefore it is eternal; for things that are of necessity in the unqualified sense are all eternal; and things that are eternal are ungenerated and imperishable." Jonathan Barnes, ed., *The Complete Works of Aristotle*, 2 vols. (Princeton, N.J.: Princeton University Press, 1985).
5. This is by no means the only traditional reading of Aristotle. Walter Ong, for example, in his important book *Ramus, Method and the Decay of Dialogue* (Cambridge: Harvard University Press, 1958), treated Aristotle's categories quite differently.

> The *Categories* or *Predicaments* of Aristotle are not a classification of things, nor of being-in-general, nor are they a classification of the whole range of human concepts as such. Neither are they categories in the modern sense of a system of classes into which items are "put." As their name indicates and a recent study confirms, they are types of predicates conceived of more or less as "accusations" (or "outcries" in the market place or assembly, *categoria*, transformed into latin as *praedicamenta*, things spoken out) which can be brought against a subject or "prime substance" (106–7).

But contrast this account to that of Manley Thompson:

> The word "category" was first used as a technical term in philosophy by Aristotle . . . . [who] held that every uncombined expression signifies (denotes, refers to) one or more things falling in at least one of . . . ten classes . . . .Each of the ten classes of entities signified constitutes a category, or genus, or entities, and each categorematic expression is said to be an expression in the category constituted by the class of entities it signifies. (*The Encyclopedia of Philosophy*, Paul Edwards, ed. [New York: Macmillan, 1967], s.v. "Categories.")

6. Dewey uses the term "technological" here in the sense he later described in *Human Nature and Conduct*. There he contrasted tools in a toolbox, passive and unused, to tools in use, actively engaged in modifying a situation. It is the passive use that he intends here.

7. Sidney Hook, *The Metaphysics of Pragmatism* (Chicago: Open Court, 1927), 29.

8. William James, *The Principles of Psychology* (Cambridge: Harvard University Press, 1983), 217.

9. Ibid.

10. Richard J. Bernstein, *John Dewey* (New York: Washington Square Press, 1967), 61.

11. Quoted in Bernstein (1967), 60.

12. Webster F. Hood, "Dewey and Technology: A Phenomenological Approach," *Research in Philosophy and Technology*, vol. 5 (1982), Paul Durbin, ed. (Greenwich, Conn.: JAI Press, 1982), 190.

13. Ibid.

14. Ibid., 191.

15. Ibid.

16. John J. McDermott, ed., *The Philosophy of John Dewey*, vol. 1 (New York: G. P. Putnam's Sons, 1973), xxiv.

17. John J. McDermott, ed., *The Philosophy of John Dewey*, vol. 2 (New York: G. P. Putnam's Sons, 1973), xxv.

18. R. W. Sleeper, *The Necessity of Pragmatism* (New Haven, N.J.: Yale University Press, 1986), 10.

19. See, for example, Sleeper (1986), 21ff.

20. See, for example, Max Horkheimer, *Eclipse of Reason* (1947; reprint, New York: Seabury Press, 1974), 171–72. See also my chapter 3, especially the responses of Stephen Pepper and Benedetto Croce to Dewey's *Art as Experience*.

21. As Bertrand P. Helm has forcefully and eloquently argued, Dewey's "temporalization" of time was virtually unique among philosophers who were his contemporaries, and his views on this matter were a source of great misunderstanding among his critics, including C. S. Peirce. (Bertrand P. Helm, *Time and Reality in American Philosophy* [Amherst, Mass.: The University of Massachusetts Press, 1985], 96ff.)

22. See Lewis S. Feuer, "John Dewey and the Back to the People Movement in American Thought," *Journal of the History of Ideas* XX (1959), 545–68.

23. Helm (1985), 117.

24. Willard Van Orman Quine, *Ontological Relativity and Other Essays* (New York: Columbia University Press, 1969).

25. James (1983), 224.

26. William James, "The Function of Cognition," in *The Writings of William James*, John J. McDermott, ed. (New York: Random House, 1967), 143.

27. For a particularly entertaining assessment of Dewey's educational program see John A. Stormer, *None Dare Call it Treason* (Florissant, Mo.: The Liberty Bell Press, 1964), 99ff. The copyright page of this book indicates that between February and July 1964 almost a million and a half copies were printed. The religious fundamentalists have not been silent since that time. In the nationally televised speech that effectively initiated his campaign for the 1988 Republican presidential nomination, the Reverend Pat Robertson singled Dewey out for criticism on three separate occasions. He was more critical of Dewey than he was of Karl Marx, whom he mentioned only once.

28. This remark is also interesting in view of the fact that some of Dewey's critics accused him of being a hard-line Baconian, of seeking to "dominate" nature.

29. There is, of course, a deep contradiction in the fundamentalist position. Christian-fundamentalist television evangelists in America cry that "man" can do nothing and that God does everything. They also rely on massive bases of electronic technology to diffuse their message. Islamic fundamentalists in Iran make the same claim. They also purchase massive amounts of military hardware on world markets.

30. Many of the situations about which Dewey complained have changed very little since his time. In *Individualism, Old and New*, Dewey expressed his disappointment that "one half of the pupils in the last years of the high school think that the first chapters of the Hebrew Scriptures give a more accurate account of the origin and early history of man that does science, and only one-fifth actively dissent" (LW5:47; ION:15). That was written in 1929. During the writing of this chapter, in 1988, the results of an informal poll among students at Texas A&M University indicated that in the event of a nuclear war, about half of those sampled would take to a bomb shelter, as their only book, a copy of the Bible. It occurred to only about 10 percent of those sampled that a copy of *The Foxfire Book* or some other technological manual might be of some use.

31. One finds this reverse instrumentality even in the work of Martin Heidegger. Especially in his later period, Heidegger seems to suggest that it is not so much that human beings use language as an instrument as it is that they become instruments for language. For the later Heidegger, it is as if language speaks humankind.

32. Ludwig Wittgenstein, *Philosophical Investigations*, G. E. M. Anscombe, trans. (New York: Macmillan, 1953), 126, 126e.

33. Ludwig Wittgenstein, *Tractatus Logico-Philosophicus*, C. K. Ogden, trans. (London: Routledge & Kegan Paul Ltd., 1986), 108 (5.1361).

34. Richard Rorty, *Consequences of Pragmatism* (Minneapolis: University of Minnesota Press, 1983), 28. Emphasis added.

35. Jean Gimpel, *The Medieval Machine* (New York: Penguin Books, 1977), 153.

36. D. P. Walker, *Spiritual and Demonic Magic from Ficino to Campanella* (1958; reprint, Nendeln, Liechtenstein: Kraus, 1976), 75 ff.

37. E. William Monter, *Witchcraft in France and Switzerland* (Ithaca: Cornell University Press, 1976), 173.

38. C. E. Ayres, *The Industrial Economy* (Boston: Houghton Mifflin Co., 1952), 52.

39. Ibid.

40. Ibid. 54.

41. Harry T. Costello, "Logic in 1914 and Now," *Journal of Philosophy* LIV (25 April 1957), 245–64.

42. Ibid., 251–52.

43. See the epilogue of this volume for Max Horkheimer's criticism of this view.

44. Siegfried Giedion (Giedion, 1969) provides an interesting example of this. The patent granted to Oliver Evans for his mechanized grain mill was challenged in 1813 by other millers. "Thomas Jefferson was called in by an expert. His opinion of Oliver Evans' devices was low. He saw only the details, not the thing as a whole. 'The elevator,' he declared, 'is nothing more than the old Persian Wheel of Egypt, and the conveyor is the same thing as the screw of Archimedes' " (p. 84). Giedion admits that if Evans's mill were split into single components, Jefferson's judgment would be correct. The point, however, is that they functioned together in ways that gave the entire assembly a new meaning. "For Oliver Evans, hoisting and transportation have another meaning. They are but links within the continuous production process: from raw material to finished goods, the human hand shall be replaced by the machine" (p. 85).

45. Bertrand Russell, *Our Knowledge of the External World*, 2nd ed. (New York:

W. W. Norton & Co., 1929), 60. Dewey's reference is to p. 56 of the first edition, published in Chicago by Open Court Publishing Co. in 1914.
46. Costello (1957), 252.

3. PRODUCTIVE SKILLS IN THE ARTS

1. Sidney Hook, *The Metaphysics of Pragmatism* (Chicago: Open Court, 1927), 53.
2. Ibid., 54.
3. Ibid, 54–55.
4. See Walter Benjamin, *Illuminations* (New York: Schocken Books, 1969) and John Berger, *Ways of Seeing* (New York: Penguin Books, 1977).
5. J. Berger (1977), 106.
6. See Robert Hughes, *Shock of the New* (New York: Alfred A. Knopf, 1982), 99ff.
7. See Leo Steinberg, *The Sexuality of Christ in Renaissance Art and in Modern Oblivion* (New York: Pantheon, 1983) for an excellent treatment of this matter.

> The assault on art in the name of propriety is one mode of iconoclasm. But a general history of the iconoclastic impulse in action remains to be written. As I see it, such a work would reveal the preservation of art as an embattled cause, intermittently threatened by waves of anti-art feeling.
> The modalities of iconoclasm are various, as are the objects of its execration. The grounds may be doctrinal (as in the classic Byzantine phase); or socio-political (as in the destruction of royalist imagery by revolutionists); or ideological (as in the proscription of "decadent" art under Hitler and Stalin); or moralistic (as in the zeal of the censor); or entrepreneurial (as in site clearing for urban development and renovation); or gustatory, the deadliest ground of all, since nothing endangers a work's survival more than a recent aversion of taste (p. 174).

Steinberg gives examples of the defacing of representations of Jesus that either cover up or chisel off the genitalia presented in the originals (pp. 174–83). He has little regard for Duchamp's treatment of the "masterworks" of the history of art—for example, his mustached Mona Lisa. But Duchamp did not deface the Mona Lisa; he merely parodied its value as a cult object by constructing what was essentially a new work of art. It would be incorrect to say that the original was left "untouched." Nevertheless, the original painting was not defaced.
8. Max Horkheimer, *Critical Theory* (New York: Continuum, 1986), 290.
9. Ibid.
10. Ibid.
11. Ibid.
12. Hook, (1927), 58n.
13. Quoted in Hook (1927), 58n.
14. See LW1:36–37 (EN:31–32). Dewey consciously uses the metaphor of banking. Theories or ends "receive their check" from the practice or means that bring them forth and by which they are tested. This is literally the "payoff." See also EW5:6: "As the philosopher has received his problem from the world of action, so he must return his account there for auditing and liquidation."
15. Hughes (1982), 243–44.
16. Ibid., 244.
17. Lynn White, "The Act of Invention: Causes, Contexts, Continuities and Consequences," in *The Technological Order: Proceedings of the Encyclopaedia*

Britannica Conference, Carl E. Stover, ed. (Detroit: Wayne State University Press, 1963), 113–14.

18. Ibid., 114.

19. See Webster Hood, "Dewey and Technology: A Phenomenological Approach," in *Research in Philosophy and Technology*, vol. 5, Paul T. Durbin, ed. (Greenwich, Conn.: JAI Press, 1981) for a good account of these "platforms."

20. See Gerald Mast and Marshall Cohen, eds., *Film Theory and Criticism*, 3rd ed. (New York: Oxford University Press, 1985). This excellent anthology contains a section of seven essays entitled "Film and Reality."

21. See Wolfgang Schadewaldt, "The Concepts of *Nature* and *Technique* According to the Greeks," in *Research in Philosophy and Technology*, vol. 2, Paul T. Durbin, ed. (Greenwich, Conn.: JAI Press, 1979), 160. Schadewaldt has provided a wonderful account of the concreteness of the demotic use of the term "nature" for the Greeks and Latins. I quote him here at length because his account casts light on Dewey's. Dewey's understanding of nature, like Schadewaldt's rendition of the Greeks', was functional and "gerundive."

> In Latin *natura* (derived from *nasci*, "to be born") originally belonged to the language of the farmer and the breeder who used *natura* in a concrete way to designate the uterine orifice of a female quadruped. Designating the place through which birth happens and from which the succession of births proceeds, *natura* was used quite early to translate the Greek *physis*, so that its original concrete meaning was expanded to include a new general content. As such it designated the creative origin of everything which is and, in another sense, the inborn character, because it also determines the constitution of the thing brought forth.

Further, the Greeks never used the term in the way that modern science and popular parlance has it, that is, to designate a realm of objects.

> *Physis* is never that "nature" out there where people make Sunday excursions, "in" which this and that occurs or this and that is such and such. *Physis* comes from the Greek verb *phyo*, which means something like "bring-forth," "put forth," "make to grow," chiefly in the botanical realm where the tree puts forth leaves, blossoms, branches, and then in the zoological realm in respect to hair, wool, wings, horns. Moreover, the noun *physis*, like all Greek constructions with *-sis* [similar to English gerunds], does not mean some object or material thing, but a coming-to-pass, an event, a directing activity, a *Wesen* [being or essence]—if we understand this word in its original active meaning, which is preserved in *verwesen*[to administer, manage].

22. Paul Arthur Schilpp, *The Philosophy of John Dewey* (Evanston: Northwestern University Press, 1939), 371.

23. Ibid.

24. John Dewey, "A Comment on the Foregoing Criticisms," in *Journal of Aesthetics and Art Criticism* 6 (1948), 207.

25. Ibid., 208.

26. Ibid. See also LW10:91 (AE:85): "Such, however, is the newness of scientific statement and its present prestige (due ultimately to its directive efficacy) that scientific statement is often thought to possess more than a signboard function

and to disclose or be 'expressive' of the inner nature of things. If it did, it would come into competition with art, and we should have to take sides and decide which of the two promulgates the more genuine revelation."
27. Dewey (1948), 208.
28. Ibid.
29. Ibid.
30. Ibid.
31. John J. McDermott, ed., *The Philosophy of John Dewey*, vol. 1 (New York: G. P. Putnam's Sons, 1973), xxv–xxvi.
32. Thomas M. Alexander, *John Dewey's Theory of Art, Experience and Nature: The Horizons of Feeling* (Albany, N.Y.: State University of New York Press, 1987), 212.
33. Dewey works out the simile of the garden in his essay "Evolution and Ethics" (EW5:34–53).
34. William James, "Conversion," lecture 9 in *The Varieties of Religious Experience: A Study in Human Nature*. The Gifford Lectures on Natural Religion delivered at Edinburgh in 1901–1902 (New York: Longmans, Green and Co., 1893), 209–10.
35. Neither Dewey nor the editors of the critical edition has provided a reference to Ayres's work.

4. FROM *TECHNE* TO TECHNOLOGY

1. Anthony Quinton, "Cut Rate Salvation," in *The New York Review of Books* IX, no. 9 (23 November 1967), 6–14.
2. Justus Buchler should be mentioned here as an exception to this generalization.
3. Chapter 7 includes a lengthy discussion of Dewey's notion of progress.
4. Edith Wyschogrod, "The Logic of Artifactual Existents: John Dewey and Claude Lévi-Strauss," in *Man and World*, vol. 14 (1981), 235–50.
5. Ibid., 235.
6. Claude Lévi-Strauss, *The Savage Mind* (Chicago: University of Chicago Press, 1966), 16.
7. I owe to conversations with Douglas Browning the suggestion that the most primitive myths may not be, as some have thought, religious stories or tales of the creation of the world. He argues instead that they are stories of individuals—the exploits of individual hunters, for example. I think that Dewey would have been quite sympathetic to this account. Human beings have a tendency to exaggerate, so accounts of the exploits of a great hunter may after his lifetime, or even during it, gradually become stories of the accomplishments of supernatural beings. Stories of the creation of the world would come later in this sequence and would be the result of maximal exaggeration of supernatural accomplishment. What greater feat could be attributed to a god? Perhaps only that he (or she) perform the task with neither materials nor instrumentation— creation *ex nihilo* and by merely willing it to be so, as in the several creation myths in Genesis.

In this same vein, some have suggested that the Osiris myth, an extremely popular story recounted throughout the Middle East in various forms for some three thousand years before the common era, is the enhanced account of an individual accomplishment. In this case the story is that of a reformer who attempted to replace certain nomadic practices with those of agriculture. For more on this subject, see Martin A. Larson, *The Story of Christian Origins* (Washington, DC: Joseph J. Binns/New Republic, 1977), 1–24.
8. This is, of course, also the "radical empiricism" of William James.
9. As usual, Dewey does not give his reference, and it is not listed in the critical

edition of *Experience and Nature*. The quote is from lines 416–20 of Hesiod's *Theogony*.

10. White's note here is H. Diels, *Fragmente der Vorsokratiker*, 6th ed. (Berlin, 1951), 171 (B.90).

11. Lynn White, "The Act of Invention: Causes, Contexts, Continuities and Consequences," in *The Technological Order: Proceedings of the Encyclopaedia Britannica Conference*, Carl F. Stover, ed. (Detroit: Wayne State University Press, 1963), 104.

12. F. E. Peters, *Greek Philosophical Terms* (New York: New York University Press, 1967), 48.

13. José Ortega y Gasset, *History as a System and Other Essays Toward a Philosophy of History*, Helene Weyl, trans. (New York: W. W. Norton and Co., 1961), 146–47.

14. C. J. Ducasse, *The Philosophy of Art* (1929; reprint, New York: Dover Publications, n.d.), 86.

15. John Dewey, *Problems of Men* (New York: Philosophical Library, 1946), 291n.

5. THEORY, PRACTICE, AND PRODUCTION

1. Alfred North Whitehead, *Science and the Modern World* (New York: New American Library, 1963), 107.

2. Nicholas Lobkowicz, *Theory and Practice: History of a Concept from Aristotle to Marx* (1967; reprint, Lanham, Md.: University Press of America, 1983). See especially p. 2

3. F. E. Peters, *Greek Philosophical Terms* (New York: New York University Press, 1967), 163.

4. Jonathan Barnes, ed., *The Complete Works of Aristotle*, 2 vols. (Princeton, N.J.: Princeton University Press, 1985), 1025b17ff., 1064a17ff.

5. Ibid., 1064a5–6.

6. Hannah Arendt, *The Human Condition* (Chicago: The University of Chicago Press, 1958), 301. "The matter is somewhat confused because Greek political philosophy still follows the order laid down by the *polis* even when it turns against it; but in their strictly philosophical writings (to which, of course, one must turn if he wants to know their innermost thoughts), Plato as well as Aristotle tends to invert the relationship between work and action in favor of work. Thus Aristotle, in a discussion of the different kinds of cognition in his Metaphysics, places dianoia and episteme praktike, practical insight and political science, at the lowest rank of his order, and puts above them the science of fabrication, episteme poietike, which immediately precedes and leads to theoria, the contemplation of truth." Arendt's reference in this material is to *Metaphysics*, 1025b25ff. and 1064a17ff.

7. Barnes (1985), 1197a9–13.

8. Lobkowicz (1983), 24.

9. Ibid., 17.

10. C. Wright Mills, *Sociology and Pragmatism*, Irving Louis Horowitz, ed. (New York: Oxford University Press, 1966), 314.

11. This is a quote in EW3:128 from St. George Stock, *Deductive Logic* (Oxford, London: Longmans, Green and Co., 1888). Neither Dewey nor the editors of the critical edition cite the page number.

12. Dewey does *not* say that writing comes out of spoken language. I do not think that he would have difficulty with a current view that holds that writing evolved from graphic arts, not from spoken language. See Roy Harris, *The Origin of Writing* (La Salle, Ill.: Open Court, 1986).

13. Willard Van Orman Quine, *From a Logical Point of View* (1953; reprint, New York: Harper & Row, 1963), 10.

14. See Dewey's 1916 paper "Logical Objects" (MW10:89 ff.) and Ralph Sleeper's excellent discussion of that essay in *The Necessity of Pragmatism* (New Haven: Yale University Press, 1987), 85ff.

15. C. S. Peirce, *Collected Papers of Charles Sanders Peirce*, C. Hartshorne, P. Weiss, and A. Burks, eds. (Cambridge: Harvard University Press, 1931–1958), 1:668. Standard references to this edition are to volume and paragraph number. Peirce said: "A useless inquiry, provided it is a systematic one, is pretty much the same as a scientific inquiry. Or at any rate, if a scientific inquiry becomes by any mischance useful, that aspect of it has to be kept sedulously out of sight during the investigation, or else . . . its hopes of success are fatally cursed."

16. Milton Fisk, *Nature and Necessity* (Bloomington: Indiana University Press, 1973), 3.

17. Ibid., 25.

18. It should be said that the conceptualists come closer to Dewey's position than to either of the other two positions, and certainly closer than he knew.

19. David Hume, *A Treatise of Human Nature*, L. A. Selby-Bigge, ed. (Oxford: Clarendon Press, 1968), 179.

20. There are, of course, uses in imaginative art for many types of quality groupings that are not instrumental outside that domain. Consider, for example, Ionesco's *Bald Soprano*.

21. Ernest Nagel, introduction to vol. 12 of *The Later Works* (LW12:xvi).

22. William James, *Principles of Psychology* (Cambridge: Harvard University Press, 1983), 968.

23. Ibid.

6. INSTRUMENTS, HISTORY, AND HUMAN FREEDOM

1. William James, "The Dilemma of Determinism," in *The Will to Believe and Other Essays in Popular Philosophy* (Cambridge: Harvard University Press, 1979), 117.

2. Richard Hofstadter, *Social Darwinism in American Thought* (Boston: Beacon Press, 1967), 40.

3. Quoted in Hofstadter (1967), 45.

4. James (1979), 117.

5. Ibid., 118.

6. Karl Marx, *The Poverty of Philosophy* (New York: International Publishers, 1982).

7. Ibid., 109.

8. Karl Marx, *Capital,* Ben Fowkes, trans. (New York: Vintage Books, 1977), 90–91. Emphasis added.

9. Marx (1982), 109.

10. Ibid., 110. Emphasis in original.

11. Ibid., 186.

12. Ibid., 187.

13. Karl Marx, "Theses on Feuerbach," in *The Marx-Engels Reader*, Robert C. Tucker, ed. (New York: W. W. Norton & Co., 1978), 145.

14. Marx (1977), 101.

15. Jacques Ellul, *The Technological Society*, John Wilkinson, trans. (New York: Vintage Books, 1964).

16. Jacques Ellul, *The Technological System*, Joachim Neugroschel, trans. (New York: Continuum, 1980).

17. Stanley R. Carpenter, review of *Autonomous Technology*, by Langdon

Winner, in *Research in Philosophy and Technology*, vol. 3, Paul T. Durbin, ed. (Greenwich, Conn.: JAI Press, 1980), 117.

18. Ellul (1964), xxv.

19. Ellul (1980), 32–33.

20. Ellul (1964), 107.

21. Ibid., xxx.

22. David C. Menninger, "Marx in the Social Thought of Jacques Ellul," in *Jacques Ellul: Interpretive Essays*, Clifford G. Christians and Jay M. Van Hook, eds. (Urbana: University of Illinois Press, 1981), 18–19.

23. Marx (1982), 185.

24. Langdon Winner, *Autonomous Technology* (Cambridge: The MIT Press, 1980).

25. Although Ellul certainly holds this view, he does not do so consistently. In places he writes as if even the state will be unable to control the juggernaut he takes the technological system to be.

26. Carpenter (1980), 120.

27. Ibid., 120–21.

28. Note here Winner's brush with anthropomorphizing the "system."

29. Carpenter (1980), 118.

30. There is considerable debate, however, regarding just how long this pattern will continue, due to practices of soil use that some analysts regard as deplorable.

31. An excellent introduction to Habermas's work is Rick Roderick, *Habermas and the Foundations of Critical Theory* (New York: St. Martin's Press, 1986).

32. Langdon Winner, *The Whale and the Reactor* (Chicago: University of Chicago Press, 1986), 55.

7. PUBLICS AS PRODUCTS

1. Harriet Alice Chipman, whom Dewey married in July 1886, undoubtedly was instrumental in turning his attention in this direction. See George Dykhuizen, *The Life and Mind of John Dewey*, Jo Ann Boydston, ed. (Carbondale and Edwardsville: Southern Illinois University Press, 1973), 53ff.

2. Lewis S. Feuer, "John Dewey and the Back to the People Movement in American Thought," in *Journal of the History of Ideas* XX (1959), 553.

3. Dewey was also prescient in realizing that Stalin's version of Marxism and the various types of European Fascism of the 1930s were cut from the same cloth. In "Why I Am Not a Communist" (1934) he wrote: "As an unalterable opponent of Fascism in every form, I cannot be a Communist" (LW9:93).

4. C. Wright Mills, *Sociology and Pragmatism* (New York: Oxford University Press, 1966), 394.

5. Ibid.

6. Ibid.

7. John Rawls, *A Theory of Justice* (Cambridge: Harvard University Press, 1971). See page 11: "My aim is to present a conception of justice which generalizes and caries to a higher level of abstraction the familiar theory of the social contract as found, say, in Locke, Rousseau, and Kant."

8. Robert Nozick, *Anarchy, State, and Utopia* (New York: Basic Books, 1974).

9. An excellent example of the superiority of the public/private functional distinction over the individual/social structural one appeared in *The New York Times* during the writing of this chapter. The United States Supreme Court was asked to decide whether large private male-only clubs could legally continue to exclude women. Club members argued that this was a case of individual rights pitted against the abrogation by society of those rights. Those seeking admission argued that it was not an issue of individual versus society at all, but

whether putatively "private" clubs were in fact so. The Supreme Court ruled that the clubs, including The Century Club and The University Club, were private in name only, that is, that their function was primarily a public one. As the *Times* reported (21 June 1988, p. 12, national edition), "Justice White's opinion noted that some clubs might have a First Amendment right to discriminate, especially if they can prove that they were formed primarily for religious or free speech purposes or that their members do not use them for business or professional discussions."

The *Times* also pointed out that "New York law provides that clubs are not 'distinctly private,' and thus are 'public accommodations' covered by the city's 1965 Human Rights Law, if they have more than 400 members, provide regular meal service and regularly receive income for use of the facilities by nonmembers "for furtherance of trade or business."

10. An interesting example of this phenomenon is in the courts at the time this chapter is being written. *The New York Times* (21 June 1988, p. 13, national edition) reports attempts by abortion rights advocates to obtain "church records for use in a suit to strip the church of its tax-exempt status. The groups charge that the Roman Catholic church had been using tax-deductible contributions illegally to support political candidates who oppose a right to abortion." The issue, of course, is the extent to which a putatively "private" organization creates publics and is therefore subject to the same rules as other public organizations.

11. "The particular form a convention takes has nothing fixed and absolute about it. But the existence of some form of convention is not itself a convention. It is a uniform attendant of all social relationships. At the very least, it is the oil which prevents or reduces friction" (LW13:37; EE:67).

12. Mills (1966), 381.

13. Earl James Weaver, "John Dewey: A Spokesman for Progressive Liberalism" (Ph.D. diss., Brown University, 1963), 3.

14. Dewey echoed the metaphors of this polarity in *Human Nature and Conduct*: "The significance of morals and politics, of the arts both technical and fine, of religion and of science itself as inquiry and discovery, all have their source and meaning in the union in Nature of the settled and the unsettled, the stable and the hazardous. Apart from this union, there are no such things as 'ends,' either as consummations or as those ends-in-view we call purposes. There is only a block universe, either something ended and admitting of no change, or else a predestined march of events. There is no such thing as fulfillment where there is no risk of failure, and no defeat where there is no promise of possible achievement" (LW4:194–95; QC:244).

15. Quoted in Richard Hofstadter, *Social Darwinism in American Thought* (Boston: Beacon Press, 1967), 40n.

16. Ibid., 60.

17. Ibid., 45.

18. Ibid., 123.

19. Ibid., 125.

20. Thomas H. Huxley, "Evolution and Ethics," in *Collected Essays,* vol. X (1902; reprint, New York: Greenwood Press, 1968), 46 ff.

21. Robert N. Bellah *et al., Habits of the Heart* (New York: Harper and Row, 1985). One finds Dewey's instrumentalism around every turn of Bellah's book, although he is never mentioned.

22. Robert B. Reich, *Tales of a New America* (New York: Vintage, 1988).

23. Reinhold Niebuhr, *Moral Man and Immoral Society* (New York: Charles Scribner's Sons, 1932).

24. Ibid., xii.

25. Ibid., xiii.

26. Ibid., xv.

27. Ibid., xv.
28. Ibid., xvi.
29. Ibid., xxii.
30. Ibid., xxiii.
31. Ibid., 35.
32. Ibid., 57.
33. Ibid., 179–80.
34. Ibid., 212.
35. Ibid., 213.
36. Joseph Ratner, ed., *Characters and Events,* vol. 2 (New York: Henry Holt and Co., 1929), 782–89.
37. On the subject of passive resistance and the pragmatists, see K. Ramakrishna Rao, *Gandhi and Pragmatism* (Calcutta: Oxford & IBH Publishing Co., 1968), especially chapter 4, "The Experimentalism of John Dewey."
38. "Humanist Manifesto I," in *The New Humanist* VI, no. 3, (May/June 1933).
39. Karl Mannheim, *Freedom, Power, and Democratic Planning*, Adolph Lowe *et al.,* eds. (New York: Oxford University Press, 1950).
40. Ibid., 303.
41. Ibid.
42. Mills, 358. See also page 391. "The general type of action and thought which Dewey most pervasively utilizes and which forms his positive model in large part may be termed *technological*."
43. Ibid., 392–93.
44. Ibid., 405.
45. Ibid.
46. In 1917, the year that the United States became a belligerent in the First World War, a disaffected Randolph Bourne also characterized Dewey's variety of pragmatism as a type of straight-line instrumentalism, even though as late as 1915 he seemed to have grasped the extent to which that was a poor reading of Dewey's work. See Randolph Bourne, "John Dewey's Philosophy," in *The New Republic* II (13 March 1915), 154–56. This article is reprinted in Randolph Bourne, *The Radical Will: Randolph Bourne Selected Writings 1911–1918*, Olaf Hansen, ed. (New York: Urizen Books, 1977), 331–35. See also R. Bourne, "Twilight of Idols," in *Seven Arts* II (October 1917), 688–702. This article is reprinted in Bourne (1977), 336–47.

Mills quotes Bourne (Mills, 410), but misidentifies his article as being from *The Dial* and gives no more specific source. Bourne's disaffection with Dewey is palpable.

> To those of us who have taken Dewey's philosophy almost as our American religion, it never occurred that values could be subordinated to technique. We were instrumentalists, but we had our private utopias so clearly before our minds that the means fell always into its place as contributory. And Dewey, of course, always meant his philosophy, when taken as a philosophy of life, to start with values. But there was always that unhappy ambiguity in his doctrine as to just how values were created, and it became easier and easier to assume that just any growth was justified and almost any activity valuable so long as it achieved ends. The American, in living out this philosophy, has habitually confused results with product, and been content with getting somewhere without asking too closely whether it was the desirable place to get. It is now becoming plain that unless you start with the vividest kind of poetic vision, your instrumentalism is likely to land you just where it has landed this younger intelligentsia which is so happy and busily engaged in the national enterprise of war. You must have your

vision and you must have your technique. The practical effect of Dewey's philosophy has evidently been to develop the sense of the latter at the expense of the former. Though he himself would develop them together, even in him there seems to be a flagging of values, under the influence of war (Bourne [1977], 343–44).

This passage from the 1917 article in *Seven Arts* foreshadows Mills' criticism of Dewey, although Bourne, unlike Mills, seems to have had some second thoughts about his analysis by the end of the passage.

Of course, Dewey's reply to criticism of this sort was already well developed by his 1903 *Studies*. But in his 1920 *Reconstruction in Philosophy* he put his point even more plainly: "When we take means for ends we indeed fall into moral materialism. But when we take ends without regard to means we degenerate into sentimentalism. In the name of the ideal we fall back upon mere luck and chance and magic or exhortation and preaching; or else upon a fanaticism that will force the realization of preconceived ends at any cost" (MW12:121; RP:73).

47. Either Mills or his editor, Horowitz, has given as a reference for this quotation Dewey's *Essays in Experimental Logic*, pp. 1–2. It does not appear on pp. 1–2 of the 1916 University of Chicago Press edition.

EPILOGUE: RESPONSIBLE TECHNOLOGY

1. John J. McDermott, *The Culture of Experience: Philosophical Essays in the American Grain* (New York: New York University Press, 1976), 220.
2. Edwin A. Burtt, "The Core of Dewey's Way of Thinking," in *The Journal of Philosophy* LVII, no. 13 (23 June 1960), 406.
3. Ibid. Emphasis in original.
4. Peirce, *Collected Papers*, 8:240.
5. Ibid.
6. Richard Rorty, *Consequences of Pragmatism* (Minneapolis: University of Minnesota Press, 1982), xliii.
7. Ibid., 208.
8. Ralph Sleeper, *The Necessity of Pragmatism* (New Haven: Yale University Press, 1986), 1.
9. Thomas Sheehan, "Heidegger and the Nazis," in *The New York Review of Books* (16 June 1988), 41–47. This is a lengthy critical review of Victor Farias, *Heidegger et le nazisme*, Myriam Benarroch and Jean-Baptiste Grasset, trans. (Paris: Editions Verdier, 1988).
10. Sheehan (1988), 46.
11. Ibid., 41.
12. Gary Bullert, *The Politics of John Dewey* (Buffalo, NY: Prometheus Books, 1983), 35.
13. Max Horkheimer, *The Eclipse of Reason* (1947; reprint, New York: Seabury Press, 1974), 46.
14. Ibid., 45.
15. Ibid., 46.
16. Ibid., 48.
17. Ibid., 46–47.
18. Ibid., 75.
19. C. E. Ayres, "The Significance of Economic Planning," in *Development of Collective Enterprise*, Seba Eldridge and Associates, ed. (Lawrence, Kan.: University of Kansas Press, 1943), 479.
20. Hans Jonas, *The Imperative of Responsibility*, Hans Jonas and David Herr, trans. (Chicago: University of Chicago Press, 1984), 43.

Index